ENGLISH SENTIMENTAL DRAMA

ENGLISH
SENTIMENTAL
DRAMA

by

ARTHUR SHERBO

MICHIGAN STATE UNIVERSITY PRESS

1957

★
  ★
★
  ★
  ★

FOR ALFRED HARBAGE

PREFACE

THE IDEA of the historical or chronological continuity of literary forms, their origins, their development, and their transmutations is a commonplace in literary studies. It is equally a commonplace, of course, that literature is an expression of the human being, his environment, his feelings, his deepest convictions, and the intellectual circumstances of his place in time. These, like the literary forms in which they are embodied, are marked by the same pattern of growth, development, and modification. But while it is true that an idea or emotion may be expressed in any literary genre, the material upon which a writer draws is basically and eternally the same; it is the experience of the human race. And even in literature of a decidedly inferior order the fact is inescapable that some part of that same vast reservoir is being tapped. The poetaster who hymns the beauty of a tree or the joys of a mother as she contemplates her child has not, by very definition, produced poetry, but he has touched an audience which is ready for, and appreciative of, his limited capacities. Good literature always, and bad writing often, both have their roots in something durable; failure of adequate and authentic expression is only a matter of individual talent or, sometimes, the deliberate exaggeration of some fundamental aspect of human nature. Thus, to take the first example that suggests itself, love and honor can and have been treated with dignity and verisimilitude, but in the heroic play of the Restoration they have been so distorted and magnified that the results cannot be literature of lasting excellence. That Dryden succeeded with the genre to the point of producing plays, or parts of plays, which are still read with pleasure does not alter the fact that the end product is recognized as something artificial, foreign to human nature as we know it. The subject of a heroic play is true, the treatment is false. Nor would anybody argue seriously that the heroic play, whatever its origins, flourished for a few years because Englishmen of the Restoration were more preoccupied with nice questions of love and honor than Englishmen of the first Elizabeth's reign or, indeed, than continental Europeans of the sixteenth, seventeenth, or any other century.

Sentimental drama, like the heroic play, is a debased literary genre, incapable of producing literature of any marked degree of excellence. It is artificial; it exaggerates and distorts human nature and emotions; and it is conceived in terms of a view of life which is absolutely inconsistent with reality. Yet many sentimental plays enjoyed great popularity in their day, and one cannot ignore the very real fact that the genre was taken seriously. A few playwrights, it may also be granted, were probably sincerely interested in the sentimentalism that formed the basis of their efforts. Although it is difficult to achieve any great degree of detachment in reading these sentimental plays today, the usefulness of subjecting them to a close scrutiny cannot be doubted. At least one positive result will emerge from this examination of a body of inferior literature: the faults to be avoided will be laid bare. The reader is asked to lay aside prejudices of taste and assist in what may be thought of as an experiment in the laboratory. Two specimens are exhibited—drama that is sentimental and drama that is not. They show points of similarity, yet the differences are greater than the likenesses. One must isolate differences, analyze them, and give them a name of some sort—if only for the sake of subsequent convenience.

No claim of exhaustiveness can be made for the appended bibliography; it is, however, still the most complete available bibliography of writings on sentimental drama. There has been no attempt to list all the discussions, usually short, that appear in introductions to anthologies (or introductions to separate plays therein) or in histories of English literature or English drama. The amount of original thinking to be encountered in these works is small; most of those written after 1915 rely heavily on Ernest Bernbaum's *Drama of Sensibility*, published in that year. The bibliography, furthermore, does not include every work cited or quoted in the text or notes. Thus, while the plays of Thomas Heywood afford a striking example of the difference of opinion on the sentimental status of some Elizabethan drama, the reader will not find the many articles and books on Heywood's plays in the bibliography. If he is interested in those I have used, he can find them readily with the aid of the index. References to Allardyce Nicoll's three volumes on the English drama from 1660 to 1800 appear in the text, abbreviated as *1660-1700, 1700-1750,* and *1750-1800.* Throughout, London is the place of publication unless otherwise indicated.

I owe debts of gratitude to the following friends and scholars: Oscar James Campbell, James Lowry Clifford, Daniel Dodson, Alan Holaday, and Joseph Wood Krutch. My greatest obligation is to the man whose name appears in the dedication.

CONTENTS

Chapter I. SENTIMENTAL DRAMA "DEFINED"

LITERARY CRITICISM in the present century has displayed a thoroughly commendable reluctance to categorize and pigeonhole literary movements. The tendency to make use of convenient pegs upon which to hang works of literature has been, in great part, a fault (crime seems too harsh) which can be laid at the door of the maker of anthologies. In the pure sciences categorization is logical and valuable—even inevitable. The possession of certain properties in a chemical marks it as acid or base, and there can be no doubt of the identity of the chemical; unfortunately, literature has no method of identification analogous to the litmus test. Indeed, some of the so-called New Critics have even questioned the validity of terming certain works prose or poetry. This seems an over-refinement, but there are certain convenient labels which have been more justly subjected to critical analysis with the result that they have either been discarded or looked upon with suspicion. Actually, it is difficult to do away with a term that has endeared itself through constant usage, and there can be no question that certain of these terms much simplify the teaching of literature. A case in point is the term "romanticism," the attempted definition of which has occasioned an impressive body of critical writing in recent years. The word has really ceased to have any meaning, and that because of the multiplicity of meanings that have been given or denied it. It is still permissible—and highly convenient—to speak of the romantic movement in English poetry, but now it is also necessary to sound a warning when the word "romantic" or any of its derivatives is used.

Another term which has been loosely used and many times defined, and which is beginning to be looked upon with growing distrust, is "sentimentalism." In the present study the emphasis is on the use and abuse of that word in its application to English drama. Here, as with "romanticism," there is the further complication that the word is used in a loose, almost colloquial sense—indeed, from the time that it first makes its way into popular usage to the present day it has been used in a number of ways to describe a number of things. In 1749 we find Lady Bradshaigh writing to Samuel Richardson:

Pray, Sir, give me leave to ask you (I forgot it before) what, in your opinion, is the meaning of the word *sentimental*, so much in vogue amongst the polite, both in town and country? In letters and in common conversation, I have asked several who make use of it, and have generally received for an answer, it is —it is—*sentimental*. Everything clever and agreeable is comprehended in that word; but am convinced a wrong interpretation is given, because it is impossible everything clever and agreeable can be so common as this word. I am astonished to hear such a one is a *sentimental* man; we were a *sentimental* party; I have been taking a *sentimental* walk.[1]

In 1749 "sentimental" denotes "everything clever and agreeable." The following year it makes its first appearance in a dramatic context in the prologue to William Whitehead's *The Roman Father*. Interesting confirmation of the newness of the word is to be seen in the manner in which it is set off. It is the only word in the entire prologue in roman type; all the others are in italic. The limited sense in which the word is used is noteworthy.

> *Nay, even each moral,* sentimental *stroke,*
> *Where not the character but poet spoke,*
> *He lopp'd as foreign to his chaste design;*
> *Nor spared a useless, though a golden line.*

Allardyce Nicoll comments on Whitehead's use of the word:

A "*Moral,* Sentimental, *Stroke,*" for Whitehead was the utterance of the poet *in propria persona,* not part of dramatic dialogue, and this explains to a certain extent the numbers of "sentimental sentences" which abound in the drama of this time. (*1700-1750*, p. 180)

Two years later (1752) the Reverend Philip Francis' *Eugenia* was acted and published. In it occur the phrases "some sentimental merit" and "the sentimental language." By this time, then, it seems that the word had passed into common usage in the drama, not needing to be pointed out or explained. "Sentimental" is henceforth frequently met with in plays and in dramatic criticism, but very soon a reaction against the word and what it stands for sets in.

While it is not pertinent to present purposes to attempt a complete history of the battle against sentimental comedy, it may be pointed out that in 1775 George Colman the Elder, could write:

But the most offensive weapon of Modern Criticism is some *reigning word,* with which every literary Rifleman arms himself, and does dreadful execution. The two leading monosyllables of the House of Commons are not more powerful than such a *word,* be it what it may, while it remains formidable by being in fashion. I am old enough to remember when the word Low was this Scare-crow. *Genteel* Comedy, and the *politest* Literature, were in universal request; and every writer who attempted to be *comick,* dreaded the imputation of buffoonery. If a piece had strong humor—Oh, Sir, it's damned *low!*—was its sentence of condemnation. At length, however, the word Low has been restored to favour, and the term SENTIMENT in its turn has fallen into disgrace. "To anatomise a character, and see what breeds about the heart," had formerly its merit; but now this dissection of the human mind has lost its advocates and admirers; *Sentimental stuff* is the phrase; and he who dares to approve a scene, where the course of the story apparently leads the author to exhibit Passion rather than Humour, is condemned for an old-fashioned dunce and a coxcomb. Gross drolleries, or dull moralities, (*moralities* let me call them!) are equally reprehensible: but Humour is not to be censured merely because it is *low*, nor *sentiment* to be banished when it seems to exhibit the workings of the heart.[2]

Some twenty years later Mrs. Hannah Cowley, herself a writer of sentimental comedies, deprecates the predilection of audiences for mirth rather than instruction or sentiment:

The combinations of interest, the strokes which are meant to reach the heart, we are equally incapable of tasting. LAUGH! LAUGH! LAUGH! is the demand: Not a word must be uttered that looks like instruction, or a sentence which ought to be remembered.

What mother can now lead her daughters to the great National School, THE THEATRE, in the confidence of their receiving either polish or improvement? Should the luckless bard stumble on a reflection, or a sentiment, the audience yawn, and wait for the next tumble from a chair . . .

O! GENIUS of a polish'd age, descend!—plant thy banners in our Theatres, and Bid ELEGANCE AND FEELING take place of the *droll* and the *laugh* . . .[3]

And not too long ago William Archer, in a review article entitled "Elizabethan Stage and Restoration Drama," redirects attention to the question of sentimentalism again:

The ill-omened word "sentimentalism" has often played havoc with critical common sense, but few have yielded so tamely as Mr. Nicoll to its mischievous influence. It is surely time that a stand should be made against the cant which glorifies as "intellectual" all sorts of brutal cynicism, and despises as "sentimental" everything which betrays the smallest touch of human feeling.[4]

It is evident from this that "sentimentalism" and all it stands for has continued an object of critical disputation.

In the latter half of the eighteenth century two schools of dramatic writing are conspicuous: that which favors sentimental drama, and that opposed to it. Making allowances, as one must, for the allegiance to one or the other of these two opposed camps, some insight into the nature of the genre can be gained by looking at eighteenth-century discussions of sentimental drama. The purpose is to discover what sentimental drama was thought to be, not to decide on its merit or lack of merit. Although most of the strictures on sentimental comedy are to be found after 1750 there is at least one criticism before that date worth quoting. Edmund Burke points to one of the great weaknesses of sentimental comedy, and uses the adjective "weeping," an adjective that was to appear frequently later, to describe it.

. . . our Authors reverse the Business of the Drama, and are fond of introducing Scenes of Distress in Comedy. Who were the first Inventors of this Weeping Comedy, I cannot tell.

. . . our Modern Stage Directors think Satyr the greatest Fault in a Comedy, and as they know the Relish of the Town, give high Encouragement to Plays that abound with Characters insipidly perfect, where Virtue is painted in an unnatural, and consequently an unamiable Manner.[5]

The dissatisfaction with the "insipidly perfect" characters of "Weeping Comedy" which Burke expressed was to be echoed again and again. Not too long after Burke's essay Arthur Murphy, yet to have his first play produced, elected to comment upon the same aspect of sentimental comedy.

Should the several persons, represented in the drama, be in their conduct correct and regular, of amiable manners, and upon all occasions governed by principles of honour and virtue, such pieces, in their judgment, may be considered as legitimate. To this notion it is that we owe that new fangled species of the drama, called sentimental or pathetic comedy, of late years highly applauded in *France* . . . Compositions of this kind, while they give a transcript from real life, may claim their share of praise; but whether the mass of mankind afford, with probability, those select groups of virtuous characters, may be questioned.[6]

Murphy's essay appeared in 1754, only five years after Lady Bradshaigh's letter which saw "everything clever and agreeable" comprehended in the word "sentimental." The word had already taken on more than a hint of the pejorative in its application to the drama.

Reference to the hand-list of plays appended to Allardyce Nicoll's *Eighteenth Century Drama, 1750-1800* reveals that the author (adapter or translator would be more accurate) of the first play to bear the words "A Sentimental Comedy" on its title page despaired of any success on the stage and designed his work for readers. In the preface to his play, *The Man of Family* (1771), the Reverend Charles Jenner, adapting Diderot's *Le Père de Famille* for an English reading public, makes state-

4

ments which show all too clearly that sentimentalism in the drama still had its opponents. The Reverend gentleman

. . . is conscious that refined sentiments, which perish if they are not sown in a warm and genial soil, and even characteristic humour, to which nothing but observation can give a relish, have very little chance of amusing an audience, who go not to the theatre to think or feel.

And, he adds,

The author purposely forbears entering into any discussion of the merits of sentimental or characteristic comedy, compared with the comedy of Stage-trick and Decoration: he will not lament that the cast of the times is so *frivole,* as to have banished both nature and sentiment from the stage in such a manner, that the amusements of that and the closet cannot be brought to coincide.

These remarks take on added interest when one notes that Richard Cumberland's *The West Indian,* one of the better-known English senti-mental comedies, was first acted on January 19, 1771. The huge success of Cumberland's play would seem to contradict the truth of Jenner's statements, but the two can be reconciled.

The best-known eighteenth-century essay on the whole question is Oliver Goldsmith's *Comparison Between Sentimental and Laughing Comedy,* published in the *Westminster Magazine* for January, 1773. Gold-smith's role in the war against sentimental comedy is a peculiar one, but it is not germane to the present discussion to inquire into his position.[7] What is of importance are his remarks, the core of whose relevancy is contained in the following quotation:

. . . a new species of dramatic composition has been introduced under the name of *sentimental comedy,* in which the virtues of private life are exhibited, rather than the vices exposed; and the distresses rather than the faults of man-kind make our interest in the piece. . . . In these plays almost all the charac-ters are good and exceedingly generous; they are lavish enough of their tin money on the stage; and though they want humor, have abundance of senti-ment and feeling. If they happen to have faults or foibles, the spectator is taught not only to pardon, but to applaud them, in consideration of the goodness of their hearts; so that folly, instead of being ridiculed, is commended, and the comedy aims at touching our passions, without the power of being truly pathetic.

He then gives a satiric formula for the writing of sentimental comedy.

But there is one argument in favor of sentimental comedy which will keep it on the stage, in spite of all that can be said against it. It is of all others the most

5

easily written. Those abilities that can hammer out a novel, are fully sufficient to raise the characters a little; to deck out the hero with a riband, or give the heroine a title; then to put an insipid dialogue, without character or humor, into their mouths, give them mighty good hearts, very fine clothes, furnish a new set of scenes, furnish a pathetic scene or two, with a sprinkling of tender melancholy conversation through the whole, and there is no doubt but all the ladies will cry, and all the gentlemen applaud.

Later, examination of twentieth-century definitions of sentimental drama will show some scholars insisting that the characters be drawn from "the ordinary walks of life." This is a refinement whose origins can be traced to the study rather than to actual practice. Many sentimental plays recruit their personages from the middle class, but there is no hard and fast rule in this respect. Goldsmith's remarks are directed to the particular variety of sentimental drama that was being written in the 1760's and 1770's. There is no insistence that the *dramatis personae* be recruited from the middle and lower classes; the hero is decked out with a riband, the heroine has a title. Certain basic elements of sentimentalism, that sentimentalism which does not depend on accidental and ephemeral vogues, are, however, present. The characters are to be possessed of "mighty good hearts"; there are to be pathetic scenes; and the appeal to the emotions will be effected both by the pathetic scenes and the "sprinkling of tender melancholy conversation through the whole."

While no critical preeminence can be claimed for the work from which the following passages are taken, it is evidence of another writer's dissatisfaction with this "bastard tragedy" (Goldsmith's term) which was enjoying so much popularity. William Cooke declares roundly that

. . . whoever will make the comparison between that comedy left us by antiquity, and so ably continued to us by several of our English poets with this sentimental comedy, will find the features too dissimilar to claim the most distant references; in the former, we have a fable founded on the laws of probability, and nature; characters speaking the language of their conformation, and the whole stage reflecting the manners of the world; in the latter, names instead of characters, poetical egotisms for manners, bombast for sentiment, and instead of wit and humour, (the very essence of comedy) a driveling species of morality, which as a term generally applied to ethics, may properly enough be called *good*, but from being falsely applied to comedy (however it may excite the *piety* of the crowd) must nauseate men of sense, and education.[8]

A passage or two further on Cooke makes another statement which points to the unreal nature of sentimental comedy in which "the principal figures are tricked out in all the brilliancy of virtue, without the least shade of mortality." (p. 145) And he returns to the attack with a vigorous passage in which he, like Goldsmith, furnishes a satiric formula for the ready composition of sentimental comedies:

Comedy being thus debauched, like an unhappy female, began to be viewed in the light of *common game*, by those poets who dare not look up to her in the days of her chastity; such finding the intercourse easy, and the profits great, immediately hired themselves in her service. The success of one fool drew many; they had nothing to do but change the *vis comica* for the pathetic, and substitute tame individual recital for natural dialogue; in short, a novel furnished them with the plot; a servile allusion to all the little chat of the times, for wit, and humour; and the Whole Duty of Man, Pamela, or the Oeconomy of Human Life, for sentiments. (pp. 143-44)

One must bear in mind that Cooke's work, published in 1775, appeared during the period which has been said to have witnessed the "final triumph of sentimental comedy."[9] Nor were Goldsmith and Cooke alone in attacking the genre in this period (1773-1780) of its triumph. The elder George Colman's strictures, written in 1775, have already been quoted. Charles Dibdin, historian of the stage, had no liking for "sentiment," in the latter half of the eighteenth century an almost indispensable concomitant of sentimental comedies. Seizing upon Hugh Kelly (died 1777) as a particularly obnoxious practitioner of "sentiment," he delivers himself upon that playwright with considerable vehemence:

Kelly . . . happened, fortunately for himself, and unluckily for the public taste, to take advantage of the rage that then prevailed for sentiment. Everything was at that time sentiment. It was the only secret of writing for success. If a man was to be hanged, or married, out came a sentiment. If a rogue triumphed, or was tossed in a blanket, what an opportunity for a sentiment! If the butler was drunk, or the chambermaid impertinent, listen to a sentiment! In short, if the alderman ate too much custard, or his wife frequented too many routs; if the vice was gaming in the Alley, or at Brooks's, wenching, or drinking; if fortune came unasked, or was deaf to solicitation; if the subject was health or sickness, happiness or misery; hooraw for a sentiment![10]

Simple justice demands that Kelly be permitted to answer in his own defense. In the preface to his sentimental comedy, *The School For Wives* (1773), Kelly vindicates his championship of the sentimental school of dramatic composition. Speaking of himself in the third person, he states that

His chief study has been to steer between the extremes of sentimental gloom, and the excesses of uninteresting levity; he has some laugh, yet he hopes he has also some lesson; and fashionable as it has been lately for the wits, even

7

with his friend Mr. Garrick at their head, to ridicule the Comic Muse, when a little grave, he must think that she degenerates into farce, where the grand business of instruction is neglected, and consider it as a heresy in criticism, to say that one of the most arduous tasks within the reach of literature, shou'd, when executed, be wholly without utility.

Kelly aligns himself with the less extreme proponents of sentimental drama, and anyone who has read widely in late eighteenth-century drama will conclude that Dibdin's remarks might more justly have been directed at any one of a score of other playwrights. And Kelly, it will be remarked, affords evidence of the fashionableness of ridiculing sentimental comedy in this period. "Robert Heron" [John Pinkerton], in an essay "On Comedy" in his *Letters of Literature* (1785) states that "Sentimental Comedy bore a very short sway in England. Indeed it was incompatible with the humour of an English audience, who go to comedy to laugh, and not to cry." (p. 46). For him *The Jealous Wife* and *The Clandestine Marriage* represent a "happy medium" (p. 47).

Other strictures on sentimental drama exist, of course, but the passages selected for quotation are sufficient to indicate where the attackers of sentimentalism concentrated their attention. A definition of sentimentalism in the drama of the eighteenth century can be established by noting what features came in for comment most frequently. Dibdin fastens on the excessive use of "sentiments," and Burke and Murphy object most strongly to the improbability of characters of such signal virtue as appear in sentimental comedy. Goldsmith and Cooke agree with Burke and Murphy in condemning the unreal characters of sentimental comedy. They object to the lack of wit and humor and they point out that the "distresses rather than the faults of mankind" furnish the principal interest. Both find that goodness is the fundamental characteristic of the figures of sentimental comedy; both speak contemptuously of the use of the "pathetic." Throughout there is bitter condemnation of the artificial nature of sentimental comedy.

Of course sentimental comedy had its defenders. Bishop Hurd accepts, with minor reservations, the basic assumption of sentimental comedy, the legitimacy of pathos in comedy. He will allow that "all *distresses* are not *improper* in comedy; but such only as attach the mind to the *fable*, in neglect of the *manners*, which are its chief object." He repeats, "my idea of comedy requires only that the *pathos* be kept in subordination to the *manners*." And he has still another reservation which may seem surprising: "After all, I fear the *tender and pitiable* in comedy, though it must afford the highest pleasure to sensible and elegant minds, is not perfectly suited to the apprehensions of the generality."[11] Actually, this is an observation that comes up again and again in eighteenth-century discussions of sentimentalism. It seems that the capacity to react sentimentally was thought of as something peculiar to men and women of birth and culture. Hannah More's *Sensibility: An Epistle to the Honourable Mrs. Boscawen* may serve to prove that Bishop Hurd's fears about "the apprehensions of the generality" were not peculiar to himself alone. Here are a few lines from the poem:

> Let not the vulgar read this pensive strain,
> Their jests the tender anguish would prophane.
> Yet these some deem the happiest of their kind,
> Whose low enjoyments never reach'd the mind.[12]

And, in 1805, in his review of Thomas Morton's *Speed the Plough*, Thomas Holcroft, himself termed a writer of sentimental drama, remarks that "There is a mixture of virtue and vice, in all men . . . and when servants, bailiffs, jailors, and all classes of people, are described as sentimental . . . these precious qualities become too common."[13] This, to anticipate slightly, is strangely at odds with the fairly widespread scholarly view that tragedy must be domestic to be sentimental. And yet it seems safe to assume that there is not one kind of sentimentalism in comedy and another kind peculiar to tragedy. Another writer, Richard Cumberland's first biographer, William Mumford, proves a less reserved champion of sentimental comedy than Bishop Hurd. There is no hesitance, no qualifying phrase, in his defence.

The vehement censures which some critics, and especially those of France, have fulminated against the sentimental comedy, partake more of bigotry than reason. Laughter and ridicule they consider as the legitimate weapons of comedy; but, if virtue can be inculcated through the soft influence of tears; if, by awakening the heart to tenderness, we can dispose it to the admission of moral truth, he who would deny to comedy this privilege may be pronounced an enemy to human happiness.[14]

Even more revealing is this next passage which demonstrates clearly what Mumford thought the chief features of sentimental comedy.

Such incidents as belong to sentimental comedy, those touching scenes of domestic woe which spring from domestic follies, vices or misfortunes, are as much the picture of what may be found in society by actual inspection, as anything which has hitherto been pronounced the legitimate topics of comic drama. Everyman's experience confirms this; and while tragedy, therefore, calls forth our tears alone, let it be the province of comedy to mingle them with our smiles, to awaken the serious as well as the cheerful affections of our nature, and to enforce the practice of virtue, by making us laugh at folly, and weep for the consequences of vice. (pp. 282-83)

It becomes apparent that both defenders and attackers of sentimental comedy agreed on its fundamental characteristics; they are both talking about the same thing. That their points of view diverge so sharply is, of course, another matter.

There is also a kind of middle ground between the two violently opposed schools of sentimentalism and its opponents. The spokesman for this middle group, selected here because of his position in the best society of his age rather than for any great critical acumen, is Horace Walpole. Walpole does not object to the content of sentimental drama; he is even inclined to sympathize with its aims. What seems to trouble him is the name given to the new species. Had sentimental comedy been called something else, Walpole, presumably, would have been satisfied. It is the word "comedy" which will not go down with him. His words are sufficiently interesting to warrant full quotation.

The enemies of *sentimental comedy* (or, as the French, the inventors, call it, *comédie larmoyante*) seem to think that the great business of comedy is to make the audience laugh. *That* may certainly be effected without nature or character. A Scot, an Irishman, a Mrs. Slipslop, can always produce a laugh, at least from half the audience. For my part, I confess I am more disposed to weep than to laugh at such poor artifices. The advocates of merry comedy appeal to Moliere. I appeal to him too. Which is his better comedy, The *Misanthrope*, or the *Bourgeois Gentilhomme*? The *Tartuffe*, or The *Etourdi*? In reality, did not Moliere in The *Misanthrope* give a pattern of such comedy? What is finer than the serious scenes of Maskwell and Lady Touchwood in The Double Dealer? I do not take the *comédie larmoyante* to have been so much a deficience of pleasantry in its authors, as the effect of observation and reflection. Tragedy had been confined to the distresses of kings, princesses, and heroes; and comedy restrained to making us laugh at passions pushed to a degree of ridicule. In the former, as great personages only were concerned, language was elevated to suit their rank, rather than their sentiments; for real passion rarely talks in heroics. Had tragedy descended to people of subordinate stations, authors found the language would be too pompous. I should therefore think that the first man who gave a *comédie larmoyante*, rather meant to represent a melancholy story in private life, than merely to produce a comedy without mirth. If he had therefore not married two species then reckoned incompatible, that is tragedy and comedy, or, in other words, distress with a cheerful conclusion; and, instead of calling it *comédie larmoyante*, had named his new genus *tragédie mitigée*, or as the same purpose has since been styled, *tragédie bourgeoise;* he would have given a third species to the stage.[15]

Elsewhere Walpole criticizes the sentimental comedies of Richard Cumberland, but he had conceived a cordial dislike for that dramatist, and his criticism of the latter's plays are colored by that prejudice.[16]

Some examination of twentieth-century studies of sentimentalism in drama must also be undertaken in order to arrive at a tentative working definition that can be used as a point of departure. Upon the basis of such examination it will be possible to determine the common denominator. Using this lowest common denominator, it should be logically possible to examine any play in the confident expectation of being able to term it sentimental or not, with some degree of accuracy. If this check system prove fallible, then, of course, other factors, not covered in the existent definitions, must be taken into consideration.

Ernest Bernbaum's *The Drama of Sensibility*, published in 1915, has continued to be the standard work on English sentimental drama; Joseph Wood Krutch's *Comedy and Conscience After the Restoration* (1924) deals more exhaustively with the causes of its appearance in the early years of the eighteenth century only. Other scholars have dealt with particular aspects of the rise of sentimentalism or have limited their discussions to a particular period: Bernbaum attempts to examine it from its origins to its "final triumph" in the late years of the eighteenth century. There have been numerous articles and short treatments (chapters in histories of the drama, for example) which have concerned themselves with the meaning of the term "sentimental drama," the relative place of one or another dramatist in the rise of this literary phenomenon, and the origins of the form. Twentieth-century definitions of sentimental drama have, however, included a number of points upon which there is fairly common agreement. And it is not remarkable that these later definitions should so often parallel the views of the eighteenth-century writers quoted earlier. Bernbaum's definition is useful and may serve as a model against which other definitions can be tested for differences of opinion or additional elements. "The drama of sensibility," he writes

which includes sentimental comedy and domestic tragedy, was from its birth a protest against the orthodox view of life, and against those literary conventions which have served that view. It implied that human nature, when not, as in some cases, already perfect, was perfectible by an appeal to the emotions. It refused to assume that virtuous persons must be sought in a romantic realm apart from the everyday world. It wished to show that beings who were good at heart were found in the ordinary walks of life. It so represented their conduct as to arouse admiration for their virtues and pity for their sufferings. In sentimental comedy, it showed them contending against distresses but finally rewarded by morally deserved happiness. In domestic tragedy, it showed them overwhelmed by catastrophes for which they were morally not responsible. A new ethics had arisen, and new forms of literature were thereby demanded. (p. 10)

In a discussion of Steele's *Conscious Lovers* another point of importance is made.

In earlier sentimental comedies improbabilities were present, but not prominent. Their personages were ideal, but their action was on the whole realistic. The further development, one of the most important contributions by Steele to the type, was a natural, almost an inevitable, one. That perfectly virtuous people come to a happy issue out of all their afflictions is, alas, a theory not so plausibly illustrated in a world resembling the real one as in a realm of beneficent coincidence. In such a region the conscious lovers moved; and sentimental comedy, though still affecting truth to life, departed therefrom still further. As Steele's method in this particular was often followed, improbability of plot became henceforth a frequent, though not a constant, attribute of the genre. (p. 136)

Although there are other points made in the course of his analysis of particular plays, the essential elements that Bernbaum finds in sentimental drama are present in these two quotations.

Only domestic tragedy, with its characters drawn from the middle or lower classes, is allowed possible sentimental status by the critic just quoted; hence a brief digression is necessary. The argument that people of *any* class are proper subjects for sentimental drama is based on the belief that audiences will respond to drama and its appeals both when the figures on the stage are kings and nobles and when they are of the middle or lower classes. The thrill or response that is evoked by drama is essentially a vicarious one. There is an inevitable—conscious or unconscious—identification of ourselves with one or more of the characters of the play. Even deeper than this often perceptible identification is the realization that one is part of humanity and that the men and women whose images are thrown on the stage—the real men and women who might be actually enacting a part of their lives before our eyes—are part of the race of which one is also a member. That the personages on the stage are of exalted position means little when the audience sees a king reunited to his daughter, long thought dead, or when a princess, patiently bearing the cruelties and infidelities of the prince, her husband, is able to bring about his reformation by some signal act of devotion. Can anyone maintain for a moment that the tradesman who had paid his penny to stand in the pit of an Elizabethan theatre was not moved by such situations merely because the actor wore royal attire? If a special theory of vicarious experience is to be set up along class lines, the burgher responding only to the sorrows of his fellow burgher as represented on the stage, then further qualifications of sex, age, creed, and the like might just as logically be set up. The notion is, of course, untenable. One does not respond to a play solely because one or more characters are recognizably of one's class, sex, age, creed, and so forth. There should not, therefore, be any difficulty in accepting a play as sentimental in which the characters are not middle class or lower. This is not to say that the sentimental play which does employ common folk may not, partly because of that fact, affect the audience more profoundly. In fact, given two sentimental plays of equal merit, the one which presents bourgeois characters should be more effective than that which presents royalty —to the popular audience. The converse is equally true. An audience composed entirely of royalty (to make the analogy extreme) would surely show more sympathy for the sufferings of a king than for those of a tradesman. But surely the sufferings of King Lear did not leave our Elizabethan tradesman dry-eyed.

A survey of other modern analyses of sentimental drama,[17] to return to the point of departure, reveals only a few disagreements with Bernbaum's major premises; additional characteristics of the genre have been insisted upon by other scholars, but these are also few. Allardyce Nicoll makes the surprising statement that a sentimental play "may exist in and for itself with characters wholly unrelieved by any virtue or humane sense of justice" (*1700-1750*, p. 182), and F. W. Bateson makes the even more startling statement that "there is nothing essentially false or essentially second-rate in the conception of sentimental comedy. It need only be in feeble hands" (*English Comic Drama*, p. 148). One is tempted to ask which hands that have labored with sentimental comedy have not been feeble. Since the majority opinion is so decidedly against these two extreme positions, they may be safely recorded and forgotten. Interest centers rather upon the points of agreement. The presence of the moral element, called the moral problem by Nicoll, has been universally agreed upon, directly or by implication. There is equal awareness of the greater appeal to the emotions than to the intellect. The suggestion that sentimentalism partakes of the artificial, or the exaggerated, or the improbable has found its way into most of the definitions. Bateson's is the dissenting voice here. With the notable exception of Nicoll the idea of the essential goodness or perfectibility of human nature has been regarded as a necessary characteristic of sentimental drama. Most of the writers on the subject have pointed out that there is an emphasis on pity; that tears are solicited for the spectacle of the sufferings of the good and admiration for the virtuous.

A number of other characteristics have been urged, now by one critic, now by another, but these may be considered as embellishing rather than contributing basically to the idea of sentimentalism. Nicoll's suggestion that there is a "return to a highly artificial love of natural scenery and rural landscape" (*1700-1750*, p. 179), and Bernbaum's insistence that sentimental drama must observe native setting (pp. 37-38) and contemporaneity of action (pp. 46-47), may be discounted. The condition that the characters be from "the ordinary walks of life" has had more than one champion. The point has been discussed already, and although the condition is frequently satisfied, it is by no means a necessary one. Examples of sentimental plays of the eighteenth century in which the principal characters are of the titled nobility abound. Here, as elsewhere in this work, a play may be called sentimental because it has been termed so by other critics, but that does not necessitate one's own acceptance of it as such. Indication will be given of the present writer's acceptance of a play as sentimental when such indication is called for. The restriction of the characters of sentimental drama to those drawn from "domestic life," a term of no little ambiguity, may also, then, be regarded as a refinement. Of first importance are the points of agreement that have been established, for it is from these that the present work must proceed.

Chapter II. THE "DEFINITION" TESTED

INDULGENCE IN EMOTION for its own sake, luxuriating in grief, excessive yet shallow emotion, vicarious enjoyment of happiness or grief (it is, of course, possible to enjoy grief, our own and others')—all these are related phenomena which do not belong peculiarly to any time, people, or class. They are probably coeval with man and will, conceivably, always continue to have a place in his make-up. It would be presumptuous to state that these psychological phenomena came into being at one particular time in a certain locale. Such a statement would be manifestly absurd. Almost equally absurd, one feels, is the statement that these phenomena, so integral a part of sentimentalism, found their way into English drama at one determinable time, and thereupon gave birth to a new dramatic genre. Yet it has been said, and that often, that sentimentalism in the drama came into being in England at one specific, ascertainable time. Scholars have suggested different dates for the first appearance of the genre, but most of them seem agreed that a date can be arrived at. It must be admitted, however, that most of these same scholars have said something about early manifestations of sentimentalism in the drama; yet their comments have only served to point up the startling emergence of sentimentalism in the late seventeenth and early eighteenth centuries. Bernbaum's is an extreme statement of such a belief: "Such being the orthodox theory and practice, the appearance in 1696 of sentimental comedy was, in the true sense of a much abused term, revolutionary" (p. 71). The "orthodox theory and practice" referred to is the Restoration dramatists' adherence to classical authority which demanded "unity of tone within each genre," and their "distrust of ordinary human nature." Allardyce Nicoll is more conservative: "All through the Restoration period sporadic attempts had been made to chasten the drama but the more pronounced 'moral' works did not make their appearance in any numbers until after 1680" (*1660-1700*, p. 252). Both scholars, it should be added, remark that sentimentalism in the English drama had its origins much earlier than its manifestations in the last years of the seventeenth century. The observation needs no great elaboration. The view that the drama demonstrates a continuous development, that sports, in the biological sense, are rarely, if ever, to be found in this development, has become a commonplace of criticism, and it is not necessary to defend its appositeness in relation to sentimental drama.

In an examination of "the beginnings and significance of sentimental comedy" another, and later, writer develops the idea of the early origins of sentimentalism more fully.

The first traces of sentimental comedy are to be found as far back as the Morality Plays. In the majority of these pieces we follow the vicissitudes of the fortunes of Mankynd or Everyman, or some other abstract hero through a series of phases of good and evil. We see him sent into the world a model of virtue; soon he is beset by Pleasure, Sensuality and Vice, and starts on the downward grade, plunging deeper and deeper into evil, until he is finally reclaimed either by his own conscience or by the intervention of one of the virtues. It is the expression, in a very concrete form, of the fundamental goodness of human nature and the triumph of virtue over vice, the reformation of the accomplished rake. This, one of the usual themes of the eighteenth century sentimental comedies, was the stock subject of most of the morality plays.[1]

And Felix Schelling, writing in 1908, speaks of the breaking off of single plays from the great mystery cycles in these terms:

In the fortitude of Judith, the repentance of Mary Magdalene, or the sufferings of Job, men read themselves and felt a sympathy in the doings of such protagonists which could not always have animated them among the deeper mysteries symbolized in the life of the Saviour.[2]

This raises a question which is provocative, but not vital to the present discussion. How much did religious feeling interfere with the spectator's identification of himself with one of the personages of the mystery cycles? To put the question in another way: How much did religious feeling tend to absorb into itself the emotional response of the spectator? And was there an emotional response other than the religious, an emotional response similar to that evoked by later, sentimental drama? Schelling's statement indicates that he believed in the existence of this kind of response, and one is inclined to agree with him. On the basis of this belief it is even possible to speak of the seeds of sentimentalism existing in the religious cycles. Some scholars have remarked that dramatic treatments of the Prodigal Son theme show evidences of sentimentalism, and it is not difficult to equate the Prodigal Son with the repentant rake who is so familiar a character in sentimental drama. One could easily take the bare outlines of one of these Prodigal Son plays, furnish the characters with real names (in place of the abstract ones they bear), tone down the religious-didactic note, cut out the broad comedy which obtains (in some plays of the type), and one would have a sentimental comedy. The point need not be argued further; there is no real disagreement on it.

The preceding discussion may serve to show that elements of sentimentalism have been recognized in the morality plays. The sentimental response, it can be stated with confidence, is greater when the spectator identifies himself with a character who bears a name and surname like his own rather than with one who loses some of his immediacy because he is called Everyman or Mankind. One should expect, then, to find this early sentimentalism passing into the English drama when the moralities gave way to drama of a more secular nature. Two quotations will help to demonstrate the validity of such an expectation. The first is from a discussion of the eighteenth-century novel, but it is quite *apropos* here.

Although the words which describe them are new, sentiment and sensibility are as old as human nature. The desire to be moved by fictitious sorrows is a healthy instinct which has sought satisfaction in every age. . . . The need for an emotional outlet was acknowledged frankly by the Elizabethan and Jacobean dramatists. The age which produced *Dr. Faustus* and *The Broken Heart* had no self-conscious mistrust of feelings.[3]

The second emphasizes the presence of sentimental features in Restoration drama, but also glances at the Elizabethan period.

But recognizing, as every student of Elizabethan drama must, that all the conventional features of sentimental comedy had been for generations the common property of English playwrights, we need not be surprised to encounter, even in the very midst of the Restoration period, sporadic performances combining enough of these features to qualify them as accepted specimens of the type.[4]

It seems evident, hence, that sentimentalism had its place in Elizabethan drama. Many writers have seen fit to apply "sentimental" or one of its derivatives to single characters, situations, isolated passages or scenes, and even to whole plays in the period up to the closing of the theatres. Often the words are used loosely, or in a restricted sense; less frequently they are used in the stricter sense in which they appear in discussions of sentimentalism in drama—that is, in the sense of the definitions already studied. An application of these words in their loose employment is to be seen in references to Shakespeare and to Fletcher. Examples of the stricter use of "sentimental," etc., are frequent in comments on some of Thomas Heywood's plays.

Before listing a number of references which show the use of "sentimental" and its derivatives in various comments on Elizabethan dramatists, a warning must be sounded. There is no intention to criticize the use of these terms by the scholars from whose work they have been wrenched bodily. Such criticism of a single phrase detached from its context is manifestly unjust. Rather, it is the purpose of this procedure to indicate that some features of the drama before 1660 have been thought of as sentimental, and that an examination of Elizabethan drama will prove helpful in a study of sentimentalism. That is to say, the conclusion that certain Elizabethan plays, or scenes from plays, are or are not sentimental can be of great importance, and the fact that other students have chosen to apply the term "sentimental" to them becomes then of significance. No thought, however, of using these chance references as evidence for determining the sentimental or non-sentimental status of any dramatist is intended.

Since a slight suggestion of opprobrium attaches to our modern use of "sentimental," and an almost indefinable hint of lack of emotional control is associated with the word, critics of Shakespeare have been almost unanimously chary of applying it to him. Some critics, however, have thought it necessary to defend him from the charge of being a senti- mentalist. Discussing Shakespeare's treatment of love and marriage, C. H. Herford says:

He was no sentimentalist; his pathos is never morbid; but it is in imagining souls of texture fine and pure enough to be wrought upon to the most piteous extreme by slander from the man they love that Shakespeare found most of his loveliest yet most authentically Shakespearian characters of women; Hermione and Hero, Desdemona and Imogen, are to his graver art what Rosalind and Beatrice and Portia are to his comedy.[5]

This statement can be accepted without comment. There have been, however, some uses of "sentimental" in connection with Shakespeare's plays. Here are a few: Alwin Thaler speaks of "the sentimental Olivia and the super-sentimental Duke"; O. J. Campbell of "the sentimental story of Viola, Orsino, and Olivia"; and John Palmer of "Orsino who is an exquisitely comic man of sentiment as suitor to Olivia." The last-named writer thinks of the Christians in *The Merchant of Venice* as "impulsive, sentimental, and wayward"; and he calls the encounters of the lords and ladies in *Love's Labour's Lost* "sentimental." Frank Chapman Sharp calls Macbeth "a sentimentalizing dealer in phrases"; E. E. Stoll mentions the "sentimentality" of Jacques; and George H. McKnight adds Romeo to the list of Shakespeare's "sentimental" characters. Schucking attaches the adjective "sentimental" to Romeo, Troilus, and Helen (of *All's Well That Ends Well*). Edward Dowden, asserting that "the melancholy of Jacques is not grave and earnest, but sentimental," also enrolls Hamlet's mother and Richard II in the muster of Shakespeare's "sentimental" characters. A. H. Thorndike even goes so far as to speak of some of Shakespeare's plays as sentimental comedies.[6] It will be noted that the term "sentimental" has been used most frequently of characters in the plays, and not of Shakespeare as a dramatist. Shakespeare portrays sentimental characters; he is not, himself, a sentimental writer.

The tragicomedies of Fletcher and his various collaborators have had certain aspects labeled sentimental. An extreme instance of the fondness for "sentimental" and its derivatives appears in A. H. Thorndike's *The Influence of Beaumont and Fletcher on Shakespeare*. On one page (116) there occur no less than eight uses of "sentimental": "sentimental love" (three times), "sentimental" bliss, devotion, emotions, comedy, and "sentimental and tragic interest." F. H. Ristine acknowledges his indebtedness to Thorndike in his work on English tragicomedy, and he, too, demonstrates some fondness for "sentimental." He confines his use, generally, to the phrases "sentimental love" and "sentimental" heroes or heroines. Later writers have sometimes used the term in connection with certain of the Beaumont and Fletcher plays. Lawrence B. Wallis, discussing *Monsieur Thomas*, speaks of "the sentimental, essentially tragicomic story of Frank, Cellide and Valentine." Tucker Brooke, in the *Literary History of England* (1948), calls *Monsieur Thomas* "very uproarious and also very sentimental" and states that *The Maid's Tragedy* "is rather sentimental than tragic." Another critic distinguishes Fletcher's share in *The Two Noble Kinsmen* by, among other features, its "sentimental" craftsmanship.[7]

The Elizabethan dramatist most often called a sentimentalist, however, is Thomas Heywood; some of his plays have even been frequently called sentimental comedies. It will be sufficient for the moment to quote a number of relevant passages from various scholars without trying to conclude the relative value of each. The question whether Heywood is a sentimentalist will not be answered, although the reader will be in a better position to answer this question for himself after finishing the present work. F. T. Wood states unequivocally that

The most important and consistent exponent of sentimental comedy in the Elizabethan age was Thomas Heywood . . . in *The Fair Maid of the West* (1617), *The English Traveller* (1625, printed 1633), and *The Wise Woman of Hogsdon* . . . he struck out into comedy of a decided sentimental cast. . . . *The English Traveller* centres around the story of Mistress Wincott, who keeps herself free from all taint . . . In both of these plays [*The English Traveller* and *The Fair Maid of the West*] the heroine is sentimentally conceived.[8]

It will not escape notice that Wood speaks of Heywood as "the most important and consistent exponent of sentimental comedy in the Elizabethan age," implying, of course, that there were other Elizabethan writers of sentimental comedies. Since Wood is discussing sentimental comedies he naturally omits *A Woman Killed With Kindness*, the one play of Heywood's that has been most often referred to as sentimental. T. S. Eliot's coupling of Mrs. Frankford with the Little Em'lys of nineteenth-century fiction is well-known, but he is only one of many to regard Heywood's play as sentimental. A. W. Ward calls the play "a typical example of the sentimental family drama." A. H. Thorndike terms it a "sentimental comedy." Katherine Lee Bates says that "even its sentimentality is English." Otelia Cromwell regards the main plot of the play as "sentimental tragedy," and the "secondary action" as "sentimental comedy." Arthur Melville Clark links Heywood, in a discussion of *A Woman Killed With Kindness*, with Richardson. His words are worth quoting: "In another way Heywood may be regarded as the forerunner of Richardson, the school of sensibility, and the *comédie larmoyante* of the eighteenth century."[9]

The view that *A Woman Killed With Kindness* is a sentimental play is the favored one, but there are those who hold the contrary opinion. Philipp Aronstein absolves it from any imputation of sentimentalism.

Das stück, wohl das erste rührdrama der modernen literatur, hält sich frei von den klippen dieser gattung, falscher sentimentalität und rührseligkeit, und gehört sicherlich zu den hervorragendsten dramen der zeit.

Another defense of *A Woman Killed With Kindness* against the charge of sentimentalism is found in one of the many anthologies in which it appears.

Neither in the climactic scenes nor in the equally difficult scenes of Mrs. Frankford's repentance and death in act five, does he allow intrusion of sentimentality. Frankford indulges in no false heroics, Mrs. Frankford in no mawkish agonizings. No better illustration could be found of the difference between true sentiment and false sentimentality; the sentimental dramatists of the eighteenth century could have studied this play with profit.

Bernbaum also maintains that *A Woman Killed With Kindness* is not a sentimental play (p. 36), and Hallett H. Smith, after reviewing previous criticism of the play, concludes: "Viewed in its place in the tradition, the catastrophe of *A Woman Killed With Kindness* is not sentimental."[10] The question is obviously a vexed one. The writers cited have all been decided in their views; either they thought of Heywood as a sentimentalist or they did not. One writer, however, seems unable to decide, and one tends to sympathize with his indecision. Mowbray Velte speaks of "the tender-hearted and sentimental Heywood" and of "Heywood's sentimental mind." He calls the death of Jane Shore and her husband (*II Edward IV*) "a piece of sentimentality very characteristic of the most sentimental of Elizabethan dramatists," speaks of the "sentimentality" of *A Woman Killed With Kindness*, and says of *The English Traveller* that "the tone of the whole narrative is sentimental." Yet he concludes:

To me there is little mawkishness in Heywood's sentiment. The sophisticated may sneer at it, and call it sentimentality, but though it may verge on that it seldom if ever crosses the border-line that separates sentimentality from true feeling. Heywood was too simple-hearted himself ever to be sentimental in the worst sense of the word, and it is only a cynic that dare call him so.[11]

The many other references to Heywood and his plays as sentimental need not be catalogued. The point is clear: at least one Elizabethan dramatist has been consistently accused of writing sentimental plays and has been defended against the charge.

When another scholar can entitle one of the chapters in a book on Elizabethan and Jacobean playwrights "Sentimental Tragedy"[12] the need to scrutinize the period before 1660 becomes more and more apparent to the student of sentimental drama. Actually, it will be remembered, the numerous uses of "sentimental" that have been cited in connection with Shakespeare, Fletcher, and Heywood were listed solely to point up the necessity of such a study. No careful examination of this large corpus of dramatic literature has been made by any student of sentimentalism. The period of the Restoration, it is true, has been the subject of greater scrutiny by students of sentimental drama, but there, too, much remains to be done. It is to be hoped that new light will be thrown upon the whole question by an examination of Elizabethan and Restoration plays. The method followed is selective rather than exhaustive.

Analysis of definitions of sentimentalism in the drama has revealed certain points of agreement among various writers. Sentimental drama includes:

1. The presence of a moral element, variously designated as a "moral problem," "moral treatment," or "moral purpose."
2. An element of the artificial, illogical, exaggerated, or improbable (very often in the treatment of emotion).
3. Good or perfectible human beings as characters.
4. An appeal to the emotions rather than to the intellect.
5. An emphasis on pity, with tears for the good who suffer, and admiration for the virtuous.

Here, essentially, are what previous writers have considered the basic characteristics of sentimental drama. These features are not always all present in plays which have almost unanimously been called sentimental, but usually only one of them is lacking. That is to say, these five basic elements which have emerged from an analysis of definitions of sentimentalism have all the appearance of affording a reliable method or check system for determining whether a play is sentimental. There can be no doubt that certain of these characteristics, taken alone or in combination with others, appear in plays which have not been, and cannot be, called sentimental. The question then suggests itself: Can these features, thought peculiar to sentimental drama in their appearance together, occur together in plays which are not of the genre? If plays can be found which exhibit all the features of sentimentalism common to existent definitions, and these plays, it can be agreed, are not sentimental, the inevitable conclusion must be that there are other vital factors which have been overlooked or slighted.

A startling example of the unreliability of the definition that has been arrived at is afforded by an examination of Fletcher and Massinger's *The Custom of the Country* (c. 1620). In the "Preface to the Fables" Dryden, whose own use of bawdry in his plays qualified him to judge, declares roundly that "there is more bawdry in one play of Fletcher's called *The Custom of the Country*, than in all ours together." In 1700, the year of the Preface, such a statement gains a very dubious fame for Fletcher's play. Those who have read to any extent in the dramatists of the Restoration will realize what a remarkable claim Dryden is making. One would not, then, expect to find that *The Custom of the Country* can be called a sentimental comedy with complete accuracy, accepting the definition that has been evolved. Such is actually the case, however. There is a moral problem in Fletcher's play—indeed, there are several. The element of artificiality and the exaggerated is present to a pronounced degree. Good or perfectible human beings are present in the *dramatis personae* to the number of four or five. Finally, there is pity for the good in distress and admiration for the virtuous, and this is effected by an appeal to the emotions rather than to the intellect. The characters even partially satisfy a condition that has been found in some definitions of sentimental drama, but which has been ruled out as not essential to it: they are from the "more ordinary walks of life."

In *The Custom of the Country* a mother who does not know that her cherished son has been killed promises to help the murderer escape the pursuing officers. When the officers break into her home on the track of the murderer she learns that the murdered man is her son. The laws of hospitality demand that she shield the murderer to whom she has vowed protection, but her mother-love cries out for immediate revenge. This is a moral problem; tied up, it is true, with what may now seem a fantastic code of ethics, but a problem nevertheless. In the same play a young wife, her marriage still unconsummated, is threatened with instant death unless her husband satisfy the lust of another woman. Shall she save her life at the expense of her husband's chastity, or shall she embrace death in the knowledge that he will remain chaste? This is a second moral problem. The young husband is courted by another woman, and fed and bribed handsomely to satisfy her concupiscence. All this occurs when he has landed in a strange country, without money or friends. Shall he lapse from his chaste state (who would be the wiser?) and know that his future ease is assured, or shall he refuse the beautiful and rich stranger's advances because he would keep his virginity for his wife, who might by that time be dead or dishonored? This, like the others, is also a moral problem.

The play under discussion has a character, Count Clodio, who enjoys the privilege known as *le droit du seigneur*. He is passionately desirous of enjoying Zenocia, the exemplar of female chastity, is thwarted in his attempts, and finally gives up his pursuit of her when he suddenly reforms —even to the extent of doing away with a custom from which he derived so much pleasure and revenue. In addition to Zenocia and her husband Arnoldo, himself of an invincible chastity, there is Hippolyta, who tempts Arnoldo and tries to kill Zenocia, but who finally also reforms and promises to atone for her previous evil by a program of good works. And to complete the roll there is Duarte, a vainglorious quarrelsome young man, who seeks out the man that almost killed him in a duel, delivers him from a painful if unusual servitude, and announces his intention to turn over a new leaf. These characters satisfy the condition of the working definition of sentimental drama that insists on good or perfectible human beings.

The suggestions of plot action which have come out in the course of this discussion of *The Custom of the Country* indicate to some extent that the element of the improbable, exaggerated, or artificial which has been asserted to be indispensable to sentimental drama is also present. Count Clodio's reform is both unmotivated and sudden. He leaves Italy in furious pursuit of Zenocia, assuring her wretched father that if he "miss her," the consequences will be on his, Charino's, head (II, i). On his next appearance he is comforting Charino: "Assure thyself, Charino, I am alter'd/From what I was—" (III, v). There is no reason given for this complete about-face. Hippolyta's reform is as abrupt and as mysterious as Clodio's (V, v). Duarte causes the knowledge of his recovery from his wounds to be kept from his mother who mourns him as dead, and this, it develops, merely to see how long his mother's grief will last (IV, i). This desire to refine on emotion will be subsequently remarked as one of the stigmata of eighteenth-century sentimental plays. Later Duarte tests his mother's virtue in a fashion that must strike any modern reader as unfilial, to state it mildly. Guiomar, Duarte's mother, ends a play which would seem to have had enough of the artificial and improbable in it already by marrying Rutilio, considerably her junior and practically a stranger to her. It was Rutilio who had wounded Duarte in the duel. There is little need to quote sample passages as further evidence of the essential artificiality of the play.

Finally, that all parts of the working definition be satisfied, there is pity for the suffering of the good and admiration for virtue. Zenocia and

Arnoldo are subjected to insult and injury, threatened death, and—what would be infinitely more tragic—loss of chastity in the course of the play. The end of the play sees them cured of a fatal sickness, the result of charms, by Hippolyta's conversion. Hero and heroine are so painfully good that pity for their suffering and admiration for their virtue seem an act of presumption: there is a divinity that looks out for these rare creatures. This is not, however, a feeling that is absent when one turns to contemplate eighteenth-century heroes and heroines (particularly the latter) of sentimental drama. It is quite obvious that the appeal in the play is to the emotions, hardly to the intellect.

The Custom of the Country displays all the necessary characteristics of sentimental comedy. Two conclusions are possible: either it is a sentimental comedy, and this is difficult to accept when one remembers Dryden's remark (one need only follow Rutilio's career in the "male-stews" to see what he meant), or it is not. Either conclusion leads one inevitably to a reconsideration of the working definition. In the first place there must be some attempt to reconcile bawdry and sentimentalism. (The presence of the bawdry, it must be stressed, is only one factor which prevents the play from being sentimental). Such a reconciliation is impossible, for the two are antagonistic. The spectator or reader whose lubricous nature is titillated, or whose sense of the sexually comic is appealed to, is not in the proper frame of mind to sympathize with distressed virtue. When one has been treated to the spectacle of sexual degradation, even if handled comically, it is too much to ask that one, a few minutes later, look upon a chaste heroine with the admiration that is compatible with her virtue or the pity that should be shown for her suffering. This is, however, to anticipate later discussion. If the play is not to be regarded as sentimental, it is obvious that there is something lacking in the definition that has resulted from previous investigation. There are many more plays, both of the Elizabethan and Restoration periods, that can be demonstrated to fit the working definition. One could apply the method that is being used to more modern plays with equal success. In examining a number of other plays the emphasis will be on showing how they fit the definition; explanation of why these same plays are not sentimental will have to await subsequent discussion.

The "abused wife" is no infrequent member of the *dramatis personae* of sentimental drama. Cibber, best described as a shrewd man of the theatre rather than as a sentimentalist of any demonstrable sincerity, used her almost to the point of ridiculousness. Elizabethan dramatists were fond of her, and one student of the drama of that period speaks of "a series of more than twenty extant plays dealing with the sorrows of injured wives."[13] Discussing *The London Prodigal*, one in the series, the same scholar is reminded of eighteenth-century sentimental drama.

Although it belongs to the general group ["abused wife" plays] under discussion, it has shaken off most of the devices of Italian romance and stands alone
as one of the first naturalistic dramas in English. Moreover it so nearly
approaches in theme and tone the sentimental drama of the eighteenth century
that the very real differences between it and the later plays on the same
subject are not instantly apparent. The setting is contemporary London. A
father, giving out that he has died abroad, disguises himself, enters the employ
of his prodigal son and proceeds to manage his affairs. He arranges a marriage
for him with the virtuous daughter of Sir Lancelot Spurcock but becomes so
disgusted with his son's mercenary attitude towards the match that he causes
him to be arrested for debt on his wedding day, hoping that this calamity
may bring him to terms. The prodigal is deserted by all save his faithful wife,
but her sacrifice does not alter in the least his riotous course. He blasphemes
the memory of his father, casts off his faithful servant, tries to filch from his
wife the pittance which a compassionate uncle had given and finally casts
her off . . . In the end she is the means of saving his life. Her father intends to
prosecute him for murder since she is not to be found, but her appearance at
the right moment prevents his arrest. A complete reconciliation takes place
and the prodigal is reformed. Because this moving scene is made the more joyful
by the promise of a large dowry and the prospect of material blessings for
the re-betrothed pair, an inevitable accompaniment to most eighteenth-century
dramas of regeneration, some have been inclined to call this play a genuine
sentimental drama. This important difference is to be noted. Sentimental
drama as it was known in its great day . . . assumed the fundamental goodness
of human nature as a postulate. Sin became, therefore, an aberration resulting
from evil counsel or ignorance. But the Elizabethans were far from being
Rousseauists. This particular sinner is pictured from the beginning as a
thoroughly depraved young man, utterly wanting in any tender feeling or
natural affection. His reformation comes as a kind of baptism, a giving over of
the sins of the world by the regenerative power of his wife's virtue. The
beast of original sin within him has, as it were, been slain. (pp. 91-92)

The summary of the plot indicates clearly enough that *The London
Prodigal* satisfies the conditions of our model definition, even if it does
not emerge as a sentimental play for Thorp. For him the difference between sentimental drama and this play is the fact that the play does not
assume the "fundamental goodness of human nature as a postulate." The
objection is that the hero, young Flowerdale, "is pictured from the
beginning as a thoroughly depraved young man, utterly wanting in any
tender feeling or natural affection." But Thorp loses sight of the fact
that the fundamental goodness of human nature is sometimes demonstrated
in sentimental drama by the reform of a vicious character who need not
show any evidence of that innate goodness until the play is ready to end.[14]
Thorp's remarks on *The London Prodigal* are immediately followed by
his comments on George Wilkins' *Miseries of Enforced Marriage*, and
it is surprising that he does not point out that the hero of the latter play

does satisfy the condition for sentimental drama which was wanting in the former. Young Scarborow is a good man[15] whose cruelty to his wife is the result of his being forced to marry her. As a result of this marriage Clare, with whom he had plighted troth, takes her own life.[16] If one must have an amiable, good man for sentimental hero, he is certainly present in the person of Young Scarborow. In addition there is a moral problem; the question of the justice, as well as the consequences, of forced marriages. Young Scarborow, Clare, and Katherine, Scarborow's wife, are all three fundamentally good people, and there is a definite appeal to the emotions in the death of Clare and the ill-treatment of Katherine. The element of the artificial or improbable enters in the last act with its reconciliations on all hands. *The Miseries of Enforced Marriage*, even more than *The London Prodigal*, seems to demand admission into the sentimental canon.

Domestic tragedy of the Elizabethan age would, then, seem a logical place to expect to find sentimentalism. It certainly provided eighteenth-century sentimental dramatists with very effective vehicles for their sentimental effects, and there is no reason to doubt that the genre was equally amenable to such exploitation in the late sixteenth and early seventeenth centuries. One of the most powerful domestic tragedies in Elizabethan dramatic literature is *A Yorkshire Tragedy*, of unknown authorship. The plot can be given in a few words. A husband who has gambled everything away kills two of his children, wounds his loving wife, and is apprehended as he is on his way to kill the third child. His motive for the murders was the wish to save his children from a life of beggary. Before he is executed he is reconciled to his wife and kisses the bodies of his children. The wife is pictured as loving, patient, forbearing; and she is subjected to considerable abuse and cruelty, being called whore, harlot, strumpet, and filth by her husband. Despite its sentimental possibilities—it contains most of the necessary characteristics—the play is not sentimental.

Some suggestion of the difference between *A Yorkshire Tragedy* and a sentimental drama will come out in a comparison of the Elizabethan play with two eighteenth-century plays adapted from it. Aaron Hill's *The Fatal Extravagance* (1721), a one-act play, depicts a good man coming to a bad end because of weakness rather than because of any real viciousness. Bellmour, the husband, is of tender sensibilities; he cannot bear to see others suffering. "Bellmour could ne'er behold a stranger wretched, But he partook his pain, 'till he could ease it," says his wife Louisa.[17] He is more concerned for Woodly, a friend who has signed a bond as guarantor for him and cannot now pay it, than for himself. But he has been driven to kill his merciless creditor Bargrave and has decided on suicide. Unlike his prototype in *A Yorkshire Tragedy* he loves his

wife dearly, and his decision to poison her—the most painless death
he can think of—is motivated by the desire to save her from want and
derision after his own death. Louisa and her children are saved by her
uncle's substitution of a harmless drink for the poison intended for them
by Bellmour. Bellmour dies from self-inflicted wounds as Courtney comes
in, just too late, to tell him that his rich brother, long thought dead, has
returned with a great fortune. The sentimental effect is heightened in
Hill's play by making Bellmour admirable, rather than detestable. The
husband in *A Yorkshire Tragedy* is the victim of demoniac influence[18]
and his suffering does not evoke the sympathy that is gained for Bellmour
by the dramatist's frequent references to the latter's innate goodness.

The gratuitous irony, capitalized upon by Hill, of good news arriving
too late by a matter of moments is a device which lends itself admirably
to the sentimentalist's purpose. The sense of "the pity of it all" is touched
more acutely by the realization that the solution to all difficulties was just
at hand, but did not, alas, arrive in time. One recalls the same device in
St. John Ervine's *John Ferguson* and would willingly forget its use
in many other plays. *A Yorkshire Tragedy* ends on a grim note, unrelieved by any promise of hope. The Master of the College has the final
speech:

> I must returne with griefe; my answer's set:
> I shall bring newes weies heavier then the debt.—
> Two brothers: one in bond lies overthrowne,
> This on a deadlier execution.

Although Hill's play is sentimental enough, it remained for a later playwright to supply the one twist that made a sentimental comedy out of
what had been a sentimental tragedy. Using Hill's adaptation, a late
eighteenth-century writer, seeing no reason why Bellmour should die,
took it upon himself to have Courtney arrive in time to prevent Bellmour
from stabbing himself. The same rich brother is reported in the offing,
and lest the legally-minded in the audience raise hypercritical objections
about the slaying of Bargrave, that worthy is announced to be alive,
having been only wounded. The play ends with this stage direction:
"Louisa and Bellmour kneel, in adoration of, and gratitude to Heaven;
then embrace their Uncle, and each other."[19] The sentimentalist is
confronted with a Hobson's choice: he may weep tears of sorrow at the
death of a good Bellmour in Hill's play, or he may smile through misty
eyes at the tableau which ends the later play. Neither response is possible
with *A Yorkshire Tragedy*.

Pastoral drama is, by very definition, artificial. There are invariably one
or more chaste shepherdesses or shepherds, and often there are sexually

aggressive "nymphs" and "swains" who, resorting to trickery or villainy to achieve their purposes, finally abjure their evil ways and embrace the good life. The retention of chastity even to almost pathological extremes can be assumed to imply the presence of a moral problem. The appeal is unmistakably to the emotions rather than to the intellect, and pity is aroused for suffering; admiration, for virtue. In short, the whole genre fits the definition of sentimental drama. The term "sentimental" has been used to describe pastoral drama and its creators,[20] but here it seems to suggest only a certain lushness of phrase and a readiness to indulge in emotion on the slightest provocation. Actually, of course, the latter is an important feature of sentimentalism. John Fletcher's pastoral effort, his bid for poetic immortality, is an almost direct descendant of Guarini's *Pastor Fido* which ends with chastity triumphant and the villainess of the piece, Corsica, repentant and forgiven. In *The Faithful Shepherdess* virtue is triumphant, and evil, in the persons of Amarillis, Cloe, and Alexis (representing unchaste love) is forgiven after an expression of repentance. But *The Faithful Shepherdess* is not the only pastoral of this period. Another example will emphasize the point being made. Samuel Daniel wrote two pastorals, *The Queen's Arcadia* and *Hymen's Triumph*. The first is modeled on Tasso's *Aminta* and Guarini's *Pastor Fido*, and shows obvious direct imitation. In a comparison of the same scene in the *Aminta* and in *The Queen's Arcadia* (that of the discovery by the nymph of the supposedly dead swain who has destroyed himself for love of her) W. W. Gregg suggests that

. . . if Daniel's treatment of the scene, which is typical of a good deal of his work, has the power to call a tear to the eye of sensibility, his sentiment, divested as it is of the Italian's subtle sensuousness, appears perfectly innocuous and at times not a little ridiculous.

In another place Gregg says of Daniel

. . . if his conception of virtue is more wholesome [than his Italian models], his picture of it is at times marred by exaggeration, while his sentiment for innocence is of a watery kind, and occasionally a little tawdry. His pathos, as is the case with all weak writers, constantly trembles on the verge of bathos, while his lack of humour betrays him into penning passages of elaborate fatuity.[21]

Without wishing to attach too much importance to Gregg's use of phrases which have, through constant application to sentimentalism, become associated with that phenomenon, one cannot resist noting the words used to describe Daniel's work, which has "the power to call a tear to the eye of sensibility." These are the words of one scholar applied to the work of one man, and they are not submitted as direct evidence.

Taken in conjunction with the fact that pastoral drama satisfies the terms of the definition of sentimental drama, however, they assume some significance.

There is another way in which a play may, by a kind of innocent misrepresentation, seem a candidate for sentimental honors. For example, very little of a play's individuality can be revealed by reducing it to its *sine qua non*, the story. Whether drama employs speech or only gesture it must tell some kind of story. The story is the skeleton of the play. In recounting the story of a play one is actually practicing a kind of scarification, stripping from the bones the flesh—that is, language, characterization, emotion, etc. Anyone who has been asked to tell what happens in some great play, or novel, or poem has known the sense of helplessness and inadequacy that is felt. So, too, in isolating one part of a play for comment in this discussion an injustice has been done it. Yet just such a method as this must be used to show that the presence of a number of sentimental situations and reconciliations occurring in the denouement of a play does not necessarily make that play of the sentimental genre. This fact takes on greater importance later in determining the sentimentalism of many plays of the eighteenth century. *The Spanish Gypsy* (1623) has a fifth act which involves four situations, any one of which might have been the basis for a sentimental play. A repentant rake reforms and marries the girl he has ravished. A vicious woman, appalled at the evil she had tried to do, repents and is forgiven. A son is reconciled to his father's slayer. Finally, a daughter, long believed dead, is restored to her father. The possibilities these situations have for eliciting the kind of response that eighteenth-century sentimental dramatists worked for is obvious. Indeed, there is an embarrassment of riches here; the tugs on the heart-strings come thick and fast. Actually, of course, *The Spanish Gypsy* does not provoke any such response. Familiarity with the play will suggest reasons for this seeming paradox; one's own explanation will not be wanting.

While sentimentalism in Elizabethan drama has received only cursory study by scholars, more attention has been centered on appearances of sentimentalism in the last decades of the seventeenth century. Often the attempts to read sentimentalism into some of these Restoration and post-Restoration plays seem a trifle forced. An exception occurs with Thomas Southerne whose *The Disappointment* (1684), *The Fatal Marriage* (1694), and *Oroonoko* (1696) have definite affinities with eighteenth-century sentimental drama. In the conclusion of his study of Southerne as a dramatist, J. W. Dodds says of the first play:

. . . it appears to have gone unnoticed that as early as 1684 Southerne wrote a comedy in which the entire main plot expressed the moralized emotions later known to sentimental drama. In *The Disappointment* were anticipated the characters that Cibber and Steele were to make famous: the loyal wife whose virtue triumphs in the end; the man and maid whose love was untouched by any cynical contempt of marriage; the faithful friend; the spurned mistress who is at last married to her former lover; and the rake purged just in time for the fifth-act curtain. Pathos is stronger here than wit, human nature is found to be fundamentally good, and aroused sensibilities find issue in an emotion altogether moral. The history of sentimentalism in England cannot afford to ignore this early appearance of a play that adumbrates, perhaps more clearly than any original comedy prior to *Love's Last Shift*, the approach of the new drama.[22]

Dodds has pointed out most of the features in the play that fit the definition that has been set up, but he is careful to avoid calling the play a sentimental comedy; he says only that it "adumbrates . . . the approach of the new drama." He labels a section of his chapter on *The Disappointment* "Restoration Comedy Sentimentalised," and it is this description of the play that is noteworthy. Southerne is not writing a new kind of play; he is only doing something to an old type. This is an important distinction, for it is intrinsically bound up with the larger consideration of the different emphases that will be shown to play so large a part in determining what sentimental drama is.

Enough plays have been described to warrant the assumption that the nature of the paradox confronting the student of sentimental drama is clear. Reduced to simplest terms it is this: plays which should, by definition, be looked upon as sentimental are not. Those plays which have been selected to demonstrate the existence of the paradox have represented different genres. *The Custom of the Country* is a tragicomedy. *The London Prodigal* and *The Miseries of Enforced Marriage*, not properly tragicomedies, are domestic comedies in which a large element of the serious is present. *The Yorkshire Tragedy* is a domestic tragedy, *The Faithful Shepherdess* is a pastoral (although Fletcher calls it a tragicomedy), and *The Spanish Gypsy* is closer to tragicomedy than to any other genre. There is no insistence that these designations be accepted unreservedly. It is enough if they show how various kinds of plays can be fitted into the definition that is being studied. Inevitably, because sentimental comedy, described so often as something between tragedy and comedy, partakes of the serious there is the realization that tragicomedy comes closer to the type than any other genre. Ristine suggests that many of the essentials of tragicomedy were adopted into sentimental comedy, and speaks of the latter's "generic resemblance" to the former. It is true he concludes "that there is scant lineal relation between the two forms,"[23] but he has seen, as who must not, that there are definite features held in common.

The plays which have been described are but a very few of a great number that might have been used as examples. With the definition before him the reader can himself add plays that should be sentimental, in that they satisfy the requirements, but are not. It is fairly obvious that many of the tragicomedies of Fletcher and his collaborators will suggest themselves—there is no need to enumerate them. Plays which give prominence to abused wives and repentant profligates are, of course, fruitful fields for exploration. Possibly tragedies which might very well have been something other than tragedies except for the almost mechanical decimation that occurs in the catastrophe may be studied with profit. And taking the palpably artificial emotion that informs many plays as a point of departure, one may proceed to a point-by-point comparison of the terms of the definition with elements in the plays under examination. The working method by which some plays have been tested in this chapter admits of wide application. It is one thing to apply the method; it is another to account for the results with which one finds himself. Some hints have been dropped in previous discussion, but hardly enough to permit one's reaching any justifiable decision concerning the resolution of the paradox. That such a resolution is possible is the premise which must be examined.

Chapter III. REPETITION AND PROLONGATION

REPETITION IS ONE of the most important devices for attracting and focusing attention; propagandists and advertising men fully recognize its value. The repetition *ad nauseum* which characterizes modern advertising is also encountered with great frequency in sentimental drama, and it is partly the use of repetition and prolonged treatment of certain situations or themes which causes sentimental drama to be branded inferior. Modern propaganda, particularly in World War II, has shown that the grossest perversions of truth are accepted if only they are repeated often enough and at sufficient length. The incredible is made credible simply because it has been repeated to such an extent that it becomes familiar and hence believable. So, too, in a sentimental play it is usually sufficient for the dramatist to state enough times that a particular character is really good at heart for the audience to accept him as basically good, despite visual evidence to the contrary. Thus, a character who appears very often in sentimental drama is the forlorn maiden, usually an orphan (at least for four acts), who is beset by temptation, but who maintains an impregnable chastity. The typical sentimental treatment of such a character includes references, any number of them, to her wretched, friendless state; to the parent or parents whom she never knew; to her present destitution; to her readiness to undertake any menial employment rather than compromise her chastity; and to the dangers by which she is beset. Generally these references are frequent and long drawn out. The dramatist evidently depends upon them to evoke the requisite sympathy for his distressed heroine. That there are other, far more subtle ways of arousing pity is obvious to anyone who has read the major Elizabethan dramatists with any care. One is tempted to make the sweeping generalization that a sentimental play is never a great play because the two are a contradiction in terms—that, by very definition, a sentimental play cannot be great. The improbable, the illogical, the exaggerated, or the artificial that is an inevitable concomitant of sentimentalism is always related to spurious emotion, what Krutch calls "facile and usually, shallow, illogical emotion."[1] In short, when the emotion is genuine, and not disproportionate to that circumstance which evoked it, one can no longer accurately speak of sentimentalism.

Another favorite character of sentimental drama is the "repentant rake." It is understood, of course, that these characters are not peculiar to sentimental drama. That statement has been made, but it does not merit refutation. The reader or spectator is treated to a picture of a seemingly vicious young man indulging himself in various interesting forms of dissipation, practicing physical or mental cruelty on some un-offending and good female, and endangering the lives or well-being of other persons. Sometimes the dramatist inserts little hints whose purpose is to warn one that Bellmour (there are a surprising number of Bellmours) is only sowing his wild oats and is really a decent sort of fellow at heart. Often the reader is totally unprepared for Bellmour's reform. How, then, does the playwright try to make the fifth-act reformation of his rake credible? Granting, only for purposes of argument, that any of the reformations of sentimental drama are credible, the answer is simple. The dramatist crowds into his last act as many speeches as he can give his repentant rake and still untangle all his plot complications. These speeches are wordy expressions of contrition and promises of turning over a new leaf, and they are made to every character from whom the rake feels he needs forgiveness. The rake protests so much that what he says is accepted. The viciousness of his career in the first four acts is overlooked as he kneels, vociferating feverishly, at the feet of his father, or his wife or his beloved, pleading for forgiveness.

The sentimentalist achieves certain results by the methods described above—repetition and prolonged treatment. The opposite of this method can be conveniently described as brevity of treatment; or, to put it another way, the deliberate hurrying over of an incident or circumstance or speech so that too much attention will not be focused upon it. When a situation full of sentimental possibilities is hurried over as though the playwright wanted merely to get the affair done with, the assumption is that he is not interested in sentimentalism and that his play is not senti-mental. Let the reader imagine a play in which the basic characteristics of sentimental drama are present, a play in which a young husband mis-treats his wife, deserts her, is unfaithful to her (in intent, if not in deed), but is finally reconciled to her and begs her forgiveness. The formula is a familiar one. If, in this play, much is made of the repentance and reformation of the husband, if he protests at great length that he is sorry for past misdeeds, and promises, also at some length, that things will be different in the future, there can be little doubt that the intent is sentimental. Another play, written on the same formula, shows the husband uttering a grudging request for pardon, and letting it go at that. The assumption here is that the intent is not sentimental. Shake-speare's *All's Well That Ends Well*, in its barest outlines, is a play written on the formula just mentioned. So, too, is Cibber's *Love's Last Shift*. Shakespeare's play has never, to the best of my knowledge, been claimed for the canon of sentimental comedy, but Cibber's play, with the exception of one or two dissenting voices, has not only been called a sentimental comedy but has even been claimed as the first

English specimen of that genre. The "sentimental" element in these plays, if it is present in both, is in the fifth-act conversions of Bertram and Loveless. It will be remembered that the situations in which Bertram and Loveless find themselves have definite points of similarity. Here is how Shakespeare disposes of the necessary business of the rake's conversion:

KING. Is there no exorcist
  Beguiles the truer office of mine eyes?
  Is't real that I see?
HEL. No, my good lord
  'Tis but the shadow of a wife you see,
  The name and not the thing.
BER. Both, both! O, pardon!
HEL. O my good lord, when I was like this maid
  I found you wondrous kind. There is your ring,
  And look you, here's your letter. This it says:
  'When from my finger you can get this ring,
  And are by me with child,' &c. This is done
  Will you be mine now you are doubly won?
BER. If she, my liege, can make me know this clearly,
  I'll love her dearly—ever, ever dearly. (V, iii, 305-17)

Bertram does not even have the grace to accept the truth of his wife's statement, as his hesitant "if" so clearly reveals. He is trapped, cannot extricate himself, and makes the best of things. Compare Bertram's few words to the torrent of speech that gushes from Loveless. Two speeches are quoted, but they are only part of a series in a similar vein.

LOVELESS. Oh, thou hast roused me from my deep lethargy of vice! For hitherto my soul has been enslaved to loose desires, to vain, deluding follies, and shadows of substantial bliss, but now I wake with joy to find my rapture real! Thus let me kneel and pray my thanks to her whose conquering virtue has at last subdued me. Here will I fix, thus prostrate sigh my shame, and wash my crimes in never-ceasing tears of penitence.
AMANDA. Oh rise! this posture heaps new guilt on me. How you over-pay me.
LOVELESS. Have I not used thee like a villain? For almost ten long years deprived thee of my love and ruined all thy fortune? But I will labor, dig, beg, or starve to give new proofs of my unfeigned affection.[2]

Loveless kneels, offers to weep, and even volunteers to "labor, dig, beg, or starve" (surely extreme measures for a Restoration gentleman) to prove his love for Amanda. Bertram, it is worth repeating, is taciturn and singularly undemonstrative. In both instances the ready reformation of the rake is incredible. In Shakespeare, who uses the convention of the fifth-act repentance to end his play,[3] the sentimental possibilities of the situation are deliberately overlooked. In Cibber, the reformation is capitalized upon through the equally deliberate use of repetition and prolongation. Here, then, is one of the factors that has been slighted by students of sentimental drama. Given two plays which demonstrate the same essential characteristics of sentimental drama as outlined earlier, one has been accepted as sentimental, the other has not. The difference lies in the exploitation of sentimental possibilities by repeated and prolonged emphasis on the one hand, and neglect of the same sentimental possibilities by brevity of treatment.

Criticism of the speedy fifth-act repentance which resolves all difficulties and permits the play to close on a happy note has been wide-spread. Quite naturally, most critics have justly remarked on the improbability of such reformations on the basis of the previous conduct of the rake who eventually reforms. The objection has been that there is no motivation, that one is not prepared for the happy denouement. And much of this criticism is leveled at Elizabethan last-minute reformations. Actually, of course, the use of fifth-act reformations came to be a convention of Elizabethan dramaturgy, and it should be accepted as such. The fact that rapidity of reformation was a convention does not weaken the argument that potential sentimentalism was kept under by its use. All Elizabethan plays which end with a repentance and forgiveness scene do not slight the scene by using the convention. Certainly Mistress Frankford is given plenty of time to say everything she wishes to say before she dies, and *A Woman Killed With Kindness* has been called sentimental drama more often than any other Elizabethan play largely because of its last scene. It is precisely this emphasis, this prolonged treatment of the situation which gains credibility for the scene—all consideration of the relative skill of that treatment aside. Along with this gain in credibility, even part of it, is a deepened emotional effect which is achieved by halting the action to allow the spectator to savor the emotional response that has been evoked. When the action hurries along, riding hastily rough-shod over a repentance scene, or leaving the scene out entirely and confronting the spectator with the *fait accompli*, there is no chance for an emotional bath. Omission of such a scene has been noted in Count Clodio's reformation in *The Custom of the Country;* short, hurried reformation scenes occur also in the same play with both Hippolyta and Duarte.[4] It must be understood that the credibility that is gained for reformation scenes by prolonged treatment is not the credibility of real life; it is rather a concocted credibility that belongs in the fundamentally artificial world of sentimental drama.

In the light of what has been said it is interesting to read a few comments by earlier critics who have taken exception to speedy reformations in the drama. Dryden, in his *Essay of Dramatic Poesy*, thinks the French free of this fault.

. . . the French have many other excellencies not common to us; as that you never see any of their plays end with a conversion, or simple change of will, which is the ordinary way which our poets use to end theirs. It shows little art in the conclusion of a dramatic poem, when they who have hindered the felicity during the first four acts, desist from it in the fifth, without some powerful cause to take them off; and though I deny not but such reasons may be found, yet it is a path that is cautiously to be trod, and the poet is to be sure he convinces the audience that the motive is strong enough.

He then objects to the reformation of the usurer in Fletcher's *The Scornful Lady*, who, being duped by a young gallant, forswears his covetousness. Dryden concludes: ". . . but that he should look on it as a judgment, and so repent, we may expect to hear of in a sermon, but I should never endure it in a play." Dryden's comments, and some of those to follow, do not necessarily concern themselves with plays that have been thought of as sentimental. Horace Walpole objects to the "sudden" reformations in Shakespeare, Fletcher, and Cibber.

The reformation of the termagant wife in The Taming of the Shrew is too sudden. So are those of Margaritta in Rule a Wife and have a Wife, and of Lady Townly in The Provoked Husband. Time or grace only operates such miracles.[5]

Samuel Richardson, using a literary genre which permitted him to spend as much time as he saw fit for the thorough enjoyment of sentimental effects, objected to the reform of Mrs. Clerimont in Steele's *The Tender Husband*. His spokesman is Pamela, (Letter 51): "Mr. Clerimont then upbraids her with her guilt; and what was hardly ever known in nature, she reforms *instantly* on the spot, and expresses all the signs of contrition possible." The author of *Pamela, Clarissa*, and *Sir Charles Grandison* knew the value of devoting enough time to the full exploitation of sentimental emotion. His remark supports the conclusion that brevity is inimical to sentimentalism. The next critic, Henry Fielding, has sometimes been suspected of showing some sympathy for the sentimental movement that was making itself felt in the literature of his day, but he is most often seen as a critic and satirist of sentimentalism, seldom as an advocate or practitioner of it. Some definitions of the sentimental hero, as applied to the novel, are broad enough to include Tom Jones, but he is saved from being one by the absence of the wishy-washy, sententious, and absolutely hypocritical trick of speech that distinguishes the type. In any event, Fielding has expressed his disgust with fifth-act conversions in no un-certain terms in *Tom Jones* (Book VIII, Chapt. I).

Our modern authors of comedy have fallen almost universally into the error here hinted at; their heroes generally are notorious rogues, and their heroines abandoned jades, during the first four acts; but in the fifth, the former become very worthy gentlemen, and the latter women of virtue and discretion: nor is the writer often so kind as to give himself the least trouble to reconcile or account for this monstrous change and incongruity. There is, indeed, no other reason to be assigned for it, than because the play is drawing to a conclusion; as if it was no less natural in a rogue to repent in the last act of a play, than in the last of his life; which we perceive to be generally the case of Tyburn, a place which might indeed close the scene of some comedies with much propriety, as the heroes in these are most commonly eminent for those very talents which not only bring men to the gallows, but enable them to make an heroic figure when they are there.

If there was any sympathy for sentimental drama in Fielding, it did not extend to an uncritical acceptance of the improbable endings that characterized the genre.

In view of our knowledge of Elizabethan dramaturgy and its conventions it comes as rather a surprise to find a careful scholar of the period forgetting himself to the point of applying present-day standards of taste in drama to a play of the earlier period. In a preliminary discussion of *A Cure for a Cuckold* F. L. Lucas demands a realism of that play which is incompatible with most Elizabethan dramatic literature. He writes:

. . . when after so much prate of friendship the almost incredible and repeated perfidy of Lessingham seems hardly to ruffle, at the end, even those whose lives he has tried by the lowest treachery to ruin—when this creature is dismissed to a happy marriage, as quite a good fellow after all, it is as monstrous as the end of *The Two Gentlemen of Verona* or *Measure for Measure*. There is no need to labour the point: with the customary adulations of Elizabethan criticism laid aside, let us admit that there are moments when these writers, even Shakespeare himself, strike us as insensitive and morally obtuse. For them marriage suffices to cover any multitude of sins—even such a marriage as seems to us itself the most flagrant sin of all. It is no use making mere gods of these men and adoring them with fast-shut eyes: at times their attitude is odious. If they are great, it is despite faults which would have killed the work of less vital poets once for all. And if *A Cure for a Cuckold* is less read than many other Elizabethan plays, it is not because it is baser in its ending than *The Two Gentlemen* or *Measure for Measure:* but because it has not enough of their redeeming poetry.[6]

Lucas has selected two of Shakespeare's plays to comment on, indicating that the reward of the villain in these plays is "monstrous." He might just as easily have selected literally scores of other Elizabethan plays in which this same phenomenon appears. When this sort of thing appears in playwright after playwright and in play after play, the only tenable conclusion is that audiences did not object to it, and that it was, hence, a convention. One is sure that Lucas would not even for a moment harbor the idea that villains were rewarded in actual practice in Elizabethan times.

The difference between the perfunctory repentance of the rake that brings so many Elizabethan plays to a close and the repentance of the rake of eighteenth-century sentimental comedy whose reform is one of the high points of the play may be further illustrated by comparison of other plays. When possible, plays which have some similarity of plot or situation will be compared. These similarities do not often extend to actual details. That is, the basic situation will be similar—a gamester forswearing gaming, an unfaithful husband promising unswerving fidelity, etc.—but the circumstances which lead up to that situation will often differ considerably. James Shirley's *The Gamester* (1633) depends, in its main plot, on a situation in which Wilding, desiring his ward, Penelope, insists that his wife help him to the former's bed. She pretends to comply, planning to substitute herself for Penelope. Wilding, in a winning streak at play, sends his friend Hazard in his stead, and is later tortured with the knowledge that it was his own wife, and not Penelope, who was enjoyed by Hazard. These nocturnal assignations are carried out in complete darkness. As the play ends Wilding is reassured that he has not been cuckolded, Hazard having been enlisted as an accomplice by the two women. He asks his wife's forgiveness and promises future fidelity. Shirley disposes of Wilding's repentance, request for forgiveness, and promise of good behavior in a speech of four lines (V, ii). Not so the sentimental dramatist. In Lady Wallace's *The Ton* (1788) Lord Raymond is given to gaming, and has been unfaithful to his wife. She not only secretly supplies him with money, but continues to love him despite her knowledge of his defection. Lord Raymond learns of his wife's generosity and comes to ask her forgiveness. One must further note that Lady Raymond has been suspected of infidelity by her husband, a suspicion that is based on a misunderstanding. The following is from the last act:

> Enter LORD RAYMOND
> [Lady Raymond looks cold and haughty]
> LORD RAYMOND. Can my amiable Fanny pardon a sincere penitent?
> LADY RAYMOND. Can you pardon yourself, my Lord, for supposing me capable of having deviated from what I owe my duty, however little you may feel yourself entitled to from my love.
> LORD RAYMOND.   Oh! never, never can I forgive myself, and your just reproaches will distract me.
> LADY RAYMOND. Alas, my Lord! you have none to fear. Those tears of

anguish which your unkindness caused, I never obtruded on your sight—yet secretly in my heart all their bitterness preyed unuttered, and unpitied.

LORD RAYMOND. Oh, my Fanny! remorse, tenderness, and gratitude render my feelings inexpressible. Alas! in this moment, in which I have learnt to value, as I ought, your generous heart, I tremble with the fears of having lost it for ever.

LADY RAYMOND. If hereafter you should meet a feeling soul, which cannot be seduced, either by the temptations of the world, or the feelings of resentment—Oh, rescue it from the only pang that is insupportable—which has ruined my peace for ever,—the finding myself for a moment, an object of doubt, from circumstances that alone originated in a fond wish to see you happy.

Lord Raymond then tells his wife that he has discovered her generosity in supplying him with funds through a moneylender, who demanded payment of him when he confronted the latter with his discovery. Lady Raymond is immediately ready to make another sacrifice for her husband:

This is but one of the many bad consequences which arise from treating every wretch that has plenty of money, no matter how acquired, as a friend and companion; whilst birth, honour, and every virtue are depressed by poverty. —I knew he was a vile fellow, and had you treated him with more confidence, I should have told you e'er now. But how can we procure money to pay him?—I'll fly again to my father! [Going]

LORD RAYMOND. Generous, noble girl!—Stop, he is paid—I imagined from what he said, that I owed him all that you kindly advanced me—I flew to the Israelite, and forced him to tell me to whom I was indebted—and, oh, my Fanny! words cannot express my feelings at your generous delicacy.— Your money proved very fortunate; I won back a great part of my losses; and for ever I forswear the follies of fashion, and devote the rest of my life to my sweet girl.

LADY RAYMOND. Then she will be happy beyond the reach of misfortune! This assurance has made the anguish you found me o'erwhelm'd in, give way to the most lively joy.—Let us forget the past, and by mutual confidence, for the future, study the happiness of each other.—But, indeed, you must not retain so much fashion about you, as to be ashamed to protect your poor Fanny, who has been sadly beset.

LORD RAYMOND. No.—my greatest joy and pride shall ever be to show my respect and adoration for her virtues.

LADY RAYMOND. Well then, do help me to protect poor Clara, and to support her in the paths of peace and honour. But, Heavens! what wou'd Mrs. Tender not say, did she chance to hear of your suspicions of me?

LORD RAYMOND. Fear nothing, my Fanny. Virtue may be traduced, but never can be injured. Such a soul as yours is above all praise, and far beyond the reach of malice. But we must hasten to the masquerade in our new characters of the happy man and wife.

LADY RAYMOND. Indeed, my Henry, all the world will think that you have adopted that character as the surest disguise.

LORD RAYMOND. Dissipation and indifference are only masks of fashion, which I now drop, to be myself affectionate and rational; I have too perfect a sense of what I have lost by neglecting my lovely wife, ever again to sacrifice her esteem, by following the unfeeling vices of fashion.

LADY RAYMOND. [With joy.] Then all my sombre melancholy will be turned to wild transport and gaiety. [Exeunt.]

(Clara is the woman whose gratitude for Lord Raymond's help brought about the loss of her honor.) Since it would not be enough to bring husband and wife together only to leave them indebted to a moneylender, Lady Wallace allows Lord Raymond to recoup his losses by one last venture at the gaming table before forswearing the habit for ever.

The Ton is such a delightfully poor play, so admirable a guide to what should be avoided in writing drama, that it will appear more than once in the present work. In anticipation of later discussion it might be well to point out that there are very decided attempts at wit and humor in the play. That the attempts are not successful is of secondary importance; they are there. Lady Wallace on one occasion even enlists the aid of Alexander Pope: "with each frown a reputation dies" (II, p. 29), and there are faint echoes of *The School For Scandal*. Also present in the play are a number of passages which may possibly be described as ribald, although one hesitates to use even that term in connection with so innocuous a play. Evidently some criticism of this element of the "indelicate" was brought to Lady Wallace's attention, for she defends herself against the charge in her Preface. She writes:

. . . but to be taxed with indecency of language, where no one idea tending to indelicacy was meant to be conveyed, proves the ungenerous malevolence of those who resolve to oppose it, unheard, from imagined personalities. . . . And if any expression can bear to be twisted and perverted to a double meaning, it was evidently not the intention of the author, nor observable to the most respectable and delicate minds existing; who examined the comedy before it was rehearsed. But, to guard against such misrepresentations, it perhaps requires a depraved mind accustomed to study every idea tending that way;— which is a part of study as yet unknown to the author:—therefore, if she has erred in unmeant expressions, which admit perversion, it arises from ignorance of that evil-minded grossness which leads some to misrepresent every thing, and turn it to their own corrupt ideas.

In all fairness it must be admitted that Lady Wallace's "indecency of language" is very inoffensive. The remarkable fact is that it should have aroused any comment at all. Genest notes that the play proved "very dull" on presentation—little more need be said.

It seems fairly safe, on the basis of the comparison made above, to say that Shirley did not emphasize Wilding's reformation. Had he wished to do so, he would have dwelt on it to some extent. A. H. Nason says of Shirley, however, that "in *The Gamester*, and even more emphatically in *The Example*, he places the emphasis not on the evil but on the reformation."[7] Nason is comparing these two plays to Shirley's previous dramatic work and may be justified in his remark, but it seems strange to speak of a dramatist's emphasizing a reformation in his play when he dismisses it with a meager four lines. Shirley used the convenient fifth-act repentance in many of his plays. Some of the repentance speeches are marvels of compression, the speaker asking forgiveness and receiving it in a few words. For example: in *The Royal Master*, the Duke of Florence repents with "Your pardon" and the king forgives him with "Take my bosom" (V, i). Possibly because the Duke's faults were not great, his expression of repentance is cut short. The "wild and lascivious" Lodwick of *The Grateful Servant* is tricked into repentance and abjuration of his loose ways (V, ii). His reformation is disposed of in a few lines. (When fear drives the rake to reform it is a far cry from sentimentalism.) In *Love's Cruelty* the Duke of Ferrara has tried to win Eubella to his lust, employing Hippolito to work her to his desires. Hippolito reforms, enjoins Eubella to remain chaste, and is overheard by the Duke. After some furious recriminations the Duke cries out.

> Tomorrow, if I live, I'll see you both—Married.
> —Thou excellent maid, forgive my passion!
> Accept him freely, thou hast overcome
> With chastity, and taught me to be a prince,
> Which character my lust had near defaced.—(IV, ii)

No one will miss the surprise that Shirley springs. One expects the Duke—no evidence to the contrary having been given—to say that he'll see the two hanged or killed, but instead he says he'll see them married. Although *Love's Cruelty* is a tragedy, it is only accidental that it is not a tragicomedy. It is usual with Shirley that one is never sure whether to expect the happy ending of tragicomedy or the "tragic" ending.

The fact that Shirley's tragicomedies display most of the characteristics of the genre as written by Fletcher and by Massinger has not gone unrecognized.[8] One of those characteristics, already mentioned, is the use of surprises, many of them. Often all other considerations are sacrificed for the sake of a sudden twist that takes the spectator completely unaware. Such a surprise occurs in *The Duke's Mistress* and evokes the following comment from Nason: ". . . where is the scene in which Pallante achieves the reformation of the duke? To secure a surprise—the duke's unexpected escape and reformation—Shirley has sacrificed an unusual opportunity for a scene of character-development" (p. 286). The Duke, a cruel and unfaithful husband throughout, appears in V, iv, as a completely changed man, and not a word has been said to prepare one for this change. At one moment he is the lustful tyrant, at his next appearance he is the repentant husband. Shirley has not only neglected an opportunity to emphasize "character-development"; he has deliberately overlooked the chance to exploit a potentially sentimental situation. That Shirley could exploit such a situation is obvious to anybody who has read *The Example*.[9]

Very few Elizabethan dramatists of importance fail to avail themselves of the convention. Webster's use of it in *A Cure for a Cuckold* has already been noted. Lucas, it will be remembered, objected to the moral "obtuseness" shown in dismissing a villain with the reward of a happy marriage rather than giving him his just deserts. Nothing was said of the rapidity of Lessingham's reform, or of the brevity with which it is dispatched. Lessingham says, briefly and rather coldly

> Can you forgive me? some wilde distractions
> Had overturned my own condition,
> And spilt the goodness you once knew in me,
> But I have carefully recovered it,
> And overthrown the fury on't. (V, i)

and he is free to join in the festivities which end the play. Thomas Middleton's *A Trick to Catch the Old One* ends with Jane, "a Courtesan," kneeling to promise fidelity to her newly acquired husband. She is followed by Witgood, the rake, who, also kneeling, promises to live a good, clean life. Both enumerate the various interesting forms of vice and excesses they intend to forswear. The treatment is hardly serious. The reformation of Young Scarborow in Wilkins' *Miseries of Enforced Marriage*, while a trifle longer than such scenes in Elizabethan drama, is not given the prominence it would have enjoyed at the hands of an eighteenth-century sentimental dramatist. The King of Scotland in Robert Greene's *James IV*, after treachery and the attempted murder of his wife by a hireling paid by him, craves pardon of his father-in-law (the King of England), of his wife, and of his nobility, whom he had wronged. All this is accomplished in seven lines. One of the reasons that *The London Prodigal* is not a sentimental comedy is the brevity of Young Flowerdale's reform. Saved from probable execution by his wife, he acknowledges his faults with:

> Thy chastitie and vertue hath infused
> Another soule in mee, red with defame,
> For in my blushing cheekes is seene my shame.

42

He asks his father's pardon, upon the former's throwing off his disguise, in a speech of two lines.

> My father! O, I shame to looke on him.
> Pardon, deare father, the follyes that are past.

And he promises to forsake his evil ways in one line.

> Heaven helping me, ile hate the course as hell. (V, i)

Evidently this scene is not, as in sentimental drama, the scene toward which the whole—or most—of the previous action has been building. The reform of Young Flowerdale is the most convenient way to bring the play to a close and still have a happy ending. It is decidedly not a scene in which a sentimental response is expected of the audience. To miss this difference is to miss one of the important distinctions between the sentimental and the non-sentimental in drama. Instances of unlooked for, and summarily disposed of, reformations abound in Elizabethan drama. Further listing of them would make dull reading, and is not necessary. One can find a list of plays containing penitent rakes in R. S. Forsythe's *The Relations of Shirley's Plays to the Elizabethan Drama*.[10] The reader can decide for himself whether potentially sentimental plays in that list have been affected by the length or brevity of treatment given those passages in which the penitence and forgiveness take place.

Plays after 1660 also tend to neglect fifth-act reformations; that is, until it became popular, with the advent of plays like those of Cibber and Steele, to exploit their possibilities. Southerne's *The Disappointment* involves a husband's suspicion of his wife's fidelity, her threatened death at his hands, and his eventual realization of her innocence—with his request for forgiveness and a promise of future faith as an inevitable consequence. Another, but related, action contains the rake, Alberto, who had seduced and cast off Juliana. He, too, reforms in Act V, and takes her to wife. The first reformation takes place when so many proofs of Erminia's, the wife's, innocence have been brought forward that not even the most perverse of jealous husbands could continue to suspect her. Alphonso, the husband, addresses Erminia, whom, a few moments before he had reviled and attempted to kill:

> O let me thus make sure of happiness!
> Thus panting, fold thee in the arms of love,
> 'Till my repenting thoughts, and subd'd fears,
> Confessing thy dominion in my heart,
> Make room to entertain thy triumph there.

43

Erminia, it might be noted, accepts this somewhat tardy expression of repentance and renewed love with silent gratitude—for she does not say a word in answer. Here, too, was missed an opportunity for a final statement of wifely joy and love at her complete restoration into the good graces of her husband. Alberto's reform is equally short. Struck by Juliana's unswerving love for him, he asks her forgiveness, and then asks pardon for his attempts on Erminia's chastity.

> Thy story, Juliana, has subdu'd
> My wilder thoughts, and fix'd me only thine;
> But oh! instruct me how I shall appear
> Before that injur'd fair, whose innocence,
> Too late I find, I have unjustly wrong'd
> Beyond a hope of pardon

It is not usual at the period in which Southerne wrote his play (1684) to find a rake accepting his cast-off mistress as his wife, voluntarily, and for reasons of conscience. Southerne was looking forward to sentimental drama, but his neglect of sentimental situations, seen in the brevity of treatment accorded scenes like those above, is one reason why it would be improper to term his play a sentimental comedy.

The reformation scene in Tom D'Urfey's *The Virtuous Wife* (1680) is short and quite unemotional, and in his *Love for Money* (1691) the "sentimental hero," really a hard-headed hypocrite,[11] has nothing of which to repent. In Theophilus Cibber's play, *The Lover* (1731), the reform of the rake Modely is dispatched in a polite speech that must have been accompanied by two introductory bows and a graceful third when he turns to address Harriet, whom he had hoped to seduce. This elegant request, not really for forgiveness for moral looseness, but, it would seem, for pardon for a breach of manners—such little account is taken of it—is phrased as follows:

MODE: Sir John, Your Servant; Ladies, your most obedient. Hearing from your Servant the joyous Affairs were going forward, we chose rather to make two aukward Figures then decline paying our Respects, and joyning the Congratulations of your Friends. Since Madam, [To Harriet] I can never have it in my Power to offend, I hope you'll condescend to pardon what is past.
HARRIET: This is a Day of general Jubilee, Sir. (V)

Harriet's few words might very well have been addressed to a casual stranger who had jostled her in a crowd, and not to the man who had had designs on her honor. A maiden whose honor has been threatened or reflected upon does not dismiss the subject so frivolously—at least in full-fledged sentimental drama. Nor are repentant rakes allowed to ask forgiveness for attempted seduction as though they were apologizing for

44

inadvertent clumsiness at the tea table. The reform of Charles in Charles Shadwell's *Irish Hospitality or Virtue Rewarded* (1720) is brought about more by fear of discovery than by latent goodness. It remained for later writers to show how such scenes could be worked for all they were worth.

A great deal of time has been devoted to this discussion of fifth-act reformations and the difference with which they are treated by various writers, sentimental and not sentimental. The prominence that has been given this aspect of the whole question is justified by the fact that so many plays end in such reformations, that the concluding scene—the one with which the spectator is left—is of considerable importance. Again, the importance of the last scene or act with its reformations differs with the playwrights of different periods. In the Elizabethan age, as I have stressed, the play was neatly brought to a close, the plot-threads woven together (the degree of artistry or credibility varying, and a minor consideration really), and the happy ending achieved by the convention of the repentant rake or villain. The use of the convention brought the action to an end. In the late eighteenth century, sentimental dramatists also wound up their plays with last-minute reformations, but they had prepared the ground for the final scene and managed to gain a credibility of sorts for their denouement. This gain in credibility by repetition and prolonged treatment, and the heightened emotional effects that are possible by extensive treatment, form the chief differences between the playwright who consciously works for sentimental effects and the dramatist who is not interested in them.

A recent critic has suggested that "The virtue of compassion in Shakespeare's characters never has an air of display. Any suggestion of sentimentality is eliminated by the spontaneity and brevity of expression."[12] Brevity in the treatment of potentially sentimental situations characterizes most of Shakespeare's plays. Dr. Johnson recognized this, and observed, of *As You Like It*:

By hastening to the end of his work, Shakespeare suppressed the dialogue between the usurper and the hermit, and lost an opportunity of exhibiting a moral lesson, in which he might have found matter worthy of his highest powers. (General Observation)

Oliver's conversion in the same play is also dispatched with speed. In *Two Gentlemen of Verona* Proteus asks forgiveness of Valentine in a short simple speech which contains no flourishes or posturings. Angelo's admission of guilt and desire for immediate execution in *Measure For Measure* is, whatever one thinks of his previous actions, seemingly sincere and forthright. Again Shakespeare elected to overlook the opportunity for a gratuitous tug on the heartstrings by limiting Angelo to a few lines of unadorned speech. Claudio, of *Much Ado About Nothing*, told by Leonato of Hero's death and of the deception that has been practiced, expresses his penitence thus:

> I know not how to pray your patience;
> Yet I must speak. Choose your revenge yourself;
> Impose me to what penance your invention
> Can lay upon my sin. Yet sinn'd I not
> But in mistaking. (V, i)

One may be pleased to call this the masculine reticence of a military man, but it emerges as a cold, unfeeling expression of sorrow when contrasted to the wealth of self-reproaches, the offers of immediate self-destruction, and the deluge of tears that would be lavished on the situation by a sentimental hero. Claudio even attempts some self-justification; he appeals to Leonato's reason to exculpate him from full responsibility for Hero's death. This sort of thing is simply not done in sentimental drama.

Another comparison may serve to show more clearly how Shakespeare's treatment of a situation differs from the sentimental dramatist's treatment of the identical situation. The "child-recovered" theme is used in plays of every genre; Shakespeare uses it more than once, and sentimental dramatists are particularly fond of it. There is a difference, however, in the way in which the theme is used by Shakespeare, and the way in which it is used by the sentimentalist. Cymbeline hears Belarius' story of the kidnapping of the little princes, and speaks

> Thou weep'st and speak'st.
> The service that you three have done is more
> Unlike than this thou tell'st. I lost my children.
> If these be they, I know not how to wish
> A pair of worthier sons.

Cymbeline seems overly reluctant to credit Belarius' story, and it is only when Guiderius is shown to have a mole on his neck that he accepts the two lads as his sons, with these words:

> O, what am I?
> A mother to the birth of three? Ne'er mother
> Rejoic'd deliverance more. Blest pray you be,
> That, after this strange starting from your orbs,
> You may reign in them now! (V, v)

Edward Moore's *The Foundling*, not so often read as his *Gamester* nor so popular as an acting vehicle, met with great success at its presentation in 1748. Nicoll looks upon it "as the connecting link between the sentimentalism of the early and the sentimentalism of the late eighteenth century" (*1700-1750*, p. 207). As might be guessed from the title, there is a scene in which a long-lost child is restored to her parent. That the difference between the sentimental and the non-sentimental treatment of the same theme may be shown graphically the whole of the reunion in *The Foundling* is quoted. The plot particulars are not especially important.

SIR CHARLES. —You have often told me, Sir, [To Belmont] that I had an interest in this lovely Creature—I have an Interest!—An Interest, that you shall allow me!—My Heart doats upon her!—Oh, I could hold no longer! —My Daughter!—my Daughter!

[Running to Fidelia, and embracing her.]

FIDELIA. Your Daughter, Sir!

SIR CHARLES. Oh, my sweet Child!—Sir Roger!—Mr. Belmont, my Son!— these Tears!—these Tears!—Fidelia is my Daughter!

COLONEL RAYMOND. Is't possible?

SIR CHARLES. Let not Excess of Wonder over-power you, Fidelia—For I have a Tale to tell that will exceed Belief.

FIDELIA. Oh Sir!

SIR CHARLES. Upbraid me not, that I have kept it a Moment from your Knowledge—'Twas a hard Trial!—and while my Tongue was taught Dissimulation, my Heart bled for a Child's Distresses.

BELMONT. Torture us not, Sir—but explain this Wonder!

SIR CHARLES. My Tears must have their Way first—O my Child!—my Child! —[Turning to Sir Roger and the rest] Know then—That wicked Woman, so often mentioned, was my Fidelia's Governante—When my mistaken Zeal drove me into Banishment—I left her an Infant to her Care—To secure some Jewels of Value, I had lodged with her, she became the Woman you have heard—My Child was taught to believe she was a Foundling—Her Name of Harriet changed to Fidelia—and to lessen my Solicitude for the Theft, a letter was dispatched to me in France, that my Infant Daughter had no longer a Being—Thus was the Father robbed of his Child, and the Brother was taught to believe he had no Sister.

FIDELIA. Am I that Sister, and that Daughter?—Oh Heavens! [Kneels.]

BELMONT. [Running to her, and raising her.] Be composed, my Life!—A Moment's Attention more—and your Transports shall have a Loose— Proceed, Sir!

SIR CHARLES. Where she withdrew herself, I could never learn—At twelve Years old, she sold her, as you have heard—and never, till Yesterday, made Enquiry about her—'Twas then, that a sudden Fit of Sickness brought her to Repentance—She sent for Villiard—who told her minutely what had happened—The Knowledge of her Deliverance gave her some Consolation —But more was to be done yet—She had Information of my Pardon and Return—and ignorant of my Child's Deliverer, or the Place of her Conveyance, she at last determined to unburden herself to me—A Letter was brought to me this Afternoon, conjuring me to follow the Bearer with

47

the same Haste that I would shun Ruin—I did follow him—and received from this wretched Woman the Story I have told you.

FIDELIA. Oh, my Heart!—My Father! [Kneels] Have I at last found you!—And were all my Sorrows past, meant only to endear the present Transport—'Tis too much for me!

SIR CHARLES. Rise, my Child!—To find thee thus virtuous, in the Midst of Temptations, and thus lovely, in the Midst of Poverty and Distress!—After an Absence of eighteen melancholy Years, when imaginary Death had torn thee from my Hopes!—To find thee thus unexpected, and thus amiable! is Happiness that the uninterrupted Enjoyment of the fairest Life never equalled!

FIDELIA. What must be mine then!—Have I a Brother, too! [Turning to the Colonel] Oh my kind Fortune!

COLONEL. My Sister! [Embracing her.]

FIDELIA. Still there is a dearer Claim than all—and now I can acknowledge it—My Deliverer!—

BELMONT. And Husband, Fidelia!—Let me receive you, as the richest Gift of Fortune! [Catching her in his Arms.]

ROSETTA. My generous Girl!—The Pride of your Alliance is my utmost Boast, as it is my Brother's Happiness.

SIR ROGER. I have a Right in her too—for now you are my Daughter, Fidelia. [Kisses her.]

FIDELIA. I had forgot, Sir—if you will receive me as such, you shall find my Gratitude in my Obedience.

SIR CHARLES. Take her, Mr. Belmont, and protect the Virtue you have tried. [Joining their Hands.]

BELMONT. The Study of my Life, Sir, shall be to deserve her.

FIDELIA. Oh, Rosetta!—Yet still it remains with you, to make this Day's Happiness compleat—I have a Brother that loves you.

ROSETTA. I would be Fidelia's Sister every Way!—So take me while I am warm, Colonel! [Giving him her Hand.][13]

In this, and in similar situations, the dramatist's lingering over the scene is not because he needs to gain credibility for it, but because he wishes to capitalize on the emotion he has aroused.

Examples of the "child-recovered" theme treated with brevity are plentiful. In Fletcher's *Monsieur Thomas*, Valentine listens to Francisco tell a story which proves definitely that the latter is his long-lost son. Francisco finishes his tale with the words "Now ye have all," and Valentine's joy at the recovery of his boy is dispensed with in two lines (V, x). Fernando's recovery of the long-lost Costanza, his daughter, is hurried over with almost equal speed (*The Spanish Gypsy*, V, iii). Shakespeare gives Pericles only a few lines in which to express his happiness at finding the lost Marina (V, i). Perdita is restored to Hermione after many years and is questioned by her mother who wants to know all that has happened to her child. At this point Shakespeare has Paulina interrupt to say that there is plenty of time for that later, and the scene is cut short, the play ending after a few more lines (*The Winter's Tale*, V, iii). The brevity of treatment that characterizes the dramatists' handling of the "child-recovered" theme in the plays mentioned may be compared to the more prolonged treatment that is seen in such plays as Steele's *The Conscious Lovers* (V, iii), George Colman's *The English Merchant* (III), and Mrs. Charlotte Lennox's *The Sister* (II). In this last play a brother recovers his sister.

There are many other themes, scenes, and situations which can be used to show that sentimental effects are achieved by dwelling on their pathetic possibilities. Adulterous women in Elizabethan drama are usually killed or commit suicide—it will be remembered that Mistress Frankford starves herself to death; she does not die of a broken heart. The idea that the husband's honor could be restored only by summary vengeance on his unfaithful wife was what we today would call a cliché of the theatre. Actually, there was legal machinery for obtaining divorces in such cases, and husbands did not murder unfaithful wives with impunity—except on the stage. Frankford's forbearance is unusual; Heywood had added a new twist to a familiar situation. But Heywood had already shown an injured husband forgiving an adulterous wife. In the second part of *King Edward the Fourth* he had told the story of Jane Shore, once mistress to a King, who had died a pathetic death of starvation under persecution. Before her death Jane was forgiven by her husband, and the two die in a scene that has been called sentimental by some scholars.[14]

SHORE.   Ah, Jane! now there is none but thou and I,
  Look on me well, Know'st thou thy Matthew Shore?
JANE.   My husband! then break, heart, and live no more!
                           [Swoons and he supports her.]
SHORE.   Ah, my dear Jane! comfort thy heavy soul!
  Go not away so soon; a little stay,
  A little, little while, that thou and I,
  Like man and wife, may here together die.
JANE.   How can I look upon my husband's face,
  That sham'd myself, and wrought his deep disgrace?
SHORE.   Jane, be content! Our woes are now alike.
  With one self rod thou see'st God doth us strike.
  If for thy sin, I'll pray to Heav'n for thee,
  And if for mine, do thou as much for me.
JANE.   Ah, Shore! is't possible thou canst forgive me?
SHORE.   Yes, Jane, I do.
JANE.   I cannot hope thou wilt
  My fault's so great, that I cannot expect it.
SHORE.   I'faith, I do, as freely from my soul,
  As at God's hands I hope to be forgiven.

JANE. Then God reward thee! for we now must part:
I feel cold death doth seize upon my heart.
SHORE. And he is come to me. Lo! here he lies;
I feel him ready to close up my eyes.
Lend me thy hand to bury this our friend,
And then we both will hasten to our end.
 [They put the body of Ayre into a Coffin, and then he sits down on one
 side of it and she on the other.]
Jane, sit thou there! Here I my place will have!
Give me thy hand! thus we embrace our grave!
Ah, Jane! he that the depth of woe will see,
Let him but now behold our misery!
But be content! this is the best of all,
Lower than now we are, we cannot fall!
JANE. Ah, I am faint! how happy, Ayre, art thou!
Not feeling that which doth afflict us now!
SHORE. Oh, happy grave! to us this comfort giving!
Here lies two living-dead! here one dead-living!
Here for his sake, lo! this we do for thee!
Thou look'st for one, and art possess'd of three.
JANE. Oh, dying marriage! oh, sweet married death!
Thou grave, which only should'st part faithful friends,
Bring'st us together, and dost join our hands.
Oh, living death! ev'n in this dying life!
Yet, ere I go, once Matthew! kiss thy wife!
 [He kisses her, and she dies.] (V, ii)

It is not necessary to pronounce on the sentimentality of Heywood's treatment. Comparisons of this scene with a similar one from sentimental drama will indicate how the situation is exploited by the thoroughgoing sentimentalist. One could compare Heywood's treatment of the death of Jane Shore and her husband with that of Rowe (*The Tragedy of Jane Shore*, Act V) and show how Rowe managed to get even more pathos out of the same situation, but there is a late eighteenth-century sentimental comedy which makes the point more obvious.

August von Kotzebue's *Menschenhass und reue*, translated as *The Stranger* by Benjamin Thompson, was produced at Drury Lane in 1798. It is out-and-out sentimental drama, centering about an adulterous wife who has run away from her husband, but who is finally forgiven by him and restored to his love. The wife has early repented and sought to atone for her sin by a program of good works. In this effort she much resembles Jane Shore. Unlike the Jane Shore story, however, which ends with Jane's death and that of her husband (in Heywood), *The Stranger* ends on a happy note. The climactic scene is that in which husband and wife meet again for the first time in three years. Full quotation is necessary.

Enter MRS. HALLER, COUNTESS, and BARON

MRS. HALLER. (Advances slowly and in a tremor. Countess attempts to support her) Leave me now, I beseech you. (Approaches Stranger, who with averted countenance and in extreme agitation awaits her address) My lord!

STRANGER. (With gentle, tremulous utterance and face turned away) What would you with me, Adelaide?

MRS. HALLER. (Much agitated) No, for heaven's sake! I was not prepared for this. Oh, that tone cuts to my heart! Adelaide! No! For heaven's sake! Harsh tones alone are suited to a culprit's ear.

STRANGER. (Endeavoring to give his voice firmness) Well, Madam?

MRS. HALLER. Oh! If you will ease my heart, if you will spare and pity me, use reproaches.

STRANGER. Reproaches! Here they are upon my sallow cheek, here in my hollow eye, here in my faded form. These reproaches I could not spare you.

MRS. HALLER. Were I a hardened sinner, this forbearance would be charity; but I am a suffering penitent and it overpowers me. Alas! then I must be the herald of my own shame. For where shall I find peace till I have eased my soul by my confession?

STRANGER. No confession, madam! I release you from every humiliation. I perceive you feel that we must part forever.

MRS. HALLER. I know it. Nor come I here to supplicate your pardon; nor has my heart contained a ray of hope that you would grant it. All I dare ask is that you will not curse my memory.

STRANGER. (Moved) No, Adelaide, I do not curse you. No, I shall never curse you.

MRS. HALLER. (Agitated) From the inward conviction that I am unworthy of your name, I have, during three years, abandoned it. But this is not enough; you must have that redress which will enable you to choose another,—another wife, in whose untainted arms may heaven protect your hours in bliss! This paper will be necessary for the purpose; it contains a written acknowledgement of my guilt. (Offers it trembling.)

STRANGER. (Tearing it) Perish the record forever. No, Adelaide, you only have possessed my heart, and without shame I confess it, you alone will reign there forever. Your own sensations of virtue, your resolute honor, forbid you to profit by my weakness; and even if—Now, by heaven, this is beneath a man! But—Never, never, will another fill Adelaide's place here.

MRS. HALLER. (Trembling) Then nothing now remains but that one sad, hard, just word,—farewell!

STRANGER. A moment's stay. For some months we have without knowing it lived near each other. I have learned much good of you. You have a heart open to the wants of your fellow creatures. I am happy that it is so. You shall not be without the power of gratifying your benevolence. I know you have a spirit that must shrink from a state of obligation. This paper, to which the whole remnant of my fortune is pledged, secures you independence, Adelaide: and let the only recommendation of the gift be that it will administer to you the means of indulging in charity the divine propensity of your nature.

MRS. HALLER. Never! By the labor of my hands must I earn my sustenance. A morsel of bread moistened with the tear of penitence will suffice my wishes and exceed my merits. It would be an additional reproach to think that I served myself, or even others, from the bounty of him whom I had so basely injured.

STRANGER. Take it, madam, take it!

MRS. HALLER. I have deserved this. But I throw myself upon your generosity. Have compassion on me!

STRANGER. (Aside) Villain, of what a woman hast thou robbed me! (Puts up the paper) Well, madam, I respect your sentiments and withdraw my request, but on this one condition, that if you should be in want of anything, I shall be the first and only person in the world to whom you will make application.

MRS. HALLER. I promise it, my lord.

STRANGER. And now I may at least desire you to take back what is your own,—your jewels.   (Gives her the casket)

MRS. HALLER. (Opens it with violent agitation and her tears burst upon it) How well do I recollect the sweet evening when you gave me these! That evening my father joined my hands and joyfully I pronounced the oath of eternal fidelity. It is broken. This locket you gave me on my birthday. 'Tis five years since. That was a happy day! We had a country feast. How cheerful we all were! This bracelet I received after my William was born. No! I cannot keep these, unless you wish that the sight of them should be an incessant reproach to my almost broken heart.   (Gives them back)

STRANGER. (Aside) I must go. My soul and pride will hold no longer. (Turning towards her) Farewell!

MRS. HALLER. Oh, but one minute more! An answer to but one more question. Feel for a mother's heart! Are my children still alive?

STRANGER. They are alive.

MRS. HALLER. And well?

STRANGER. They are well.

MRS. HALLER. God be praised! William must be grown?

STRANGER. I believe so.

MRS. HALLER. What! Have you not seen them! And little Amelia, is she still your favorite? (The Stranger, who is in violent agitation throughout this scene, remains in silent contention between honor and affection) Oh, if you knew how my heart has hung upon them for these three long, dreadful years, how I have sat at evening twilight, first fancying William, then Amelia, on my lap! Oh, allow me to behold them once again. Let me once more kiss the features of their father in his babes and I will kneel to you and part with them forever.

STRANGER. Willingly, Adelaide. This very night. I expect the children every minute. They have been brought up near this spot. I have already sent my servant for them. He might before this time have returned. I pledge my word to send them to the castle as soon as they arrive. There, if you please, they may remain till daybreak tomorrow. Then they must go with me. (A pause)

(The Countess and Baron, who at a little distance have listened to the whole conversation with the warmest sympathy, exchange signals. Baron goes into the hut and soon returns with Francis and the children. He gives the boy to the Countess, who places herself behind Mrs. Haller. He himself walks with the girl behind the Stranger)

MRS. HALLER. In this world then—we have no more to say. (Summoning all her resolution) Farewell! (Seizing his hand) Forget a wretch who will never forget you. (Kneels) Let me press this hand once more to my lips,— this hand which once was mine.

STRANGER. (Raising her) No humiliation, Adelaide! (Shakes her hand) Farewell!

MRS. HALLER. A last farewell!

STRANGER. The last.

MRS. HALLER. And when my penance shall have broken my heart, when we again meet in a better world—

STRANGER. There, Adelaide, you may be mine again.

(Their hands lie in each other; their eyes mournfully meet each other. They stammer another "Farewell" and part; but as they are going she encounters the boy and he the girl)

CHILDREN. Dear father! Dear mother!

(They press the children in their arms with speechless affection; then tear themselves away, gaze at each other, spread their arms, and rush into an embrace. The children run and cling round their parents. The curtain falls) (V, ii)

Putting aside the extra appeal to the emotions gained by the presence of the children in *The Stranger*, it is easy to see how the eighteenth-century play exploits an emotional situation by according it sufficiently prolonged treatment, allowing the audience to relish its emotional response by drawing out the scene as much as possible. Heywood's treatment is much briefer, neglecting to capitalize on the emotion that has been evoked. And Heywood follows the death of Jane and her husband with another scene; *The Stranger* ends on the tableau—no other considerations were permitted to disturb the sentimental appeal of that final touching picture of the errant wife clasped in the embrace of her forgiving husband, their two children clinging about them.

As has been remarked from the closing scene of *The Stranger*, one situation or spectacle which is sure to evoke a sentimental response is that of a child—or children—making a plea for a parent; expressing fear, hunger, or love; or just appearing on the stage to form part of a tableau. Plenty of Elizabethan and Restoration plays use children for some desired effect or other—usually pathetic. Sometimes the children are allowed to speak by the dramatist; sometimes they say nothing; sometimes they are only referred to. The best effects are obtained by bringing the child on the stage and giving him something to say. Addison comments on the use of children for pathetic effect on the stage in *Spectator* No. 44. He says nothing about their prattling, only commenting on the greater possibility for pathetic effects as the number of children on the stage is increased. Obviously, if Addison thought the practice worth satirizing, the abuse must have been a very real one. He writes:

A disconsolate mother, with a child in her hand, has frequently drawn compassion from the audience, and has therefore gained a place in several tragedies. A modern writer, that observed how this had took in other plays, being resolved to double the distress, and melt his audience twice as much as those before him had done, brought a princess upon the stage with a little boy in one hand and a girl in the other. This too had a very good effect. A third poet being resolved to out-write all his predecessors, a few years ago introduced three children with great success: And as I am informed, a young gentleman, who is full determined to break the most obdurate hearts, has a tragedy by him, where the first person that appears upon the stage is an afflicted widow in her mourning weeds, with half a dozen fatherless children attending her, like those that usually hang about the figure of charity. Thus several incidents that are beautiful in a good writer, become ridiculous by falling into the hands of a bad one.

Many years later, in 1763, three young Scots wits, or would-be wits, who clubbed together to write *Critical Strictures on the New Tragedy of Elvira, Written by Mr. David Malloch* remembered Addison's essay and quoted it in their pamphlet. Malloch had brought two children on the stage in his last act, and James Boswell, Andrew Erskine, and George Dempster suggested "to Mr. *Malloch* the useful Hint of introducing in some of his future Productions, the whole Foundling Hospital, which with a well painted Scene of the Edifice itself would certainly call forth the warmest Tears of Pity, and bitterest Emotions of Distress" (p. 19). Elizabethan playwrights, unlike their eighteenth-century brethren, often prefer to keep children in the background, either mute or given a word or two. Like all generalizations this statement admits of exceptions—the reader may supply them himself. For the purpose of comparison one may take a few plays in which a potentially sentimental situation which involves children is slighted by hurried treatment, and one in which the dramatist knows that the presence of a prattling child on the stage is effective for his purposes and, therefore, allows him to remain until he has had his say. In *The Miseries of Enforced Marriage* Scarborow's children are brought on stage in the fifth act to help soften their father's heart. He calls them bastards; they answer, "Father"—and are heard from no more. In *A Yorkshire Tragedy* the little boy chides his father for interfering with his playing:

Enter his little son with a top and a scourge.
SON. What, aile you father? are you not well? I cannot scourge my top as

long as you stand so: you take up all the roome with your wide legs. Puh, you cannot make mee afeard with this; I fears no vizards, nor bugbeares.

HUSB.   *takes up the child by the skirts of his long coate in one hand and drawes his dagger with th'other.*

HUSB.   Up, sir, for heer thou hast no inheritance left.

SONNE.   Oh, what will you do father? I am your white boie.

HU.   Thou shalt be my red boie: take that   [*strikes him.*

SON.   Oh, you hurt me, father.

HU.   My eldest beggar! thou shalt not live to aske an usurer bread, to crie at a great mans gate, or followe, good your honour, by a Couch; no, nor your brother; tis charity to braine you.

SON.   How shall I learne now my heads broke:

HU.   Bleed, bleed rather than beg, beg!   [*stabs him.*

Shortly after this the husband appears before his wife and stabs the child she is holding. This passage is relatively brief, but there is another factor that must be noted. The little boy speaks like a little boy; he is believable. There is no forced sentimental effect, no spurious emotion evoked. This should be borne in mind in reading the sentimentalist's use of a child's words. In Dryden's *All for Love* Antony's children are brought in to make all the more clear to him how he has neglected his family for a light woman. The children are used rather effectively, but they, like the children in Wilkins' play, say only, "Father." These examples will be enough to contrast with fuller treatment of children, used for sentimental purposes.

John Banks has been recognized as one of the first writers of what Rowe later was to call "she-tragedies."[15] His literary descendants—despite chronological proximity—include Southerne, Otway, and Rowe; and he has been the subject of study in connection with "pathetic tragedy."[16] Banks works conscientiously to move the emotions of his spectators or readers by the spectacle of distressed virtue. In his prolonged treatment of certain situations designed to evoke an emotion in excess of what should be aroused he is an early sentimentalist. And Steele (*Tatler* No. 14) testifies to Banks's ability to draw tears despite the poorness of his plays. A scene in *Anna Bullen or Vertue Betray'd* (1682) shows Anna's child, the little Princess Elizabeth, pleading with the King for her mother's life. Here is how the sentimentalist gains his effects:

KING.   What wouldst thou have, my little Betty, say?

CHILD.   But will you promise me that you'll not frown,
           And cry aloud, Hough, and then indeed I'le tell you.

KING.   I do. Come, let me take thee in my Arms—

CHILD.   No: but I'le kneel: for I must be a Beggar,
           And I have learn't, that all who beg of you,
           Must do it kneeling.

. . . .

KING.	Well then, what is't my little Pratler, say?
CHILD.	I'm told that streight my Mother is to die,
	Yet I've heard you say, you lov'd her dearly:
	And will you let her die, and me die too?
KING.	She must die, Child; There is no harm in death;
	Besides the Law has said it, and She must.
CHILD.	Must! is the Law a greater King than you?
KING.	O yes. But do not cry my pretty Betty:
	For she'll be happier when she's dead, and go to Heaven.
CHILD.	Nay, I'm sure shee'l go to Heav'n.
KING.	How art thou sure?
CHILD.	Somebody told me so
	Last night when I was in my sleep.
KING.	Who was it?
CHILD.	A fine old man, like my Godfather Cranmer.

There then occur some speeches in which the child confesses her dislike for the Pope, but will not accept the designation "heretic." She returns to her plea:

	. . . But you forget your Child.
	Dear Father, will you save my Mother's life?
KING.	You must not call me Father: For they say
	Y're not my Daughter.
CHILD.	Who's am I then?
	Who told you so? That ugly old, bald Priest?
	He tells untruth. I'm sure you are my Father.
KING.	How art?
CHILD.	Cause I love none so well as you—
	But oh you'l never hear me what I have to say,
	As long as He, that Devil there, stands by
	Your Elbow.

There are a few lines against Wolsey, spoken by the child, and the King orders her taken away:

CHILD.	Oh, but they dare not:
	Father, will you not let your Betty kiss you?
	Why do you let 'em pull me from you so?
	I ne're did anger you:
	Pray save my Mother, Dear King-Father do;
	And if you hate her, we will promise both,
	That she and I will go a great, huge way,
	And never see you more.
KING.	Unloose her: hough!
	Hence with her straight: I will not hear her prate
	Another word. Go y'are a naughty Girl.

CHILD.   Well, I'm resolved when I am grown a Woman,
          I'le be reveng'd, and cry, Hough, too.

Shortly after this meeting, the Queen takes her farewell of her daughter, and it is she who describes the child's grief:

> See, see, Diana, by my Wrongs it weeps,
> Weeps like a thing of Sense, and not a Child;
> Like one well understood in Grief, the Tears
> Drop sensibly in order down its Cheeks;
> And drowns its pretty Speech in thoughtful Sorrow.
> Nothing could shoot Infection through my Breast,
> But this; and this has done it—
> Why weeps my Child: Ah, what a Question's that? (V)

The description of the child's tears is clearly designed to call forth tears in the audience.

Banks's *Anna Bullen* was published in 1682; about one hundred years later dramatists were still capitalizing on the emotional possibilities inherent in references to children in situations of distress, present or envisaged. In Lady Wallace's *The Ton* (1778) a mother tells of the death of her child from hunger,

Oh, had you seen my little blooming boy, when perishing, with its little wan face looking up to ours, transfixed with horror! and when we wept in silent anguish, he cried, Papa, dear Mamma, what distresses you thus? Why, Oh! why don't you give me to eat? Indeed, indeed, I shall die. Alas! we had it not to give, and the drooping innocent murmuring at our seeming cruelty, fainted and expired. (IV)

A character in James Nelson's *The Affectionate Father* (1780) describes Sir Charles Allgood (notice the name) as

Gazing one day on Miss Allgood's infant beauty . . . he broke out into an affecting ejaculation: 'Ah! lovely babe! he cries,' emblem of innocence! sweet resemblance of your sweet mother! who, now she is gone, shall comfort you in your infant years! who attend your dawn of reason! who cultivate your opening mind, and regulate the motions of your heart? who, above all, shall guard your innocence, and protect you from the wiles, the artifices, and the snares of baseness, design and treachery? (I, ii)

Banks's verse and his treatment of the distressed child are almost dignified when compared to the dripping sentiment of Lady Wallace's and James Nelson's prose. But neither Banks nor these eighteenth-century sentimentalists deserve to be mentioned in the same breath with the anonymous author of *A Yorkshire Tragedy*. The difference may be even more clearly seen in this final quotation, from the Reverend Charles Jenner's *Man of Family* (1771). A character implores his father's forgiveness and reconciliation: "I shall recover your love: my Charlotte's tears, my own entreaties, my children stretching out their little hands to you, you will not, you cannot spurn us all from you!" These little outstretched hands are somewhat gratuitous; the speaker is not yet married.

Many situations, sure to arouse genuine emotion when handled skillfully, can be easily made to serve sentimental ends. Movie-goers have observed—or experienced—the blowing of noses and furtive wiping of eyes which accompany those scenes in which a parent visits a son condemned to die in prison, or, in some locales, on the way to execution. Steele's second play, *The Lying Lover*, has such a scene. So, too, has *The Witch of Edmonton*, by Dekker, Rowley, and Ford. In Steele's play Young Bookwit lies in prison, held for killing a man in a duel. Old Bookwit, his father, enters:

> Oh, my dear child! Oh, Tom! are all thy aged father's hopes, then, come to this, that he can't see thee, his only son, but guarded by a gaoler? Thy mother's happy that lived not to see this day. Is all the nurture that she gave thy infancy, the erudition she bequeathed thy youth, thus answered? Oh, my son! my son! rise and support thy father! I sink with tenderness my child; come to my arms while thou art mine.

Y. BOOK.   Oh, best of fathers!
> Let me not see your tears,
> Don't double my afflictions by your woe—
> There's consolation when a friend laments us, but
> When a parent grieves, the anguish is too native,
> Too much our own to be called pity.
> Oh, sir, consider; I was born to die.
> 'Tis but expanding thought, and life is nothing.
> Ages and generations pass away,
> And with resistless force, like waves o'er waves,
> Roll down the irrevocable stream of time
> Into the insatiate ocean for ever—Thus we are gone.
> But the erroneous sense of man—'tis the lamented
> That's at rest, but the survivor mourns.
> All my sorrow vanish with that thought,
> But heaven grant my aged father patience!

O. BOOK.   Oh, child   [Turning away.]

Y. BOOK.   Do not torment yourself, you shall promise not to grieve.
> What if they do upbraid you with my death?
> Consider, sir, in death that our relation ceases;
> It matters not whether by law, or nature, 'tis I die.
> What, won't my father hear me plead to him?

> Don't turn from me—
> Yet don't look at me with your soul so full.

O. BOOK. Oh, my child! my child! I could hear thee ever
> 'Twas that I loved thee that I turn away;
> To hear my son persuade me to resign him,
> I can't, I can't. The grief is insupportable. (V, iii)

It is not necessary to quote the whole scene; the excerpt quoted is almost exactly one-half the entire dialogue between Young Bookwit and his father. Compare, however, the almost identical scene in *The Witch of Edmonton*. Frank Thorney is being led to execution for murder. As he comes upon the scene, his father says

> Here's the sad object which I yet must meet
> With hope of comfort, if a repentant end
> Make him more happy than misfortune would
> Suffer him here to be.

FRANK. Good sirs, turn from me:
> You will revive affliction almost killed
> With my continual sorrow.

O. THOR. O, Frank, Frank!
> Would I had sunk in mine own wants, or died
> But one bare minute ere thy fault was acted!

FRANK. To look upon your sorrows executes me
> Before my execution.

A number of other people speak, and Frank finally turns to his father again:

> . . . Lastly to you, sir;
> And though I have deserved not to be called
> Your son, yet give me leave upon my knees
> To beg a blessing.   [Kneels]

O. THOR. Take it; let me wet
> Thy cheeks with the last tears my griefs have left me.
> O, Frank, Frank, Frank!

FRANK. Let me beseech you, gentlemen,
> To comfort my old father, keep him with ye . . . (V, ii)

This dialogue, with the old man's poignant repetition of his son's name, is enough to evoke the desired emotional response; there is no necessity to dwell on the scene to the extent that Steele does in his play. Young Bookwit and his father indulge in an emotional orgy, and the effect loses rather than gains intensity because of the dramatist's reluctance to let well-enough alone. The visits of Trueman and Thorowgood to George Barnwell, in prison for murder of his uncle, afford another example of the dramatist's use of prolongation for sentimental effect (*The London Merchant*, V, ii). The situation in Lillo's play is much the same as that in *The Lying Lover* and *The Witch of Edmonton*, although the relationship between Barnwell and his visitors is not so close as it is in the other two plays.

One of the most effective ways of bringing out the essential nobility of a character is to show that character faced with the necessity of making a choice between personal interest or adherence to an ideal, and choosing to sacrifice his own happiness for that ideal. There are a number of scenes in Elizabethan drama in which a lover renounces his interest in his beloved in favor of some other person. Usually, the lover is motivated by loyalty to an ideal which transcends considerations of love between the sexes, and usually he gives up his mistress to his beloved friend or to his ruler. Friendship and loyalty to one's sovereign generally take precedence over love for woman in Elizabethan drama. Shakespeare's use of the theme is probably best remembered in the ending of *The Two Gentlemen of Verona*, that scene in which Valentine offers to surrender Sylvia to Proteus (V, iv). Shirley's *The Grateful Servant* is based on the story of a loyal subject who voluntarily renounces his love for his mistress in favor of his ruler. The same theme is the basis for Lodowick Carlell's *Osmond the Great Turk: or, The Noble Servant*, and it appears in many other plays before 1660.[17] Here is the "renunciation" speech given to Vernon by the anonymous author of *The Life and Death of Captain Thomas Stukely*:

> Here, dear Tom Stukely, all the right I have
> In fair Nell Curtis I resign to thee
> Be but her parents pleased as well as I
> God give you joy as man and wife, say I.[18]

This is short and unemotional but representative of the usual treatment of such situations by Elizabethan writers. Late eighteenth-century dramatists did not, however, worship the ideal of friendship that became almost a fetish for men of the Renaissance. In this later period love of country, tied up, of course, with love of the king, came to be substituted for older ideals. Hence, it is not surprising to find a hero of an eighteenth-century play choosing rather to fight for his country than to stay quietly at home, secure in the love of his mistress. In James Fennell's *Lindor and Clara* (1791)[19] the hero is confronted with the choice of marrying his beloved and staying in England or going off to war and being obliged to lose her. He chooses to fight for his country. The scene is set before the monument of Clara's brother, killed in battle. Sir Edward, Clara's father, addresses Lindor:

. . . Hark ye, young man, you well remember, when I consented to receive
you as my son-in-law, the first agreement on your part was, that you should
resign your commission, and reside at home, to supply to me the loss of my
poor boy Harry: that point agreed to, the marriage articles were signed. Remember the conditions, for upon those only will I now consent.

LINDOR.   My country sir, was then at peace.

SIR EDWARD.   Well sir—

LINDOR.   And with that prospect before me, I thought it no dishonour to resign a
commission for which I had then no use. But now sir, when my country is insulted, while its proud foes are glorying in the affront they have offered to our
flag, I should think myself unworthy of the commission I bear, could interest
or happiness, or any consideration in the world, tempt me to forget that
greater duty I owe my country and my king; and such a king! whose noble
and amiable virtues have so much endeared him to his people, that I am persuaded I should be the only officer in his army, that would not triumph in
this opportunity of shedding his heart's last drop to serve him.

SIR EDWARD.   Hark ye, sir, I have the same feelings for my king and country as
you have; and I know every Briton who enjoys the blessings of such a king
and such a country must have. I served him while I had the power—Heaven
sent me two crutches to support my age; the one I lent my king and (*point-
ing to the monument*) there he lies: the other he may surely spare me, to
assist my age-worn carcass to its last home.—Besides, sir, the king wants
not officers, and brave ones too, who are able and willing to supply your
place and who have not those interests and affections to detain them at home
that you have.

LINDOR.   I should be sorry, sir, if interest, or even affection, could detain me at
home, when my king, placing both in a light secondary to that love he bears
his subjects, can consent to risk the lives of his own sons in their defence.

SIR EDWARD. (Aside.)   Damme if I can help liking him better than ever; but I
don't like his going—though, zounds I believe I should do the same on this
occasion myself, if I was as young as he is.—If he will go, he shall not marry
my daughter, I am resolv'd; I can't lose both.

CLARA.   O Lindor! pause a moment on the dangers you are rushing to! Think
of those fatal scenes, which once presented themselves to you, when my poor
brother, your first, your dearest friend, sunk beneath the arms of opposing
enemies: think on those deadly wounds, which when you saw gashing his
manly breast, your arm in vain defending him, struck, for the first time, terror
to your shuddering soul: think on his sufferings, his piercing anguish, and his
wasting death: then pause a moment, Lindor, and reflect his fate may soon
be yours. (I, i)

The reader may be spared further quotation. The scene continues in the
same vein for three more pages. Can there be any doubt which of the two
plays quoted should be called sentimental, and for what reasons?

Another of the ways in which the essential goodness of human nature
is demonstrated is through the spectacle of a wronged person forgiving

or trying to exculpate one who has wronged him. Desdemona's last words come immediately to mind. Emilia asks her who has done the deed, and Desdemona replies:

> Nobody—I myself. Farewell
> Commend me to my kind lord. O, farewell! (V, ii)

As so often in Shakespeare, there is no straining for emotional effect by the device of resuscitating a dying person long enough to allow for a wordy forgiveness speech. Angelo is forgiven by Mariana and Isabella in very few words (*Measure For Measure*, V, i), and Hermione's forgiveness of Leontes is accomplished without her saying a word (*The Winter's Tale*, V, iii). This phenomenon is by no means peculiar to Shakespeare. Bellafront's plea that Matheo go unpunished is kept down to a bare four lines (*II Honest Whore*, V, ii). Perillo, the little murdered boy of Robert Yarington's *Two Lamentable Tragedies*, forgives his murderer with: "Oh, I am slaine, the Lord forgive thy fact!/And give thee grace to dye with penitence" (IV). Anabel, "the abused wife" of *The Fair Maid of Bristow*, forgives her husband in one short speech (V, iii). Evanthe, whose brother, Sorano, has tried to get her to prostitute herself to Frederick, kneels before the King to plead that Sorano be forgiven. Her plea is contained in two lines (*A Wife For a Month*, V, iii). Such brief expression of forgiveness is very common in Elizabethan drama.

Examination of the crimes or injuries which are forgiven so tersely in the plays mentioned results in a roll which includes actual murder (*Othello* and *Two Lamentable Tragedies*), attempted murder (*The Fair Maid of Bristow*), and intended rape (*Measure For Measure*). The abuse that Bellafront suffers at the hands of Matheo is almost negligible in contrast to these other crimes. One would think that the enormity of the crimes would give rise to lengthier expressions of forgiveness on the part of the victims—if a sentimental effect were desired by the dramatist. It is no good arguing that Desdemona and Perillo are dying and, consequently, have time for only a few words. Elizabethan dramatists were not reluctant to give their dying characters long death speeches. But, in sentimental drama, the opportunity of emphasizing the remarkable goodness and forbearance of the injured party is not slighted. In Hugh Kelly's *False Delicacy*, to limit oneself to a single example, Colonel Rivers, hurt by the knowledge that his daughter intends to elope contrary to his wishes, voluntarily gives her the twenty thousand pounds which he had promised her as a marriage gift. His recriminations and his parting gift to his daughter are delivered in a veritable spate of words. Only his first and last speeches are quoted but there are three others of equal length.

Little, Theodora, did I imagine I should ever have cause to lament the hour of your birth; and less did I imagine, when you arrived at an age to be perfectly acquainted with your duty, you would throw every sentiment of duty off. In what, my dear, has your unhappy father been culpable, that you cannot bear his society any longer? What has he done to forfeit either your esteem or your affection? From the moment of your birth to this unfortunate hour, he has labored to promote your happiness. But how has his solicitude on that account been rewarded? You now fly from these arms which have cherished you with so much tenderness when gratitude, generosity, and nature should have twined me round your heart.

One thing more, Theodora,—and then farewell forever. Though you came here to throw off the affection of a child, I will not quit this place before I discharge the duty of a parent, even to a romantic extravagance, and provide for your welfare, while you plunge me into the most poignant of all distress. In the doting hours of paternal blandishment, I have often promised you a fortune of twenty thousand pounds, whenever you changed your situation. This promise was, indeed, made when I thought you incapable either of ingratitude or dissimulation, and when I fancied your person would be given where there was some reasonable prospect of your happiness. But still it was a promise, and shall be faithfully discharged. Here then in this pocket-book are notes for that sum. . . . Take it,—but never see me more. Banish my name eternally from your remembrance; and when a little time shall remove me from a world which your conduct has rendered insupportable, boast an additional title, my dear, to your husband's regard, by having shortened the life of your miserable father. (V, ii)

Colonel Rivers reviews everything he has done for his daughter, reminds her what a fond parent he has been, assures her that he will not prevent her elopement, gives her twenty thousand pounds, and goes off in a paroxysm of self-pity. Hugh Kelly obtained his sentimental effect in this scene by allowing Colonel Rivers to speak at great length. Analogous scenes in Elizabethan plays are saved from being sentimental by the rapidity with which they are dispatched.

The spectacle of death and the grief attendant upon it offers rich opportunities for emotional effects. Here, as in other situations examined, the difference between the sentimental and the non-sentimental is easily seen. Great sorrow is seldom vocal. Confronted with the unexpected news that one we have loved is dead, we do not analyze and weigh our emotion—at least, not aloud. It is this artificial description of his grief by the person most nearly concerned in the catastrophe that rings false, and it is this very feature which is found in sentimental plays. It is as though grief had to be evinced in audible and unmistakable terms that it might prove its presence. One scholar has likened sentimentalism to the emotional orgy that accompanies an Irish wake,[20] and the analogy is apt. Although

Thomas Heywood has been called a sentimentalist by many critics, it does not follow that he is always concerned to capitalize on the pathos of potentially sentimental situations. When Old Wincott in Heywood's *The English Traveller* learns that his wife has died, he can say only one word—"Dead!" (V, ii). Obviously there is no attempt to make much of the old man's sorrow. Had Heywood wished to exploit the emotional possibilities of the scene he might have given Old Wincott speeches similar to those of Old Wilmot in George Lillo's *Fatal Curiosity* (1736). In this latter play Old Wilmot, desperately poor, has murdered his son, long absent and changed to such an extent that neither his father nor mother recognized him. When he learns the enormity of his action, and hears the grief of his son's friend, he cries out

<blockquote>

What whining fool art thou, who would'st usurp
My sovereign right of grief?—Was he thy son?—
Say! Canst thou shew thy hands reeking with blood,
That flow'd, thro' purer channels, from thy loins?

EUST.   Forbid it heaven! that I should know such Guilt:
Yet his sad fate demands commiseration.

O. WILMOT.   Compute the sands that bound the spacious ocean,
And swell their number with a single grain;
Increase the noise of thunder with thy voice;
Or when the raging wind lays nature waste,
Assist the tempest with thy feeble breath;
Add water to the sea, and fire to Etna;
But name not thy faint sorrow with the anguish
Of a curst wretch who only hopes for this
                      [Stabbing himself.]
To change the scene, but not relieve his pain.

RAND.   A dreadful instance of the last remorse!
May all your woes end here.

O. WILMOT.   O would they end
A thousand ages hence, I then should suffer
Much less than I deserve. Yet let me say,
You'll do but justice, to inform the world,
This horrid deed, that punishes itself,
Was not intended as he was our son;
For that we knew not, 'till it was too late.
Proud and impatient under our afflictions,
While heaven was labouring to make us happy,
We brought this dreadful ruin on ourselves
Mankind may learn—but—oh!—   [Dies] (III)

</blockquote>

Still other examples suggest themselves. Massinger and Field's *The Fatal Dowry* contains a scene in which Novall, Sr., comes upon the body of his son. All the grief-stricken father can say is "My son, my son," and then he turns to thoughts of revenge (IV, iv). Aaron Hill's *The Insolvent*, adapted from *The Fatal Dowry*, omits the scene in which the father sees his dead son, but adds another in which a father, thinking his daughter dead, gives vent to his grief.

> . . . Oh! 'twas a black return—to me, who lov'd him!
> What, tho' he knew not half her claims to pity,
> He shou'd have felt for me. I lov'd—I watch'd her;
> Rais'd her from prattling infancy, to wonder!
> She touch'd my charm'd (perhaps too partial) heart.
> I priz'd her own sweet bloom—still more endear'd,
> By her dead mother's likeness. He shou'd have stopp'd,
> When his fell point was rais'd, and thought whose pangs
> Were to partake his suff'rings. (V, i)

The reader may wish to compare this with the similar scenes in *The Fatal Dowry* and in Nicholas Rowe's *The Fair Penitent*.[21] In all three plays the grief of the father at the death of his daughter is used for sentimental purposes. Rowe's treatment, it will be observed, strikes one as the most sentimental because the scene is longest, and because it is principally concerned with the father and daughter (before her death) who occupy the stage most of the time and speak most of the dialogue.

The number of situations which invite sentimental treatment is great. A situation frequently encountered in plays of all periods is that in which a character chooses death rather than disloyalty to a belief or ideal. This is, of course, the theme of martyrdom, and it is as potentially fraught with tears and emotion as any other theme one can think of. As will be seen, however, there is a way to exploit the emotional possibilities of such a theme; and there is also a way to avoid excessive emotion. The sad story of the ill-fated Lady Jane Gray has attracted more than one playwright. Her story is told in *The Famous History of Sir Thomas Wyatt* by Dekker and Webster, in John Banks's *The Innocent Usurper*, and in Nicholas Rowe's *Lady Jane Gray*. *The Famous History* makes no mention of the choice offered Lady Jane Gray and her husband before their execution. They are given the chance to renounce Protestantism and live, or continue in their faith and die. Both Banks and Rowe, however, introduce the choice. In Banks's play Lady Jane has been told that she can save her own life and the lives of her husband and father by renouncing her religion. She speaks to Gilford, her husband:

> Ay, my Love!
> Would'st thou for some few years of Life? perhaps
> Some days may finish what we prize so dearly;
> Would'st thou consent that I shou'd forfeit Heav'n,

My Spotless, Innocent, and Bosom Faith,
Forsake the Truth that was so lov'd by me,
And lose the Joys of Immortality?

GILF.   I know what I wou'd act were I my Jane;
Were Gilford's safety only in the Ballance.
O all you Saints that wear Immortal Crowns!
Spirits of Martyrs that bright Angels are!
Not Racks, nor Tortures, burning Pincers, Fires,
Shou'd make me leave this Faith the most Divine,
Which adorns thee, and thou hast made to shine.

JA.   O Young, O Good! O Youth belov'd of Heav'n!

GILF.   But when I see a Father's Agonies,
Sweating cold Drops with terrour, to behold
The Heads-man diving in thy Gilford's Bowels,
And in the Hearts of four unhappy Brothers—
But oh! and which is more than all the Lives
Of all the Sons and Daughters of Mankind,
Thy precious Life, if that's a Crime to save!
You Heavenly Powers, if then 'tis Sin to change!
The Fact itself wou'd from your doom appeal,
And quash Damnation with the very mention.

NORTHUMBERLAND.   Ay, there my Son; do, press her, hold her there.

JA.   What is my Husband Traytor to my Soul!
Then I may say, as Caesar did to Brutus,
Dost thou too, Gilford, stab me to the Heart!

NORTH.   Come, prostrate fall with me—Lo, at your Feet
The Sad and Miserable Dudley lies;
See on the Ground the Father and the Son,
Thy Husband too that shou'd Command thee all,
And reign the Conq'ring Rival of thy Soul.
O say the word, thou Woman most Divine!
Quick, e'er they come to fetch thee and my Children,
Like a dumb Drove with Pantings to the Shambles.
First they begin with him, and in thy sight,
Fasten his Manly Body to the Sledge,
Which ne'er was bound before, but in thy Arms,
Then see the Villain with a Butcher's Knife
Ripping his Bowels open to the Throat,
And tearing thence the Heart, he holds to view,
That Heart which did so oft in silent Language
Whisper the Story of your Faithful Loves;
But now insenc'd, leaps in the Ruffin's hand,
And cries more fierce, the cruelty of Jane.
Then, then it stabs, and e'er I come to die,
Breaks his poor Father's Heart, and all the Standers by.

JA.   What must be done, must then be done this Moment.
The time is suddain; but the Gate of Heav'n

> Is easie to be lock'd, yet hard to open,
> It has a Spring without a Key, which when
> We shut too rashly, we no more can enter—
> I am resolv'd—

NORTH.   Of what?

JA.   Not to be chang'd till I am dead,
> For all the Blood that's threaten'd to be shed,
> Not for the Crown took lately from this Head.

After further fruitless entreaties, Northumberland goes off in a fury, cursing Jane. Gardner, Bishop of Winchester, enters and tries to persuade Jane to save her life by paying at least lip-service to Catholicism. Again Jane answers, at some length, that she will not forsake her faith. Finally, as Jane is led to execution, she repeats her determination to die rather than embrace Catholicism. She is shown the bodies of Gilford and the others, and speaks the closing lines of the play:

> Away with me, were they alive again,
> Shou'd Father, Mother, Kindred, all
> Joyn'd with this fatal number, with me fall,
> And in the very Moment of their Deaths,
> Shot Curses on me with their flying Breaths,
> To save their gasping Lives, I wou'd not chuse
> One hour of Immortality to lose.
> Shou'd all your torterous Racks on me be try'd;
> Broil me on Grid-Irons, turn the other side,
> Till the Abortive Infant where it lay
> Shou'd from my flaming Intrails burst its way,
> To my vow'd Faith I'll be for ever true,
> In spight of all your Roman Gods, and you.

The same situation is disposed of in the following fashion by Rowe:

L. J. GRAY.   What! turn apostate?
GUILIF.   Ha! forego my faith? (V)

Asked once more before their execution if they will renounce their religion they reply in equally curt terms. Dying for an ideal, making a martyr of oneself for a belief, becomes singularly unimpressive and emotionally unmoving when slighted as it is by Rowe. But how rich in emotional appeal is the same theme in Banks's version! This does not mean that Banks's treatment is artistically the better of the two; it means merely that Banks exploited the situation for all the emotion he could get out of it, and that Rowe did not.

There is a special use of prolongation whose effect is to arouse an emotion and keep it at a high pitch by allowing the spectator and one or more of the characters in the play to know of some impending piece of good news, and to keep the full knowledge of that good news from the character or characters whose distress will be relieved by it, doling it out a little at a time. This is indulging with a vengeance in emotion for emotion's sake. In Lillo's *Fatal Curiosity* Young Wilmot returns from sea to learn that his parents suffer from extreme poverty. He has acquired great fortune, and one would expect him to rush immediately to relieve his father and mother. But such an act does not serve the sentimentalist's purpose. Here is a chance to "refine" on emotion. Consequently, Young Wilmot decides to keep his good news from his parents for a time. He knows that he is much changed and determines to visit them without revealing his identity. His reasons, as he gives them, are these:

> My mind at ease grows wanton: I wou'd fain
> Refine on happiness. Why may I not
> Indulge my curiosity, and try
> If it be possible by seeing first
> My parents as a stranger, to improve
> Their pleasure by surprize?

The person to whom he is speaking agrees:

> It may indeed
> Inhance your own, to see from what despair
> Your timely coming, and unhoped success
> Have given you power to raise them. (II, ii)

This desire to "refine" upon or "enhance" emotion is one of the distinguishing marks of sentimentalism. The desire to enjoy his emotion not only results in Young Wilmot's murder by his parents; it also keeps the spectators emotionally tense until the murder, after several false starts (another device calculated for emotional effect), is done.

One or two other examples may be cited as indication that the use of this device is not peculiar to Lillo. The major part of *II Honest Whore* is based on Orlando Friscobaldo's expressed desire to help Bellafront, his assuming a disguise to be near her and help her when she is in need or danger, and his final unmasking in the last act. Friscobaldo deliberately puts off making himself known to his daughter, and his observation of her afflictions in the guise of a servant enhances the emotional impact of that plot. We, as spectators or readers, know that Orlando is on hand to save Bellafront from cruelty and abuse. The use of this device in *II Honest Whore* partakes more of the nature of a plot device dear to Elizabethan audiences (the disguise plot, of course), but it also performs some

68

of the function for which it was expressly used in Lillo's play. In a full-fledged sentimental comedy, Richard Cumberland's *The Fashionable Lover*, a father returns after eighteen years to find his daughter under the protection of a cynical philanthropist named Mr. Mortimer. Without revealing his identity, the father asks that Mr. Mortimer resign the girl to his care. The following dialogue occurs:

MORT.   Sir!
AUB.   Put her into my hands: I am rich, Sir, I can support her.
MORT.   You're insolent, or grossly ignorant to think I wou'd betray a trust, a sacred trust: she is a ward of virtue; 'tis from want, 'tis from oppression I protect Miss Aubrey—who are you, that think to make a traitor of me?
AUB.   Your zeal does honour to you; yet, if you persist in it, and spite of my protest hold out, your constancy will be no virtue; it must take another name.
MORT.   What other name, and why? Throw off your mystery, and tell me why.
AUB.   Because—
MORT.   Ay, let us hear your cause.
AUB.   Because I am her father. (IV)

The only conceivable reason for having Aubrey play this cat-and-mouse game is to work on the emotions by an extra demonstration of Mr. Mortimer's goodness. We know Aubrey is Miss Aubrey's father, but we are supposed to delight in seeing Mr. Mortimer's defense of the girl against a man that he believes to be a shameless libertine. Shortly after this dialogue Aubrey's daughter enters, and the whole procedure is repeated. Aubrey looks steadily at the girl, causing her to ask the reason for this strange behavior. He answers that he knew her father and was his friend. He then tells her that he has news of her father, assures her that she is not an orphan, and only after all this does he reveal his identity. This is the sort of thing that David Hume was writing about in one of his *Four Dissertations*, that "Of Tragedy" (1757):

Had you any intention to move a person extremely by the narration of any event, the best method of increasing its effect would be artfully to delay informing him of it, and first excite his curiosity and impatience before you let him into the secret. (p. 194)

Hume then cites Iago's use of this device to awaken Othello's jealousy; few sentimental writers begin to approach the "artfulness" of this scene.

An extreme use of prolongation of a somewhat different kind occurs in Southerne's *Oroonoko*. Oroonoko, the noble savage, expecting to be killed and fearing that Imoinda, his wife, will be ravished, resolves to kill her and himself. The resolution taken, one is treated to the following scene:

69

ORO. Ha! This dagger!
   Like fate, it points to me the horrid deed.

IMO. Strike, strike it home, and bravely save us both.
   There is no other safety.

ORO. It must be—
   But first a dying kiss—   (Kisses her.)
   This last embrace—   (Embracing her.)
   And now—

IMO. I'm ready.

ORO. O! where shall I strike?
   Is there a smallest grain of that lov'd body
   That is not dearer to me than my eyes,
   My bosom'd heart, and all the life-blood there?
   Bid me cut off these limbs, hew off these hands,
   Dig out these eyes, tho' I would keep them last
   To gaze upon thee: but to murder thee!
   The joy, and charm of every ravish'd sense,
   My wife! forbid it nature.

IMO. 'Tis your wife,
   Who on her knees conjures you. O! in time
   Prevent those mischiefs that are falling on us.
   You must be hurry'd to a shameful death,
   And I too dragg'd to the vile governor:
   Then I may cry aloud: when you are gone,
   Where shall I find a friend again to save me?

ORO. It will be so. Thou unexampled virtue!
   Thy resolution has recover'd mine:
   And now prepare.

IMO. Thus with open arms,
   I welcome you, and death.

       (He drops his dagger as he
       looks on her, and throws
       himself on the ground.)

ORO. I cannot bear it.
   O let me dash against this rock of fate.
   Dig up this earth, tear, tear her bowels out,
   To make a grave, deep as the center down,
   To swallow wide, and bury us together.
   It will not be. O! then come pitying God
   (If there be one a friend to innocence)
   Find yet a way to lay her beauties down
   Gently in death, and save me from her blood.

IMO. O rise, 'tis more than death to see you thus.
   I'll ease your love, and do the deed myself—

       (She takes up the dagger, he rises in
       haste to take it from her.) (V)

There is no reason to afflict the reader with any more of this scene; a brief summary of the rest of it will suffice. Oroonoko prevents Imoinda from killing herself, but they are soon aware that their enemies are approaching. Oroonoko resolves to stab her without looking at her; Imoinda asks for a last look and then makes ready to receive the blow. He arrests his hand, however, and Imoinda has finally to kill herself. Southerne's playing with the emotions of his audience seems crude to us, but it is scenes like these that evoke the emotional response necessary for sentimentalism.

It becomes very apparent, then, that one of the devices used by sentimental dramatists for obtaining a desired emotional response is prolonged treatment of potentially sentimental situations. Conversely, sentimentalism in the drama can be avoided—and is avoided—by hurried treatment of those same potentially sentimental situations. Since sentimentalism includes, among other things, indulgence in emotion for its own sake, it logically follows that greater opportunity to enjoy an emotion is brought about by the dramatist's allowing the scene or situation that evoked it to remain before his audience for some time. Previous discussions of sentimentalism in the drama have slighted or, more often, entirely neglected this important factor, and it is here offered as the first of three major considerations which, it is expected, will bring about a clearer understanding of the true nature of sentimental drama.

Chapter IV. ESCHEWAL OF HUMOR AND THE BAWDY

THE IDEA THAT COMEDY need not arouse laughter by exposing a person, or a vice, or a folly to ridicule has origins earlier than its popularization by Steele. In a note in his edition of John Dennis' critical works, Edward N. Hooker[1] discusses the matter at some length. It was Steele, however, who insisted in preface, play, and essay that comedy which introduced "a joy too exquisite for laughter"[2] was not only allowable but to be preferred to that comedy which provokes laughter "born/ Of sudden self-esteem and sudden scorn."[3] For Steele, consciously disagreeing with Hobbes's definition of laughter, comedy performed an almost therapeutic function. When one reads in the epilogue to *The Lying Lover* that "generous pity of a painted woe/ Makes us ourselves both more approve and know," there is the suggestion that our awakened awareness, as members of the audience, of our own goodness acts as a sort of medicinal bath which washes away any incipient evil. If, Steele seems to say, you can look upon goodness on the stage and recognize it and sympathize with it, you, too, are good. Possibly there was no greater compliment to Steele's *Conscious Lovers* than the tears of the General who wept for Indiana.[4] That a General should weep is significant: first, because as a military man he would be less prone to display emotion; and second, because a General would presumably be a gentleman and a person of some breeding. Steele was writing for other "Christian gentlemen" primarily, one suspects. And Steele, too, had been an officer.

Obviously, the cruel laughter consequent upon the spectacle of man in a state of moral undress is antagonistic to the kind of comedies that Steele wrote to exemplify his views. When a dramatist sets out to win the members of his audience to a warm and glowing self-approval by representing good people such as themselves on the stage, he cannot afford to have those same good people the subject of any laughter other than the very kindest. There must be no risk of chilling the warmth by allowing the intrusion of laughter which curls back the lips. Steele, writer and champion of sentimental comedy, realized that his efforts would be endangered if the wrong kind of humor found its way into his plays. That there is some delightful humor in all four of Steele's plays is undeniable, but Hazlitt's pronouncement that the former's comedies are misnamed and might rather be termed "homilies in dialogue" is not without justification. Steele was intelligent enough to recognize the excesses of sermonizing in *The Lying Lover* (he confesses it was "damned for its piety") and wrote a much more diverting play for his next, *The*

Tender Husband. Fielding's Parson Adams witnesses, however, that he lapsed again in *The Conscious Lovers.* Later writers of sentimental drama continued to soft-pedal the element of the comic in their plays, and one of the most common eighteenth-century criticisms leveled at the type was its lack of humor. Nor has modern criticism tended to make clear exactly what kind of humor is compatible with the purposes of the sentimental writer. The feeling seems to be that the subject may be dismissed by stating that sentimental drama does admit of humor—with no qualifying statement.

The purpose of sentimental drama is to arouse emotion: pity for distress and admiration for virtue. That laughter is often antithetical to emotion has already been suggested; the following, taken from Henri Bergson's *Laughter,* is the classic statement of that view:

Here I would point out, as a symptom equally worthy of notice, the *absence of feeling* which usually accompanies laughter. It seems as though the comic could not produce its disturbing effect unless it fell, so to say, on the surface of a soul that is thoroughly calm and unruffled. Indifference is its natural environment, for laughter has no greater foe than emotion. I do not mean that we could not laugh at a person who inspires us with pity, for instance, or even with affection, but in such a case we must, for the moment, put our affection out of court and impose silence on our pity. In a society composed of pure intelligences there would probably be no more tears, though perhaps there would still be laughter; whereas highly emotional souls, in tune and unison with life, in whom every event would be sentimentally prolonged and re-echoed, would neither know nor understand laughter. Try, for a moment, to become interested in everything that is being said and done; act, in imagination, with those who act, and feel with those who feel; in a word, give your sympathy its widest expansion: as though at the touch of a fairy wand you will see the flimsiest of objects assume importance, and a gloomy hue spread over everything. Now step aside, look upon life as a disinterested spectator: many a drama will turn into a comedy. It is enough for us to stop our ears to the sound of music in a room, where dancing is going on, for the dancers at once to appear ridiculous. How many human actions would stand a similar test? Should we not see many of them suddenly pass from grave to gay, on isolating them from the accompanying music of sentiment? To produce the whole of its effect, then, the comic demands something like a momentary anesthesia of the heart. Its appeal is to intelligence, pure and simple.[5]

Bergson is trying to prove that emotion is the foe of laughter. The converse is necessarily true: laughter is the foe of emotion. One remarks particularly that "highly emotional souls . . . in whom every event would be *sentimentally prolonged and re-echoed,* would neither know nor understand laughter." George Meredith, in his "Prelude" to *The Egoist,* says of Comedy: "If . . . she watches over sentimentalism with a birch-rod, she is not opposed to romance." Is it merely coincidence that these two writers speak of the pitched battle between laughter (Comedy, for Meredith) and sentimentalism?

The distressing intrusion of the comic in pathetic or sentimental scenes did not, of course, go unremarked by eighteenth-century critics. One of them, Dr. John Hawkesworth, bowdlerizer of Southerne's *Oroonoko* and dramatic critic for the *Gentleman's Magazine* and occasionally for the *Monthly Review*, sympathized with the writers of sentimental drama. His observations on the admixture of grave and gay in drama are, hence, of considerable interest. His review of Mrs. Griffith's *School For Rakes* in the *Monthly Review* (Feb. 1769) makes a preliminary and sincere bow to the sentimental aspects of the play, "This piece is not much calculated to excite laughter, but it produces higher pleasure than laughter can give" (p. 153), and then takes up the question of the mixed drama:

The mixed drama has been generally condemned upon a supposition that grave and gay scenes succeeding each other, were neutralized like acids and alcalis by mixture, and produced the proper effect of neither.

This has been controverted with great force of reason, and the mind has been shown to be capable of sadness and mirth in very sudden transitions; but there can be no apology for producing the ridiculous and the mournful in the same scene, for however the mind may be affected by each in a quick succession, it cannot certainly be affected by each at once. Some of the most tender and pathetic sentiments are uttered by the young lady, in the height of her distress, to her aunt, a ridiculous character, whose replies, which on another occasion would move laughter, must on this, for that very reason, produce disgust in the tender and sensible; and wholly preclude that melting of the heart, which is so much more luxurious than merriment, in those whom high spirits and a levity of temper render less susceptible of pity.

Another reviewer for the *Monthly Review*, John Langhorne, takes a position very close to Hawkesworth's on the mixed drama. In his review of a French defense of *comédie larmoyante*, *Du Theatre, ou Nouvel Essai sur L'Art Dramatique*, in the *Monthly*'s appendix devoted to "Foreign Literature" (January to June 1775), he takes issue with the author's championship of the genre:

The catastrophe appears to have been brought about in a hurry, so that the change of conduct and sentiment in the parties is not sufficiently accounted for. Upon the whole, however, this performance has considerable merit, and justifies the favour with which the public received it.

Hawkesworth and Langhorne were not following a fixed policy of the *Monthly Review* in their comments on sentimental comedy; rather they were expressing a critical objection widely held at that time. It remains now to examine a number of plays with this particular stricture in mind.

It is almost impossible to name any English play, Shakespeare's great tragedies not excepted, in which humor, wit, comedy—call it what you will—does not play a part. Even the somber *Macbeth* has its drunken porter. Occasionally, with a De Quincey, there may be some deep psychological subtlety seen in the appearance of comedy in a seemingly incongruous place. More often there is the realization that audiences expected some humor even with their serious dramatic fare. This is not a phenomenon peculiarly Elizabethan. Despite the criticism that eighteenth-century sentimental drama is devoid of humor or wit, it is the rare sentimental comedy of that period which does not include attempts at a lighter vein. That these attempts were very often feeble to a fault is explained by the fact that poor writers were trying their hands at the new and easily written genre. The number of moral ladies and Reverend gentlemen that turned their dubious talents in the direction of the stage in the half-century from 1750 to 1800 is remarkable. One has only to compare the period from 1700 to 1750 with the succeeding half-century to be struck with the greater numbers of ladies and clergymen that were profiting by an increasingly moral stage.[6] These amateurs essayed wit and humor, true, but they were heavy-handed. The little, genteel joke that was tossed from the vantage point of a pulpit was sure of an appreciative welcome by one's parishioners, but it was hardly the sort of thing that would satisfy the less elegant element in the theatres. Consequently, sentimental drama was much more successful when printed for "closet" consumption than when presented on the stage. The Reverend Charles Jenner, it may be remembered, designed his adaptation of Diderot's *Père de Famille* for the "closet." There is, then, comedy of sorts in most eighteenth-century plays. The difference between this often watery concoction and the stronger brew that was poured for Elizabethan audiences is significant. Also significant is the way in which comedy was introduced, where it occurred, and what purpose it served. The importance of these criteria may be best seen by analyzing Elizabethan and Restoration plays which lend themselves to the suspicion of sentimentalism but which escape it because of the kind of humor used, and the way in which it is used. Perhaps such analysis should be prefaced by the statement that a sentimental speech, character, or situation does not make a sentimental play; a sentimental play is one which leaves reader or spectator with the desired emotional effect unmixed with disturbingly antagonistic feelings alien to the sentimental response.

There is an Elizabethan play which demonstrates the pertinency of these introductory remarks so admirably that it seems written expressly for the purpose. The play is the "pleasant conceited comedy" of *How A Man May Choose A Good Wife From A Bad*, of anonymous authorship.

It has been sometimes attributed to Joshua Cooke because of the appearance of his name in a manuscript note on the 1602 edition of the play, and recently the work has been claimed for Thomas Heywood.[7] A brief account of the plot is necessary. Young Master Arthur, wed to the daughter of Old Master Lusam, grows tired of her, reviles her, and even strikes her in the presence of others. She is patient, loving, and faithful throughout. Young Arthur falls in love with Mistress Mary, a whore, and plans to poison his wife so that he may marry his new love. He administers a dose of what he thinks is poison (actually a sleeping potion) to his wife, and she is buried as dead. A Master Anselm, who had tried unsuccessfully to win Mistress Arthur's love, goes to the vault, discovers that she is alive, and shelters her in his mother's home. Young Arthur now discovers the true nature of his second wife, a wrangling, independent whore. To impress her with his love he tells her of the murder of his first wife, and she raises a hue and cry after him. He flees, and is skulking about hungry and penniless when he comes upon his first wife whom he does not recognize. She gives him some food and money, and leaves. He is soon taken by the police and brought to trial, and is freed only when Mistress Arthur appears. A reconciliation takes place, and Young Arthur's last speech drives home the moral that a virtuous wife is to be preferred to a fair one.

Before proceeding with a careful analysis of the comic element which obtrudes to such an extent as to destroy any sentimental potentialities which might have been exploited, a few critical comments on the play may be noted. Willard Thorp examines the play as one in the "abused wife" tradition, but his comment is brief, consisting only of a summary of the plot. There is no mention of the farcical element.[8] Bernbaum speaks of "unmistakable approaches to sentimental comedy which are found in four of the Elizabethan plays that deal with a husband who maltreats his virtuous and patient wife but who finally reforms" (p. 44). One of the four is *How A Man May Choose*; the farce liberally interlarded through the play is passed over in silence. F. T. Wood states that the play "centres around a story which contains many of the motives characteristic of the Augustan comedy of sentiment—the chaste and faithful wife, the reformed rake, and the moral object." There is an account of the action, but the broad comedy goes unremarked. A. M. Clark calls the play a tragicomedy, suggests that it was "not meant to be taken too seriously on its tragic side," and states that it presents "a delicately sentimental plot with a touch of romance in its domesticity." Ward comments on the wit and comedy present in the play.[9] Other scholars have given the plot, but little attention is paid to the play's lighter side.

Confronted with the bare outline of the plot one would conclude that *How A Man May Choose* is a typical domestic play which escapes being a tragedy through the use of the fifth-act reform of the errant husband. It would also seem to conform in all respects to the typical sentimental comedy of the eighteenth century. That such is not true will, one expects, be granted on the basis of closer scrutiny. The first distracting element is the presence of Old Master Arthur, Young Arthur's father, and Old Master Lusam, Mistress Arthur's father. They are "humour" characters whose eccentricity is a a comical indecision that constantly forces them to agree or disagree with whatever is said to them, although they are ready to contradict their immediately preceding statement if there is any opposition to it—or agreement with it. Quotation is better than explanation here. The two oldsters, on their first appearance, discuss the troubled marital life of their children.

O. ART.	If fame be true, the most fault's in my son.
O. LUS.	You say true, Master Arthur, 'tis so indeed.
O. ART.	Nay, sir, I do not altogether excuse Your daughter, many lay the blame on her.
O. LUS.	Ah! say you so? by the mass, 'tis like enough For, from her childhood, she hath been a shrew.
O. ART.	A shrew? you wrong her; all the town admires her For mildness, chasteness, and humility.
O. LUS.	'Fore God, you say well, she is so indeed; The city doth admire her for these virtues.
O. ART.	O, sir, you praise your child too palpably; She's mild and chaste, but not admir'd so much.
O. LUS.	Aye, so I say, I did not mean admir'd.
O. ART.	Yes, if a man do well consider her, Your daughter is the wonder of her sex.
O. LUS.	Are you advis'd of that? I cannot tell What 'tis you call the wonder of her sex. But she is, is she, aye, indeed, she is.—
O. ART.	What is she?
O. LUS.	Even what you will, you know best what she is.[10]

This is only a mild sample of a "humour" which the playwright exploits throughout. After a serious dialogue between Young Arthur and his wife the two old men come in to debate the advisability of entering the young couple's home, comically undecided as to the necessity of knocking at the door (I, i). The playwright is seemingly unwilling to have the serious action emphasized.

Taken alone, the "humours" of the two old men would hardly be enough to distract attention from the serious action. There are, however, a number of other characters whose presence affords so much distraction that precisely such an effect is obtained. There is a witty page, Pipkin, whose name furnishes him and others with material for numerous puns.

A delightful pedant, Sir Aminadab, appears in his official capacity as a schoolmaster and in a more ludicrous role as a lover. Also present is a Justice Reason, appealed to by the old men for advice, and later the presiding officer at the trial of Young Arthur. Listen as the sage jurist dispenses counsel to Mistress Arthur, the pathetic heroine:

Good woman, or good wife, or mistress, if you have done amiss, it should seem you have done a fault, and making a fault, there's no question that you have done amiss; but if you walk uprightly, and neither lead to the right hand nor the left, no question but you have neither led to the right hand nor the left, but, as a man should say, walked uprightly; but it should appear by these plaintiffs, that you have had some wrong: if you love your spouse entirely, it should seem you affect him fervently; and if he hate you monstrously, it should seem he loathes you most exceedingly, and there's the point at which I will leave, for the time passes away: therefore, to conclude, this is my best counsel, look that thy husband so fall in, that hereafter you never fall out. (II, ii)

In addition to these comic characters there is Master Fuller, the teller of off-color stories designed to impress his friend, Master Anselm, with the fickleness of women. It is still conceivable that a serious play might emerge despite this profusion of comedy. Such a feat might possibly be accomplished by stringing a number of serious scenes together, making certain that no obtrusive elements intervened or were contained within those serious scenes. Even then one doubts that any unity of effect could be achieved—at least enough unity of effect to arouse and maintain a sentimental response in the audience. In *How A Man May Choose* the serious is mixed indiscriminately with the broadly humorous and the bawdy. In the banquet scene in which Young Arthur administers what he thinks is poison to his wife, Master Fuller completely destroys any possibility of sustained emotional effect by telling how he gained the favors of a Puritan by pretending to be one of her sect. This banquet scene, rich in sentimental possibilities, is further made farcical by a comic grace spoken by Sir Aminadab. It is good enough to quote entire.

Gloria Deo, sirs, preface:
Attend me now, whilst I say grace.
For bread and salt, for grapes and malt,
For flesh and fish, and every dish;
Mutton and beef, of all meats chief;
For cow-heels, chitterlings, tripes, and souse,
And other meat that's in the house;
For racks, for breasts, for legs, for loins,
For pies with raisins, and with prunes,
For fritters, pan-cakes, and for frys,

> For ven'son pasties, and minc'd pies;
> Sheep's-head and garlick, brawn and mustard,
> Wafers, spic'd cakes, tart, and custard;
> For capons, rabbits, pigs, and geese,
> For apples, caraways, and cheese;
> For all these, and many mo'
> *Benedicamus Domino!* (III, iii)

Add the comic examination of Pipkin's abilities as a Latinist by Sir Aminadab to Master Fuller's "travelling-salesman" type of humor and the pedant's comic grace, and it is almost impossible for one to readjust to the seriousness requisite for the poison scene.

Sentimental comedy does not trifle with the treatment of death. Death is a serious matter, to be treated in a minor key and to the accompaniment of tears. The dead may later turn up alive and occasion great joy, but if they die within the compass of the play their death is occasion for great mourning—in the case of the death of the good and virtuous, that is. Although we, as spectators, have been told that the poison administered to Mistress Mary is really a sleeping potion, this fact is not known to any of the characters in the play except Master Fuller and Master Anselm, for they had given it to Sir Aminadab. In any event, Mistress Arthur's supposed death is the occasion for a rather remarkable outburst of grief on the part of Pipkin. After having announced the death of his mistress, Pipkin enters again, preceded by Hugh, Justice Reason's man, and delivers his grief in the following fashion:

PIP.   O, mistress!. O, Hugh! O, Hugh! O, mistress!
       Hugh, I must needs beat thee; I am mad! I am lunatic!
       I must fall upon thee: my mistress is dead!   [beats Hugh.]
HUGH. O, Master Pipkin, what do you mean? what do you mean,
       Master Pipkin?
PIP.   O, Hugh! O, mistress! O, mistress! O, Hugh!
HUGH. O, Pipkin! O, God! O, God! O, Pipkin!
PIP.   O, Hugh, I am mad! bear with me, I cannot chuse:
       O, death! O, mistress! O, mistress! O, death!   [exit.]
HUGH. Death, quotha; he hath almost made me dead with beating.

This is out-and-out farce, and there can be no doubt that the audience howled at Pipkin's words and at his pummeling of Hugh. Mistress Arthur was forgotten. What is more, when she is taken from her tomb by Master Anselm, a sufficiently solemn occasion one would think, the opportunity for incongruous merriment is not passed over by the dramatist. He has Sir Aminadab appear on the scene and flee in comic terror at the appearance of something in a white sheet (IV, i). In the trial scene that ends the play it is discovered that Young Arthur obtained the "poison" from

79

Sir Aminadab, and the latter is asked to tell from whom he had it. Sir Aminadab answers:

> A man *verbosus*, that was a fine *generosus*;
> He was a great guller, his name I take to be Fuller:
> See where he stands that unto my hands convey'd a powder;
> And, like a knave, sent her to her grave, obscurely to shroud
>   her.

For the sake of completeness Brabo, Mistress Mary's pimp and lover, and Mistress Splay, her bawd, must be mentioned. Although they appear only two or three times they, too, supply distracting elements of the comic and the bawdy.

All the foregoing must not be taken to mean that there is no sentimentalism in the play. Mistress Arthur has a number of speeches whose purpose can be no other than to arouse admiration for her loving forbearance and pity for the abuse she suffers at her husband's hands. That there be no suspicion that the play has been misrepresented by a process of selective quotation one of Mistress Arthur's most sentimental speeches is given, and others are listed in a note. Master Anselm has tried to win Mistress Arthur's love by telling her of her husband's lewd pursuits. She repulses him in no uncertain terms:

> Tempt no more, devil! thy deformity
> Hath chang'd itself into an angel's shape,
> But yet I know thee by thy course of speech:
> Thou get'st an apple to betray poor Eve,
> Whose outside bears a show of pleasant fruit;
> But the vile branch on which this apple grew,
> Was that which drew poor Eve from Paradise.
> Thy Syren's song could make me drown myself,
> But I am tied unto the mast of truth.
> Admit my husband be inclin'd to vice,
> My virtues may, in time, recall him home;
> But, if we both should desp'rate run to sin,
> We should abide certain destruction.
> But he's like one, that, over a sweet face,
> Puts a deformed vizard; for his soul
> Is free from any such intents of ill:
> Only to try my patience he puts on
> An ugly shape of black intemperance;
> Therefore this blot of shame which he now wears,
> I with my prayers will purge, wash with my tears.[11]

One must, therefore, recognize that this play, like so many others of the period, contains sentimentally conceived characters, situations, and speeches. Yet the total effect of such a play is not one which can be properly termed sentimental. Obviously the writer did not concentrate on arousing one specific emotional response by the virtual exclusion of other, antagonistic responses. Had he omitted the many comic characters and their disturbing levity, or if he had allowed only an occasional flash of humor in an intercalary scene, the story of Young Arthur and his wife would have come through as a sentimental comedy in the best eighteenth-century tradition. Bergson, speaking of people as members of theatre audiences, makes a remark which sums up very succinctly all that has been said here about this play.

There is an art of lulling sensibility to sleep . . . And there is also an art of throwing a wet blanket upon sympathy at the very moment it might arise, the result being that the situation, though a serious one, is not taken seriously.[12]

The "wet blanket" Bergson refers to is laughter. When laughter is provoked to the extent that it is in this play, there can be no thought of claiming it for the sentimental canon, even though the other, supposedly fundamental, features of the type are present.

One of the plot situations in Nathan Field's *Amends For Ladies* (1618) is a husband's test of his wife's fidelity through the expedient of exposing her to temptation. The theme is familiar to readers of Steele's plays, for it forms the basis for the serious action in his *Tender Husband*. In that play Clerimont, Sr., has his mistress disguise herself as a man and lay siege to his wife's honor. He breaks in on them when Mrs. Clerimont exhibits no great dislike for extramarital dalliance, ridicules his wife by revealing the true sex of her suitor, and then forgives her as she kneels repentant before him. The serious action is the slightest thread in an enjoyable comedy which centers about the romantically minded Biddy Tipkin. Yet *The Tender Husband* is called a sentimental comedy by practically everybody that discusses it. Nicoll's description of the play is remarkable:

In *The Tender Husband* . . . Steele continued on his sentimental career. Save for some older type of satire in the presentation of Bridget, the whole conduct of the plot is in this moralising style, a moralising style, however, which permits of such callousness as is apparent in the Fainlove episode. (*1700-1750*, p. 192)

As a matter of fact, except for the first scene in Act V, the climactic scene of the serious part of the play, Clerimont, Sr., and Mrs. Clerimont figure in only two other scenes (I, i and III, i) with any degree of prominence, and in both scenes the treatment is as much comic as serious —the second is wholly comic. In Field's play Sir John Loveall asks his friend Subtle to attempt his wife, Lady Perfect's, honor. Sir John is not satisfied with a cloistered virtue. Subtle obliges, grateful of the opportunity, desiring to enjoy Lady Perfect in earnest. She repulses him, is suspected by him of cuckolding Sir John with Bold, convinces him of her virtue, and forgives him as he kneels repentant. (The required position for the expression of penitence is, it must have become obvious by now, the kneeling.) Sir John, who has overheard all, bursts out of concealment and asks his wife's forgiveness—kneeling. One scholar remarks on Subtle's reformation:

With the coming of the drama of sensibility, added stress falls upon the idea of man's reclamation by the unassailable virtue of woman. Such a scene is found in *Amends* when Subtle is convinced of Lady Bright's [*sic*, actually, Lady Perfect's] constancy and kneels to beg her pardon.[13]

The scene definitely anticipates eighteenth-century sentimental drama, and it is worth noting that Sir John makes it easier for his wife to put aside her principles by beating her and subjecting her to abuse. None of these characters is shown in a comic light. With this action there are two others of importance. Bold, disguised as an old woman, takes service with Lady Bright, a widow, and tries to seduce her. Despite her knowledge that the affair could be kept secret so easily, and despite her love for Bold, the widow resists. Bold eventually marries her by a ruse. There is much humor, but the widow's stand against Bold's importunities and threats is seriously handled. The third situation is replete with sentimental potentialities, some of which are not slighted. Lady Honour, a virgin, loves Ingen, but plays it coy. He has it bruited about that he has married, but his bride is actually his young brother dressed as a woman. Lady Honour disguises herself as an Irish footman and enters the employ of Ingen. Her brother, Lord Proudly, missing her, demands her of him. Ingen disclaims any knowledge of her whereabouts and offers to search the world for her—this, after revealing his supposed bride's identity. Lady Honour, present in her capacity as Ingen's servant, is overcome with joy at the revelation, but her joy is tempered with sorrow, for her brother and her beloved quarrel and appoint a time for a duel. In brief, Lady Honour makes herself known on the dueling ground—not before being stabbed by her brother in a fit of anger—and goes off with Lord Proudly, who will not permit her match with the untitled Ingen. The lovers marry in the fifth act, Lady Honour feigning extreme sickness and Ingen gaining access to her disguised as a physician. The last act is predominantly comic. A number of comic characters are present in the play, and there are not a few purely comic scenes. Figuring incidentally is a citizen's wife who resists Sir John Loveall's and Lord Proudly's offers to help her cuckold her husband.

Although this Elizabethan play is largely comic and somewhat bawdy there are more reasons why it should be called sentimental comedy than Steele's *Tender Husband.* The parallel situation in the two plays—the testing of a wife's virtue—is treated more seriously and to greater length (extraneous comedy, in Steele's play, discounted) in Field's play. There is only one serious action in Steele's play; there are two in Field's play, and a third which has elements of the sentimental in it. The number of "sentimental" speeches in Field's play is far greater than in *The Tender Husband.*[14] Yet *The Tender Husband* is judged to be sentimental comedy, and *Amends For Ladies* is not. One begins to suspect that Steele's play is called sentimental comedy because it was written by him, and that Field's is not because it was written in the Elizabethan age, when such a genre supposedly did not exist. Possibly, Steele's care "to avoid everything that might look ill-natured, immoral, or prejudicial to what the better part of mankind holds sacred and honourable"[15] in *The Tender Husband* is taken to be sufficient reason for the play's inclusion in the sentimental genre. Yet Nathan Field, in some complimentary verses prefixed to Fletcher's *Faithful Shepherdess,* expresses the wish that he may himself write a play with a "morality sweet and profitable," a wish which suggests that he had some moral purpose in mind in his plays. Bernbaum, the only scholar to discuss the question of sentimentalism in connection with Field's play, decides that the serious passages are too few to allow it to be called sentimental comedy (p. 41). But *Amends For Ladies* is more serious than *The Tender Husband.* Should the former, then, also be called a sentimental comedy? Or is it possible that neither play is a sentimental comedy because the comic element is so predominant in both?

The statement, earlier made, that eighteenth-century writers of sentimental comedy were aware that they must include some humor in their plays will be accepted without question by those familiar with the dramatic literature of that period. One or two quotations may suffice to convince the skeptical. Richard Cumberland was a shrewder playwright than one may realize from a cursory reading of only a few of his plays. He knew what audiences wanted as well as any practicing dramatist of his time, as the popularity of many of his plays demonstrates. In the Epilogue to *The Impostors* (1789) he indicates his awareness of the varying appetites he must satisfy.

> Oh, rot your delicacy!—Give me fun,
> Sir Balaam Blubber cries . . .
> . . . .
> I come to laugh, or I come here no more
>
> Not so Miss Biddy—she is all for feeling,
> For Sentiment, for sighing, sobbing, kneeling;
> Rope ladders she admires and closet scenes,

Escapes, surprizes, huddlings behind screens,
And ever when two meanings mask the jest,
Miss Biddy's purity picks out the best.

Lieutenant General ("Gentleman Johnny") Burgoyne wielded pen as well as sword. The Preface to his *Lord of the Manor* (1780), a comic opera, further makes clear that mixed audiences caused dramatists to write for different tastes within the compass of a single play. The General's words also support an earlier statement, namely, that the "refined" were thought to be more susceptible to the appeals of sentimental drama than were the less elegant members of the audience. Burgoyne writes:

Continued uninterrupted scenes of tenderness and sensibility (*Comedie Larmoyante*) may please the very refined, but the bulk of an English audience, including many of the best understanding, go to a comic performance to laugh, in some part of it at least. They claim a right to do so upon precedent of our most valued plays; and every author owes it to them, so long as the merriest among them shews he is equally capable of relishing and applauding what is elevated and affecting—an observation I have always seen hold good in an English gallery.

Other such references are scattered in prefaces and prologues, in dedications, and in the text of the plays themselves. One must constantly remember that most eighteenth-century sentimental plays are not wholly devoid of humor, a fact which suggests a number of questions. When does the comic element so overshadow the serious that a play can no longer be called sentimental? Are there certain comic effects which are admissible in sentimental comedy and others which are not? Does it make any difference whether the comic and the serious occur together or are kept apart? May a play be of the sentimental genre and still contain definitely anti-sentimental features; namely, parody, and satire on sentimentalism? Is it important to determine whether humor, wit, or farce intrude at the psychologically wrong moment or merely play a subordinate unobstrusive role? With the exception of the question concerning parody and satire, an attempt will be made to put these matters in proper perspective. Differentiation between "straight" writing and parody is often quite impossible without the author's direct statement of his purpose. There is still divergence of opinion on the question of Sheridan's purpose in writing the Julia-Falkland episodes in *The Rivals*.

Often the presence or absence of humor in particular scenes and situations determines whether a play can be called sentimental. Such a criterion enables one scholar to conclude that Arthur Murphy's *The Way To Keep Him* is not a sentimental comedy.

The conclusion appeals, not to the heart, but to reason. Perhaps Lovemore's reform has led critics astray, but to err on this ground is to mistake the trees for the woods and to forget that Mrs. Lovemore also reforms . . . Murphy accomplishes the reform of Lovemore and enforces the moral of his play, not by exhortation, pathos, or sympathetic appeal—the hallmarks of sentiment—but by their antithesis—ridicule.[16]

Sometimes a critic is led astray by reading humor into the portrayal of a character or the handling of a situation when that humor is, at best, very doubtfully there. On the basis of such a misconception of the authors' purpose Elizabeth P. Stein can say of Fanny, in Colman and Garrick's *Clandestine Marriage*, that her

excess of sensibility, because it forces itself continuously upon our attention, becomes ridiculous. She does not, therefore, as heroines in distress ordinarily do in sentimental comedies, command our sympathy. On the contrary, we smile at the excess of emotionalism that she displays, for it is an emotionalism that is entirely out of proportion with the source from which it springs.[17]

Miss Stein has failed to understand that the "excess of sensibility" which "forces itself continuously on our attention" is one of the most important features of sentimental comedy. This excess stirs *our* sense of the ridiculous, but it is highly questionable that it appeared ridiculous to audiences of the latter half of the eighteenth century. Despite certain anti-sentimental notes in it, Hugh Kelly's *False Delicacy* is considered one of the most sentimental of comedies because of this very excess of sensibility, refinement, or false delicacy. The Julia-Falkland plot of Sheridan's *The Rivals*, to cite one more well-known example, is rife with sensibility, whether intended to be taken seriously or not. Sheridan did not, to the best of my knowledge, divulge his intention in writing the mawkish scenes between Julia and Falkland. Critics differ in their views, some thinking the intention satirical, others accepting it as serious. The pros and cons of a vexed question which, possibly, does not admit of solution will not be argued here. One periodical of the time, *The Town and Country Magazine*, called Julia and Falkland "the most outré sentimental characters that ever appeared on the stage," but there is no assurance that the writer was doing anything other than expressing his opinion, an opinion based solely on his personal reaction to the play. To return to Fanny and *The Clandestine Marriage*: there is nothing in the character of Fanny which distinguishes her from other heroines of sentimental comedy. Her "excess of emotionalism," rather than setting her off as a satirical portrait, marks her as one of many sentimental heroines who speaks like an extract from a guide to good letter-writing and who constantly mouths, or causes others to mouth, words like "delicacy" and "sensibility." Miss Stein states that Garrick satirizes in Fanny "the lachrymose heroines of the fashionable sentimental comedies" (p. 237). Again one must question the wisdom of such a statement. Although Garrick was an enemy of sentimental comedy, he was also a shrewd man of the theatre (a fact which Miss Stein does not neglect), ready to serve the public the plays that it called for, and not above pandering to this same sentimental vogue. And it is only three years after *The Clandestine Marriage* (1766) that Mrs. Elizabeth Griffith's sentimental comedy, *The School For Rakes* (which nobody will claim as satire), introduces Harriet, a lachrymose heroine who declares unequivocally that "joy has its tears, as well as grief" and often takes occasion to indulge in tears of both variety. Harriet is really Fanny's literary sister—they are only two of a numerous progeny—and both were meant to be taken seriously. In the "advertisement" to her play Mrs. Griffith acknowledges her gratitude to Mr. Garrick both for suggesting that she adapt Beaumarchais' *Eugénie* for the English stage (so one may interpret her words) and for helping her meet an "insuperable difficulty." We must not read twentieth-century attitudes into these plays.

The discussions of *How A Man May Choose* and *Amends For Ladies* stressed the intrusion of humor alone. In both plays, however, there is some bawdry. The second is more outspoken; its situations contain more of the comico-sexual than the first. This combination of the comic and the bawdy occurs so often in early English drama (before 1700, let us say) that it is difficult to speak of one without having to speak of the other. Sentimental comedy is disposed to eschew bawdry; sentimental plays are "moral." This consideration has not prevented a number of plays from being called sentimental despite a large element of the humorous and the bawdy in them. The idea that comedy and bawdry act as intrusive and disturbing elements inimical to sentimental effects is by no means a novel one. It has been remarked upon, but it has never been given the emphasis that it merits. Bernbaum glances at the idea a few times, perhaps never more directly than in his comments on Farquhar's *Constant Couple*.

The modest Angelica in *The Constant Couple* is rendered very unhappy by Sir Harry Wildair's profligacy; but the notable scene between them, which might easily have been made sentimental, is kept comic (and very far from "genteel") by the drunken Sir Harry's mistaken belief that she is a lady of pleasure and that her virtuous protestations are mock-heroics. (p. 85)

What was necessary to make the scene sentimental was the exclusion of the comic and the "ungenteel." What made the scene non-sentimental was the intrusion of the comic and the "ungenteel" (the bawdy, in other words). The idea admits of demonstration similar to that used in solving

86

a proposition in geometry. Incidentally, it might be pointed out that the scene referred to above is also written "sentimentally" by Farquhar and is to be found, admirable for purposes of comparison, in the Mermaid edition of that dramatist's plays, after *The Constant Couple*.

Steele has been given some prominence as an apologist for sentimental comedy.[18] One of the *Spectator* essays (No. 51) treats of the "smuttiness" that mars so many dramatic compositions. It is in this essay that a female reader calls attention to an objectionable passage in *The Funeral*. "She" writes:

I was last night at the Funeral, where a confident lover in the play, speaking of his mistress, cries out "—Oh that Harriot! to fold these arms about the waste [*sic*] of that beauteous, struggling, and at last yielding fair." Such an image as this ought, by no means, to be presented to a chaste and regular audience.

The comparatively innocuous latter part of this speech disappears in the next edition of the play. In the same essay Steele suggests a new way of writing:

If men of wit, who think fit to write for the stage, instead of this pitiful way of giving delight, would turn their thoughts upon raising it from such good natural impulses as are in the audience, but are choaked up by vice and luxury, they would not only please, but befriend us at the same time. If a man had a mind to be new in his way of writing, might not he who is represented as a fine gentleman, though he betrays the honour and bed of his neighbour and friend, and lies with half the women in the play, and is at last rewarded with her of the best character in it; I say, upon giving the comedy another cast might not such a one divert the audience quite as well, if at the catastrophe he were found out for a traitor, and met with contempt accordingly?

Smut, or the bawdy, has no place ideally in the new way of writing for the theatre, then. The new way is, of course, that which Steele attempted in his plays, and that which has come to be known as sentimental comedy.

William Popple's *The Lady's Revenge, or The Rover Reclaimed* (1734) has been described as a sentimental comedy.[19] During the course of the play one learns that the hero, Sir Harry Lovejoy, had enjoyed a young woman who later married and is now the widowed Lady Traffick. Sir Harry enjoys Lady Traffick again, seduces the very willing Betty, chambermaid to Angelica, and also despoils Maria, a young virgin, of her chastity. As a reward for his avowed intention to be a different man in the future, Angelica consents to marry him—knowing of his previous affairs. Maria is married off by a ruse, and Betty is matched with Sir Harry's man Tom, a farm being payment for his taking her to wife. Popple is carrying the principle of rewarding the repentant rake a little too far. This is the very kind of play hit at by Steele in which "a fine Gentleman . . . lies with half the women in the play, and is at last rewarded with her of the best character in it." The twentieth-century critic may call Popple's play a sentimental comedy, but one is sure that Sir Richard would not have called it such (the term had not, of course, come into being), nor would he have permitted it to be classed in the same genre with his own plays. Besides the *reductio ad absurdum* of the practice of showering rewards on repentant rakes, one is struck with the bawdry in *The Lady's Revenge*. Hazlitt once remarked that familiarizing the public with the immoral was no way to go about reforming its morals, and the only excuse for extracting bawdy passages for quotation is that such a procedure is necessary if one's point is to be made. Angelica has been interrogating Betty:

BET. —O law, Mem, I mean no Harm. He only romp'd with me a little, and thrust his Hand—

ANG. You are very free with Gentlemen, methinks.

BET. Nay, Mem, 'twas only down my Bosom a little: but it was to admire the Fineness of the Edging of the last Tucker your Ladiship was pleas'd to give me. O Gemini, how my Heart did beat, and my Bosom swell! I'm sure if he had not press'd it down with his Hand, 'twould have burst my Stays. I was never in such a Taking before. I trembled every Joint of me.—Wou'd he had stopt there! [Sighs, aside.] (II)

A few speeches later, in an aside, Betty divulges the loss of her virginity to Sir Harry. As the play is about to end Tom accepts Betty, whose past relationship to his master is no secret to him, as his wife.

TOM. . . . I'll venture to take a Lease for Life. But hark'ee, my Dear, No Husbandman but myself, d'you hear, no Labourer to help me to do my Work. I'll warrant thee, Girl, I'll keep thee in good Order myself.

BET. Well, Tom, if thou art but as good as thy Word, I promise thee thou shalt reap the Fruits of Nobody's Labour but thy own. But take heed. If like a lazy Lubbard you grow idle, and let good Land run into Common, for want of enriching the Soil as it ought, it will fall to the Lord of the Manor again, and then, you know, he has a Right to turn his own Cattle a grazing there.

There is no need to explicate.

Sometimes a play, otherwise seemingly out-and-out sentimental drama, can have its emotional effect ruined by one or more scenes or characters. Thus, Charles Johnson had the misfortune to have his play *Caelia or The Perjured Lover* (1732) acted by "a cast of neophytes,"[20] and it is prob-

88

ably due, in part, to this fact that the play ran only two nights. But Johnson himself felt that certain scenes involving a bawd, Mother Lupine, and her women were responsible for the failure of his domestic tragedy. For a better understanding of Johnson's remarks on the poor reception of his play, some knowledge of the plot is necessary. Caelia has been seduced by Wronglove, brought up to London, and eventually lodged with the bawd, Mother Lupine, when Wronglove tires of her. Caelia does not know what kind of establishment she is in. She is picked up in a raid on the house and dies in jail, broken-hearted. Wronglove is killed in a duel. Before he dies he asks that Caelia be looked upon as his wife and commits her and the child she is bearing to his father's care. This resumé excludes much, but it is enough for present purposes. Johnson says, in his "Advertisement to the Reader":

I had the Mortification to see this Play acted the first Night, and to hear the Characters of Mother Lupine and her Women disapprov'd by several of the Audience, who, as if they thought themselves in bad Company, were very severe. However necessary it was to shew the Manners of these People, in order to raise the Distress of Caelia, and to heighten her Character, and whatever Care I took, that nothing indecent shou'd be said, I must confess it was an error to let 'em appear at all—I shou'd not have made 'em necessary to my Design. I had the Pleasure, however, to hear the serious Scenes applauded, and to see some of those very Spectators, who were offended at the lower Characters, join with Caelia in her tears.

There is no reason to doubt Johnson's sincere desire to heighten the pathos of Caelia's situation by exposing her to humiliation and distress in Mother Lupine's house. One can sympathize with this playwright who may have been somewhat ahead of his times. His audience refused to accept his bawdy-house scenes, possibly causing him to abandon the theatre, for he wrote no more plays.

Johnson reveals elsewhere in his "Advertisement" that Barton Booth, one of the managers of Drury Lane, had advised him to "alter his Plan with relation to the Comic Characters," but he insisted on having the play acted without deletion. One scholar, commenting on this aspect of the play, writes:

The presence of the "low" characters . . . was chiefly responsible for the failure of *Caelia*, but that their inclusion was justified dramatically cannot be denied; the heroine's brief sojourn among them undoubtedly heightens her distress. Especially effective is the scene in which the strumpets taunt the uninvited Caelia. When one remembers that these prostitutes have become what they are by dint of such betrayals as Wronglove's it will be understood why Johnson insisted that the Lupine scenes be retained. Unfortunately, he fell foul of a growing moral fastidiousness.[21]

Johnson's purpose could have been achieved without resorting to comic effects in his treatment of Mother Lupine and her women. That there is comedy in the brothel scenes needs no proof; one need only read the play. Johnson thinks of these prostitutes as "Comic Characters," and he writes comedy into their speeches. This is not the way to arouse sympathy either for Caelia or for the prostitutes—although sympathy for prostitutes is a twentieth-century refinement read into the play, and doubtless not part of Johnson's plan. Indeed, Bernbaum makes it clear that he thinks the dramatist was satirizing Mother Lupine and her ménage (p. 162). One is inclined to be skeptical of both views. Johnson was not so far ahead of his audience as to write a play of deep sociological significance, nor was he concerned to satirize prostitution. The kind of laughter he aroused was less designed for correction than for amusement. Pathetic as is Caelia's position, and effective as the juxtaposition of betrayed innocence and hardened prostitution may be, there can be little doubt that something of the pathos of the situation is lost by the admission of the bawdy note which breaks into and lessens the effect of the sentimental. The sentimental treatment of a similar situation—an innocent young woman's presence in a house of ill-fame—can be seen in Richard Cumberland's *The Fashionable Lover*. There is no attempt to capitalize on the opportunities for suggestive dialogue in this play. Even greater difference will be found between Johnson's use of the bawdy-house and the treatment afforded the same situation and locale by a woman of sensibility. The reader is invited, with misgivings, to read Lady Wallace's *The Ton* (1788), one of the dullest plays in a genre notorious for dullness.

Johnson's *Caelia* may have failed because of the presence of Mother Lupine and her girls; the same fate almost overtook Edward Moore's *The Foundling* (1748) because of a vulgar and ridiculous fop named Faddle. The March number of the *Gentleman's Magazine* for 1748 carried a criticism of the play in which the following appears:

The character of Faddle is altogether unnatural and absurd: no woman of fashion and modesty could be supposed to suffer such liberties as he is represented to take, from so infamous, so needy, a dependent. To point out particulars in so glaring a deformity is unnecessary; and as the author shortened this character as much as possible after the first night, I should have spared this remark had not he betray'd a fondness for his Faddle, by exhibiting him in print at full length, in opposition to the just exceptions in the audience.

Although Henry Fielding wrote a defense of the play in the *Jacobite's Journal* (March 19), he, too, objected to Faddle. Another critic, writing in the May and June numbers of the *Gentleman's Magazine*, also defended the play, directing his remarks against the writer of the attack in the

March number of the same periodical. His defense of Faddle was based on the argument that his vices are useful as a foil to the goodness of other characters, but he confesses that he is not "concern'd in any fondness for this character." Mme. Riccoboni was instrumental in having *The Foundling* translated into French; some of Faddle's speeches are cut out, and a note at the end of the translation singles out his presence as the cause which almost brought about the failure of the play.[22] Faddle was decidedly *persona non grata* with the audience and the critics.

Any number of Faddle's speeches might be cited as evidence of the incongruity of his appearance in a sentimental play.[23] One situation, however, shows very well how the bawdy can cast a blight on the sentimental. Fidelia, the foundling, accused of immorality, is offered help by Sir Charles, much her senior. Faddle has stationed himself where he can overhear and makes frequent remarks aside. Because his own mind is dirty, he imputes equal lack of morals to Sir Charles, making it clear that he suspects him of designs on Fidelia's innocence. Here is a scene the sentimental possibilities of which are slighted by an author who preferred to put a leering, dirty-minded, and ridiculous fop on the stage to divert the attention of the audience. The true sentimentalist does not allow a Faddle to intrude at times like these.

Very often, as has been indicated previously, the difference between the sentimental and the non-sentimental play can be seen most clearly by comparing an early play with its eighteenth-century adaptation. Colley Cibber's adaptation and completion of Vanbrugh's unfinished *A Journey To London* ends, contrary to Vanbrugh's expressed intention to have "his imaginary fine lady" turned out of doors by her husband, in a reconciliation between the two. This is, of course, the most significant change, but it must not go unnoticed that Cibber cleaned up Vanbrugh's dialogue in a few places, shrewdly capitalizing upon the trend toward a more moral kind of comedy. For one thing Cibber cut out the entire scene in which the ladies engage in dice.[24] One bawdy remark is omitted thereby, although the intent, one would assume, was to delete a "vicious" scene from the finished play. In Vanbrugh (p. 161) Colonel Courtly, describing the coach accident in which he and Lady Headpiece were jostled together, says: "—I'm sure we rowl'd so, that my poor Hands were got once—I don't know where they were got. But her Ladyship I see will pass by Slips." Most of this is in an aside; it does not appear in Cibber. Cibber could not write an entirely moral play of course, and the bawdy is still present in *The Provok'd Husband*. Fortunately, Cibber was wise enough to keep a good deal of Vanbrugh's humor, and the play still makes enjoyable reading.

Cibber's changes in *The Provok'd Husband* are valuable primarily as indications of a trend. Succeeding adapters bowed to the demands of their audiences by cutting out the comic and the bawdy from plays which had contained those elements mixed with their more serious action. Thomas Southerne's *The Fatal Marriage* suffered drastic curtailment at the hands of Garrick, who cut out the comic-bawdy subplot of his original and produced a moral *Isabella*. In the subplot of Southerne's play one finds a son saying "I intend to put the means honestly in my mother's hands, to make my father a cuckold if she pleases." This occasioned no protest in 1694, but it would have aroused a storm in 1758. In some anonymous "Observations on the Tragedy of Oroonoko" a writer in the *Gentleman's Magazine* (April 1752) criticized Southerne's play chiefly because of the intrusive subplots: "By introducing an under plot of the comic kind, though complete in all its parts, by exhibiting mirth in one scene and distress in another, our attention is too much diverted from the main story, and our concern for those who suffer too much weakened by some quick transitions" (p. 163). A few years later, in 1759, Dr. John Hawkesworth adapted *Oroonoko* for eighteenth-century consumption; the 1774 editor of Southerne's plays explains the changes:

The late Dr. Hawkesworth, in 1759, altered this play, disgusted, and justly, with the comic scenes; he has entirely removed them; his prologue contains his reasons, and also a just character of Southerne.

> This night your tributary tears we claim,
> For scenes that Southerne drew; a fav'rite name.
> He touched your fathers hearts with generous woe,
> And taught your mothers youthful eyes to flow:
> For this he claims hereditary praise,
> From wits and beauties of our modern days:
> *Yet slave to custom*, in a laughing age,
> With ribbald mirth he stain'd his sacred page,
> While virtue's shrine he reared, taught vice to mock,
> And joined in sport the buskin and the sock.
> O haste to part them—burst th' opprobrious band,
> This art and nature with one voice demand.
> O haste to part them, blushing virtue cries.
> Thus urg'd, our bard this night to part them tries;
> To mix with Southerne tho' his verse aspire,
> He bows with reverence to the hoary sire. (I, 8-9)

The account of Hawkesworth's adaptation in the *Critical Review* (Dec. 1759) makes the same point: "That it was necessary to alter it [Southerne's original], cannot be denied: the tragic action was interrupted, not only by comic scenes, but by scenes of the lowest buffoonery, and the grossest indecency" (p. 480). The effect of cutting out the disturbing comedy and bawdry of the secondary action was, of course, to heighten the sentimental effect of the serious plot of the play. It may be worth adding that Hawkesworth was no enemy to sentimentalism, as a perusal of his *Adventurer* essays will clearly show.

Another of Southerne's plays, *The Disappointment*, discussed in an earlier chapter, was used to show how untrustworthy definitions of sentimental drama are. One of the reasons for absolving the play from the imputation of any great degree of sentimentalism is the brevity of Alphonso's repentance. Even more important is the presence of the bawdy. It will be enough to quote one or two sample passages. Lorenzo speaks to Erminia:

> Oh for the brawn! the back of Hercules!
> With all the three nights sweat his father Jove
> Spent in Alcmene's service, but to try
> If that could satisfy a lady's longing. (III, i)

A mother acts as bawd for her daughter, showing a maternal solicitude that can only be described as monstrous:

This way, this way, my lord! Now, child, but shew thyself thy mother's daughter. You will be gentle to her at the first: 'bate but a little of your lordship's vigour: she's young and tender, and cannot bear, alas! what we can bear![25]

Dodds' remarks on *The Disappointment* can now be reread with a greater understanding of why the play only "adumbrates," rather than is, sentimental comedy.[26] It is odd that this intrusion of the bawdy has not been the subject of more comment in the discussion of other plays which bear so many resemblances to sentimental drama. Again bearing in mind the hurried conversions in that play also, one may state that *The Custom of the Country*[27] does not come through as sentimental drama because of the very obtrusive presence of humor and the bawdy.

A few more examples from Elizabethan drama suggest themselves. The card game, with its wealth of double meanings, that figures in Heywood's *A Woman Killed With Kindness* will be remembered with some enjoyment. The wit is directed at the adulterous relationship between Mistress Frankford and Wendoll, but it is relatively subtle and hardly offensive. When Benjamin Victor, the treasurer of Drury Lane, adapted the Elizabethan play under the title of *The Fatal Secret* (1776) he made significant changes, chief of which was the shifting of the burden of guilt from the pathetic heroine to the villain. Lady Frankford is surprised and seduced by Cransmore, and does not cry out for fear and shame. Victor made other changes, however. One of these was the omission of any humorous or bawdy notes in his original. The card game is cut out, as are the minor characters—Nicholas, Jenkin, Roger Brickbat, Spigot, and Cicely—who provide some comedy. This practice of altering older plays for modern (eighteenth-century, that is) consumption by the exclusion of broad comedy and bawdry is encountered again and again. Rarely does one find sentimental comedies which allow those intruders to mar their serious plots. Humor, it has been seen, is very often present, but the bawdry is scrupulously avoided by the generality of writers in the genre.

A more remarkable transformation is seen when an obscure eighteenth-century playwright named Joseph Richardson took Beaumont and Fletcher's *The Coxcomb* and made a sentimental comedy of it. Richardson left out the action of the older play dealing with the coxcomb, his wife, and his friend. He took the story of Viola, who planned an elopement with her lover, Ricardo, only to be insulted by him that night as he staggered upon her, drunk and amorous, causing her to flee, and he called his own play *The Fugitive* (1792). In the Beaumont and Fletcher play Viola's flight exposes her to lewd proposals in lewd language. There is no attempt to soften the language; Elizabethan sensibilities were hardier than those of the eighteenth century. Richardson's play is not wholly free from the bawdy; compared with its model, however, it is relatively innocuous. Comparison of one situation will show the difference. Viola (Julia in Richardson) awaits Ricardo (Young Manly) at the hour and place of appointment. He appears with his drinking companions and a drawer.

VIOLA.	Oh, my dear love! how dost thou?
RIC.	'Faith, sweetheart.
	Even as thou seest.
PEDRO.	Where's thy wench?
UBERTO.	Where's this bed-worm?
VIOLA.	Speak softly, for the love of Heaven!
DRAWER.	Mistress, get you gone, and do not entice the gentlemen,
	Now you see they're drunk, or I'll call the watch,
	And lay you fast enough.
VIOLA.	Alas, what are you?
	Or what do you mean?—Sweet love, where's the place?
RIC.	Marry, sweet love, e'en here? Lie down;
	I'll feese you. [Seizes her.]
VIOLA.	Good God! What mean you?
PEDRO.	I will have the wench.
UBERTO.	If you can get her.
SILVIO.	No, I'll lie with
	The wench to-night, and she shall be yours tomorrow.

94

PEDRO. Let go the wench!

SILVIO. Let you go the wench!

VIOLA. Oh, Gentlemen, as you had mothers—

UBERTO. They had no mothers; they are the sons of bitches.

RIC. Let that be maintain'd!

SILVIO. Marry then—

VIOLA. Oh, bless me, Heaven!

UBERTO. How many is there on's?

RIC. About five.

UBERTO. Why then, let's fight three to three.

SILVIO. Content. [Draw and fall down.]

DRAWER. The watch! the watch! the watch!
Where are you? [Exit.]

RIC. Where are these cowards?

PEDRO. There's the whore.

VIOLA. I never saw a drunken man before;
But these I think are so.

SILVIO. Oh!

PEDRO. I miss'd you narrowly there.

VIOLA. My state is such, I know not how to think
A prayer fit for me; only I could move,
That never maiden more might be in love! [Exit.] (I, vi)

While Ricardo's "I'll feese you" may send some readers to the *Oxford English Dictionary*, "bed-worm," "sons of bitches," and "whore" require no lexicographical aids.

Here is how Richardson handles the same situation. Young Manly, alone and drunk, thinks the trees are about to engage in a dance. Julia, hearing his bursts of drunken song, has veiled her face and hidden behind a tree.

YOUNG MANLY. So now, let me chuse my partner.
[Catches at a tree, behind which Julia
is concealed, who shrieks.]
By all the sylvan powers, another Daphne.
[Kneels.]

Madam, behold a swain, not altogether so
musical as Apollo, I grant you, but a good honest
fellow for all that—So, madam, so—
psha, never mind more words—let us go.

JULIA. Oh, my hard fortune.

YOUNG MANLY. What do you say?—Speak out, my angel.
I know that your voice is more tuneful than
Philomel's, or mine—that your eyes are
the sparkling harbingers of love—that

95

your dimples are the chosen hiding-places
of all the Cupids—and those lips!—But
hold—rot it—I had forgot—I can't
see e'er a one of them—Never mind no
matter for that—I dare say it's all
true; and if it isn't, why then we must
mend the matter with thinking.

JULIA. Oh, heavens! is it possible!

YOUNG MANLY. No, certainly—it cannot be possible—
it isn't possible—Come, come, I know
you are kind as you are beautiful, and
so it is possible—and so, without more
waste of time, come to my arms, and—

JULIA. It is in vain to reason with him in this
state—I must endeavour to divert his
attention, and by that means escape him
if I can.—If you will permit me to be
your guide.—

YOUNG MANLY. Enough my pretty pilot; take me where
you will. We will never part any more,
shall we? No, never.

JULIA. I dare say not, sir.

YOUNG MANLY. Not, sir?—Why to be sure not, sir—Never,
never, never.

JULIA. Let us walk quickly. [Aside] Oh! heaven
assist me.

YOUNG MANLY. As quick as you please, my angel—I'll fly,
if you chuse, for I'm very steady, and very
loving.

[Exeunt] (II, i)

In the Elizabethan play Viola is taken for a whore by the drawer and,
seemingly, by all the others. Ricardo seizes her and invites her to ply her
trade on the very spot. She is called a whore, and she is quarreled over
by the drunken men, who are so unsteady that they fall down when they
draw their swords. There is no doubt that the earlier treatment of this
situation is coarser and more comic than the later. Taken in its context,
as part of a play in which the bawdy predominates, it would be rash to
declare that the very coarseness of the Viola-Ricardo meeting makes the
heroine's distress more keen, and hence more capable of exciting the
sentimental response. Such a view would be possible if one were discussing
present-day drama; it has no place in the discussion of this Elizabethan
play.

One final example may serve to drive the point home. Nicholas Rowe
was an early sentimentalist. This must not be taken to mean that his "she-

tragedies" are out-and-out sentimental drama. It rather means that it would take extremely little to make thoroughgoing sentimental drama out of some of his plays. The procedure would be one of deletion rather than of addition. Nor would there be any necessity to make his characters of the middle class. The play here selected for comment is *The Fair Penitent* (1703), chiefly because it was taken from an Elizabethan play, Massinger and Field's *The Fatal Dowry* (1619), and because there is also a later version of the same play, Aaron Hill's *The Insolvent*, acted in 1758. This allows one to draw comparisons and make conclusions which can be readily checked. It must be noted at the outset that the two earlier plays are tragedies, the third is a sentimental comedy[28]—it would have been called a tragicomedy in the Elizabethan period. *The Fatal Dowry* and *The Fair Penitent* are rather well-known, but a word may be said about *The Insolvent*. In Hill's play the heroine (Amelia) rejects the villain's (Young Aumele's) lewd advances, and is betrayed by the treachery of her maid (Florella). Amelia's husband (Chalons) finds her in a very compromising situation, assumes her guilt, and locks her in her room—having dispatched Young Aumele in fair fight. Florella, caught by Chalon's friend, La Foy, lurking about on the eventful night, confesses her guilt and her mistress' innocence, repents, and is sent for Amelia. Amelia comes in, bleeding from a self-inflicted wound, but her hurt is discovered to be slight, and there is a happy reconciliation. Young Aumele, it is important to observe, does not enjoy Amelia.

In *The Fatal Dowry* both humor and bawdry are present. Quotation of these bawdy passages becomes thankless after a time, and indication of the place where they, and comic passages, occur should be enough. Reference to II, ii; III, i to Beaumont's entrance (one might also note Charalois' first speech on page 143); and IV, i to "Exeunt all but Novall, junior, and Romont" will indicate the nature of the humor and bawdy in the play. There are at least two songs to which attention may be drawn. In II, ii (p. 119) there is a song entitled "A Dialogue Between a Man and a Woman" which ends with the line: "Let's die; I languish, I consume." The sexual significance of the word "die" has perhaps received too much attention of late, but there can be no doubt of its use in that sense here. In IV, ii (pp. 156-57) there is a song in which a courtier advises a citizen to give his wife full liberty, thus insuring the success of his trade.[29] In *The Fair Penitent* the element of the humorous and the bawdy is much curtailed. Lothario describes his seduction of Calista in unambiguous terms (I, i, pp. 449-50); there is a song by "Mr. Congreve" in II, i (p. 445) which also employs "die" in its sexual sense; and in IV, i (p. 464) Lothario enjoins the now wretched Calista to "die with joy and straight to live again" with him.[30] In *The Insolvent* Florella uses a suggestive circumlocution to tell Young Aumele that Amelia's marriage makes his enjoyment of her less susceptible to discovery (III, i, p. 358). Except for this, practically nothing else in the play may properly be called comic or bawdy. Significantly, Florella repents of her betrayal of her mistress, reiterates Amelia's innocence, and is forgiven by Chalons, Amelia's husband.[31]

The conclusion one draws from this comparison of the humorous and comic elements present in three plays of three different periods, one deriving from the other, is simply that with the passage of time and the conscious attempts at sentimental drama, plays tended to become more serious and moral. Such a conclusion is not at all new or startling nor does it pretend to any momentous significance. The procedure which allowed of such a conclusion is one which might, however, have been used in an examination of other plays which have been incorrectly ad-judged to be sentimental despite the disturbing intrusion of humor and bawdry. Of course there are not many plays which provide so convenient a method of comparison as that used above. Scholars need only be aware, however, that one—only one, of course—of the criteria to be used in determining the sentimental status of a play—is the kind and extent of humor which is employed in that play—the bawdy, as contrasted to downright obscenity, being thought of as one kind of humor. Restoration plays which have sometimes been considered sentimental may profitably be compared to their Elizabethan sources, when there are such; eighteenth-century plays to their Restoration or Elizabethan sources or analogues. Mrs. Behn's *The Town Fop* (1676), for instance, may be compared with George Wilkins' *The Miseries of Enforced Marriage* (1607); and Edward Morris' *The Secret* (1799) with Thomas D'Urfey's *Love For Money* (1691). Bearing in mind also the importance of brevity of treatment as opposed to repetition or prolongation in potentially senti-mental situations, one can test the accuracy of certain critical remarks made on these plays. Why have scholars neglected the very considerable element of bawdry and humor in Mrs. Behn's play when they have dis-cussed its sentimentalism?[32] Is it enough for a critic to state that Mirtilla in D'Urfey's *Love For Money* "is the most fully developed of D'Urfey's heroines and is exhibited in the more important relationships peculiar to sentimental drama"[33] (even if one is disposed to accept this statement in its entirety)? Should not there be the accompanying and qualifying statement that Mirtilla appears infrequently and says very little, and that the slender thread of action in which she appears is almost lost in a welter of farce and bawdry? Is it possible after reading D'Urfey's play and Morris' *The Secret*, one directly after the other, to make such a remark as the following, in reference to the Mirtilla-Meritton action of the former play: "This plot is strictly in accord with that of such a later sentimental play as Morris' *The Secret*"?[34] Does a bare account of the slight serious action in *Love For Money* justify the conclusion that the play is "a speci-men of sentimental comedy"?[35] The tendency to make conclusions about a play as a whole by examining only a part is dangerous because of the unwitting ease with which this fault is committed. Such a tendency may not be completely absent from the present work, but the endeavor has been to guard against it.

That there are plenty of pathetic situations in Elizabethan drama will not be denied. It is conceivable that the plays in which these situations appear might have been sentimental—with reference to the definition arrived at earlier—yet hardly any of these plays have been included in the sentimental canon. One of the reasons is that potentially sentimental situations are hurried over, a method contrary to that of sentimental drama, which is reluctant to leave such situations until the last extractable essence of emotion is wrung from them. Even more important than brevity of treatment, the intrusion of humor and the bawdy, enemies of sentimentalism, saves many of these old plays from becoming sentimental. In this and in the preceding chapter some of these plays have been dis-cussed or mentioned. One might add others—many others—from both Elizabethan and Restoration periods. What is more, there is no reason why one must accept another critic's decision on eighteenth-century plays; one should be in a position to judge more accurately whether a play is sentimental on the basis of what has been said up to this point. These criteria are not foolproof; none can be. There are plays in which it is a nice question whether the dramatist has devoted enough time to a sentimental situation to enable one to judge his intention. In other plays the question may arise as to the prominence afforded humorous effects or bawdy dialogue, and one must decide—not neglecting other considerations—whether these elements are so conspicuous as to dissipate a sentimental effect.

Chapter V. EMPHASIS AND DIRECTION

THE METHODS BY WHICH eighteenth-century writers of sentimental drama obtained their desired effects are easily recognizable. Two of these—prolonged treatment of potentially sentimental themes and situations, and exclusion of the disturbing elements of laughter and bawdry—have already been discussed. There is a third method or technique which is so bound up with the first two that it cannot be discussed entirely by itself. This is the matter of emphasis and direction, obviously very general and inclusive terms. The sentimental dramatist, concerned primarily to arouse pity for distressed virtue and admiration for innate human goodness, starts out with a clearly defined end in mind. This end is not lost sight of, nor is it permitted to be eclipsed for any length of time by other considerations. Rather, the dramatist keeps returning to certain ideas and keeps appealing to certain emotions to the extent that the climactic scene toward which he has been building becomes the logical and expected conclusion to his play. It is the extremely rare sentimental play whose denouement cannot be predicted well in advance of its occurrence. When one is confronted with a destitute maiden of invincible chastity and of unknown parentage, and when one has it brought constantly to his attention that she is destitute, and chaste, and ostensibly an orphan, it is reasonably safe to look forward to a fifth act in which she is happily married to the man of her choice and made wealthy by the generosity of her doting father who had given her up for lost eighteen years ago. There may be extraneous bits of action which do not further the pathetic tale of virtue in distress, but they are not emphasized and do not, hence, distract attention from the dramatist's purpose.

The emphasis laid upon the story which carries the weight of the sentimental emotion distinguishes drama that is sentimental from that which is not, and can be shown more clearly by a hypothetical example. Given two plays which tell the same tender or pathetic story, the one which tells that story and no other is capable of exploiting and emphasizing the tenderness and pathos implicit in it to a far greater degree than can the other which tells two stories and introduces elements alien to—or even antagonistic to—tenderness and pathos. Further, if the second play alternates its two stories in such a fashion that a sentimental scene is followed by one which serves to destroy the effect that has just been achieved, it is obvious that the pathetic appeal must suffer. Finally, if the tender or pathetic story is relegated to a few scenes which occupy a position of minor importance in the structure of the play as a whole, its appeal is greatly dissipated. These considerations ultimately resolve themselves into a question of emphasis. A dramatist who is concerned to emphasize the sentimental possibilities of a story will not introduce another, unrelated action, nor will he add other, disturbing elements. Again, examination of specific plays will make clear in concrete fashion what has been suggested in hypothetical terms.

The most obvious way to increase or heighten the effectiveness of potentially sentimental material is to delete that which is extraneous to that purpose. Such a practice has already been seen with eighteenth-century adaptations of earlier plays. Thus Southerne's *The Fatal Marriage* was stripped of its comic-bawdy plot (which, incidentally, was related, if clumsily, to the serious action) and produced as *Isabella*. The audience which saw Garrick's adaptation in 1758 did not have its attention diverted for a moment from the pathetic story of the unfortunate Isabella. The comedy of Fernando's revival from "death"; his gulling by his daughter, Victoria, who disguises herself as a man; his jealousy and the aggravation of it by the disguised Victoria who woos her mother before his very eyes—all these disturbing elements are cut out. Dr. Hawkesworth's adaptation of *Oroonoko* in 1759 is free to concentrate on the sorrows of Oroonoko and Imoinda without the incongruous comedy and bawdry of the efforts of two sisters to procure husbands for themselves. In Southerne's play the serious story is almost travestied by the sexual intrigues of the accompanying secondary action. Joseph Richardson takes Beaumont and Fletcher's *The Coxcomb* as a point of departure and, using only the Ricardo-Viola plot, writes *The Fugitive*. The absurd Antonio-Mercury plot, which gives the older play its name, is left out. Nicholas Rowe takes the Jane Shore story, dramatized earlier by Heywood, and writes a pathetic "she-tragedy" by telling of Mistress Shore's unhappy fate, leaving out unessential matters of state. Both Rowe and Aaron Hill strip their original, *The Fatal Dowry*, of unnecessary scenes of comedy and present their versions of the story without permitting their single effect to be weakened by distracting elements. Benjamin Victor makes a more tightly knit and unified three-act play of Heywood's *A Woman Killed With Kindness* by the simple expedient of omitting a very tenuously related subplot and dispensing with scenes which do not further his purpose.[1]

The Miseries of Enforced Marriage, despite resemblances to sentimental drama, has been declared by the present writer to be free from sentimentalism—not entirely free, to be sure, but to such an extent that it cannot be called sentimental comedy. One of the reasons for such a conclusion is the fact that the pathetic aspect of the plot is constantly obscured while other matters are being treated. The story of Sir Francis Ilford's encouragement of Scarborow's extravagances, while actually a part of the serious action, is so handled as to provide a diversion—as does the matter of Ilford's gulling at the hands of the Butler. A. M. Clark has commented on this aspect of the play in a comparison of it with *A Yorkshire Tragedy.* He writes:

The Miseries and the *Tragedy* are now poles apart. The latter is domestic, sensational, homely, terrible, pathetic, vivid, and careless of outward grace. *The Miseries* opens as a kind of city comedy with three needy gallants in the foreground waiting to pluck a pigeon and airing satirical views on women; and in the admirable tavern scenes, in the duping of Ilford, and in the robbing of Harcop it is anything but domestic and sentimental. None of the characters is really suitable for domestic drama; Clare is too lively and voluble, too much a figure from high comedy, and the rest are all out of place in a tragedy of the home. Even Scarborow is a domestic protagonist only through the misfortunes which overtake him, while the wife, instead of being a central figure as in the domestic drama proper, is kept entirely in the background.[2]

Except for the rather questionable designation of Clare as "a figure from high comedy," one can agree with Clark in his objection to the confusion of genres in *The Miseries.* Effective domestic drama remains domestic drama throughout; it does not become "city comedy" or anything else for a while, returning to domestic drama only for the denouement. Often, however, one reads that one plot of an Elizabethan play is sentimental but that the other plot—or plots—is not. This may be noted in discussions of plays like *The Coxcomb, Monsieur Thomas, The Witch of Edmonton, A Mad World My Masters,* and many others. Such a distinction between parts of a play is infrequent in discussion of eighteenth-century plays because they, with certain conspicuous exceptions like *The Rivals,* have but one plot, or attempt to relate a secondary action more closely to the main action. Plays which have two or more plots (three are not uncommon in the Elizabethan period) call for a constant alternation of mood. In a discussion of "pathetic comedy" Fred O. Nolte gives a digest of the opinions of Chassiron, a French critic. Of one of Chassiron's points he says:

Although he grants that laughter and tears are prompted by natural sensations, he protests that to laugh and cry at the same time, or to laugh during one scene and cry during the next, is altogether unnatural; in such cases, our mind is torn between conflicting emotions, and the sudden transition from joy to grief and from grief to joy subjects our attention to disagreeable violence.

Nolte further points out that a number of French writers (Diderot included) used "Chassiron's objection . . . to eliminate all humor from bourgeois dramas and to establish a consistently serious type of play," a procedure which was opposed by Fontenelle and Voltaire.[3] The necessity to keep unseemly laughter out of serious drama is only one consideration in the importance of concentration of effect. Very often in Elizabethan plays the serious action is accompanied by a comic action which prevents the creation and nurture of any lasting emotional effect. In some cases this is a fault; in others, where the play might degenerate into mawkishness, it is a virtue. Examples abound.

It becomes increasingly evident that the importance of emphasis in sentimental drama cannot be discussed without constant reference to the criteria that have been examined earlier. Some plays which have already figured in previous discussion may serve the purpose of linking together all the criteria considered. It is not positively daring to say that Cibber's *Love's Last Shift* is not properly a sentimental play. Allardyce Nicoll terms it a "moral-immoral" play, and at least one other scholar has also questioned its sentimentalism.[4] Although Loveless' reform is carried out in a fashion which was to become usual with eighteenth-century writers of sentimental comedy, it must be remarked that the Loveless-Amanda story is only one of a number of interests that demanded the attention of the spectators. The intrigues of the Worthy brothers and the posturings of Sir Novelty Fashion claim their share of notice. Another consideration of importance is the place of the repentance scene, the only sentimental scene in the whole play, in the action of the fifth act. Act V opens with the deception practiced on Sir William Wisewoud by Young Worthy; the next scene is that in which Loveless reforms. Immediately on the heels of this sentimental scene Snap, Loveless' man, and Amanda's woman are hauled out of the cellar into which the former had fallen, and into which the latter had been pulled—for what purpose it is hardly necessary to state. Snap was played by the popular low comedian Pinkethman. A little later Snap is told by Loveless that he must marry Amanda's woman. He replies, "Marry her! Oh, Lord, sir, after I have lain with her? Why, sir, how the devil can you think a man can have any stomach to his dinner after he has had three or four slices off of the spit?" Loveless thereupon promises to give the girl one hundred pounds dowry, and to settle thirty pounds a year on him. Snap accepts, saying

Ah, sir, now I understand you. Heaven reward you! Well, sir, I partly find that the genteel scenes of our lives are pretty well over, and I thank heaven that I have so much grace left that I can repent when I have no more opportunities of being wicked. Come, spouse! (She enters) Here's my hand; the rest of my body shall be forthcoming. Ah, little did my master and I think last night that we were robbing our own orchards. (V, iii)

Snap's words are the best commentary on the sentimentalism of the play in which he appears. Loveless is spared the necessity to "labor, dig, beg, or starve" by Amanda's revelation that she has two thousand a year; Snap accepts Amanda's maid with her dowry and thirty pounds a year promised by Loveless, and thanks heaven he has grace enough left to repent when opportunities for being wicked are no more. It can be said with some degree of assurance that the sentimental element in *Love's Last Shift* is so small and so juxtaposed with intrigue, comedy, and the bawdy that it becomes somewhat misleading to speak of the play as sentimental comedy without some accompanying and qualifying statement.

Traditional criticism of *Love's Last Shift* is so strongly intrenched that one cannot leave discussion of the play without saying something about the circumstances which have caused so many scholars to speak of it as the first English sentimental comedy. Cibber's first play appeared at a time when reform was in the air. Joseph Wood Krutch has discussed the appearance and rise of the "Societies for the Reformation of Manners," and John Harrington Smith has suggested that Thomas Shadwell had something to do with efforts toward a more moral stage. The latter scholar has also said that the growing feminine attendance in theatres wielded an influence which made for less immorality in dramatic writing.[5] Jeremy Collier was to issue his blast soon after the presentation of *Love's Last Shift*. The time was ripe for something new in the drama, and Cibber's play seems to have supplied the need. The reception that the play met and the impression it made on contemporary audiences and critics are brought together in R. H. Barker's study of Cibber.[6] Barker's comments on the play show that he recognizes the undue emphasis placed on the sentimental element in *Love's Last Shift*, but he, too, has had to bow to tradition (p. 22). From all this it would seem that *Love's Last Shift* was so successful because it provided that something new for which the time was propitious. The new element was the spectacle of a rake brought to see the error of his ways by a devoted wife. Actually, of course, the situation itself was not new; it was only the greater degree of prominence given to the final reformation of the rake that was new. This is the scene which Tom Davies was later, much later, to say caused "honest tears" to be shed,[7] and it is very largely on the evidence of Davies' statement that it is permissible to speak of the sentimentalism of Cibber's play. Contemporary writers could praise the greater morality of Cibber's play, but it was not to be until 1783 or thereabouts that anything was to be said about Cibber's first-night audience dissolving into tears at Loveless' "remorse and penitence." There should be a statute of limitations on this kind of evidence which is submitted after the passage of so many years. Davies, almost one hundred years after the event, is the only writer to point to a definite sentimental response at the acting of *Love's Last Shift*, and Davies' accuracy often leaves much to be desired. It must be further noted that the play attracted enough attention for Vanbrugh to answer it with *The Relapse*; and Cibber, years later when he came to write his *Apology*, remarked of his play that "by the mere moral Delight receiv'd from its Fable, it has been, with the other, [*The Relapse*] in a continued and equal Possession of the Stage for more than forty years."[8] Cibber also said in the *Apology*, however, that the success of the play depended as much on the character of Sir Novelty Fashion, acted by himself, as it did on its intrinsic merits as a play (I, 212-14).

It is possible that the titular priority of Cibber's play in the history of sentimental drama is justified; my own reservations have been stated. There is still the question: where, or how, did Cibber get the idea of introducing this new element so prominently into his play? The comments on the play's "purity of Plot, Manners and Moral"[9] must serve as justification for speaking of the prominence of the fifth-act reformation. The suggestion has never been advanced that Cibber may have been influenced, directly or indirectly, by Thomas Southerne. Cibber, discussing *Love's Last Shift* in the *Apology*, informs us that "Mr. Southern, the Author of *Oroonoko*, having had the Patience to hear me read it to him, happened to like it so well that he immediately recommended it to the Patentees" (I, 212). Cibber had known Southerne for at least five or six years, acting in the latter's *Sir Anthony Love* (1690), possibly his first part on the stage.[10] During the period from the acting of *Sir Anthony Love* to the appearance of *Love's Last Shift* Southerne wrote four plays, two comedies and two tragedies. One of the comedies, *The Wives' Excuse* (1691) contains "one character that links the play directly with later sentimental drama. Mrs. Friendall, the wronged wife, courageously patient and unwaveringly pure, is a moral type strangely incongruous in her setting, and blood sister to the sentimental heroines who were to follow her."[11] The play was a failure, and the presence of Mrs. Friendall seems to have elicited no comment from contemporary writers. Evidently audiences of the year 1691 were not ready for the appearance of "sentimental comedy." Both of Southerne's tragedies in this period, *The Fatal Marriage* (1694) and *Oroonoko* (1695) were tremendous successes and both have been discussed in terms of sentimental drama. What suggests itself is that Cibber either recognized that the right moment had come for the introduction of those elements which he had observed in Southerne's dramatic work of this period, or that Southerne himself gave the young author some suggestions which developed into or gave more prominence to Loveless' reform in Act V. This is of course highly conjectural, but the combination of a dramatist who had demonstrated some interest in the inclusion of sentimental elements into his work listening to and recommending the first play of a comparative unknown, who thereupon produced "the first sentimental comedy," is warrant enough for conjecture.

Steele's *The Tender Husband*, earlier defended from the persistent charge that it is sentimental comedy,[12] is amenable to examination similar to that accorded *Love's Last Shift*. The Clerimont-Mrs. Clerimont action is only a small part of a play which concentrates on Biddy Tipkin and her delightfully fantastic notions. What is more, within the slight serious action there are comic and bawdy notes which destroy the singleness of effect that a sentimental dramatist depends upon to evoke his response. *The Tender Husband*, to take a leaf from Collier's book, is actually a misnomer; the plot which involves "the tender husband" is far less important than the Biddy Tipkin plot, and Clerimont is hardly a "tender" husband anyway. Calling *The Tender Husband* a sentimental play is like calling a building conceived and executed in one style of architecture by the name of another style, only because there is present one feature (imperfect, at that) of the second.

Another way to apply the criterion of emphasis and direction is to examine two plays; one sentimental, the other, not. Analysis of these plays will make it possible to see more immediately the difference being studied. The sentimental play chosen is an extreme example of the humorless, sententious, unrelievedly dull sentimental comedy which found its way into print for the consumption of many readers, but which never saw stage presentation. In Allardyce Nicoll's hand-list of plays at the end of his *Late Eighteenth Century Drama, 1750-1800*, only three plays in the second half of the eighteenth century are actually labeled "sentimental comedy" by their authors: the Reverend Charles Jenner's *The Man of Family*; Samuel Foote's *Handsome Housemaid, or Piety in Pattens*, a satire on sentimental drama; and James Nelson's *The Affectionate Father* (1786). Neither Jenner's nor Nelson's play was acted. Nelson's play has been selected for analysis and for comparison with the second part of *The Honest Whore*. Familiarity with both parts of the Elizabethan play is presumed, although it is hardly vital.

The Honest Whore, Part II has undeniable sentimental possibilities. The scholar whose edition of *The Honest Whore* is used speaks of "the portrait of Orlando Friscobaldo," "with its whimsey and its heartache,"[13] and it is in the picture of the disguised Friscobaldo acting as servant to his dishonored daughter's husband—as well as in Bellafront's stand against Hippolito's advances—that the pathos of the play lies. The plot of *The Affectionate Father*, the less accessible and deservedly neglected play, can be summed up very briefly. Lord Moreland, purely for considerations of fortune, wishes his son, Mr. Moreland, to marry Maria, the daughter of Sir Charles Allgood. But Mr. Moreland does not wish to marry, and Maria's heart is fixed on Mr. Walmesley, a young man whom Sir Charles has befriended. When Mr. Walmesley asks permission in a letter to pay court to Maria, Sir Charles is struck with the young man's goodness and sense of the proprieties. He believes, however, that Maria is in love with

Mr. Moreland, and he is unwilling to force Maria to marry against her own wishes. When Maria confesses her love for Mr. Walmesley the two are joined by Sir Charles. A secondary action serves as a foil to set off Sir Charles's goodness. Lord Moreland refuses to let his daughter marry Colonel Brownlow, who has no fortune, but he is brought to renounce his mercenary views by Sir Charles and gives his consent to his daughter's marriage to the Colonel. The play is a long one, running to one hundred seventy-nine pages, but it is without action. Everything is effected by long sententious speeches, and one will search in vain for humor or the slightest suggestion of the risqué. Besides the seven characters named above, three others figure in the plot: Lady Moreland; Mr. Gage, Sir Charles's friend; and Mrs. Peers, companion to Maria. No character or discordant note takes away from the sentimental appeal of the play. The extreme generosity of Sir Charles and his unselfish love for his daughter are constantly being described by others or made evident in what Sir Charles himself says. In one scene Sir Charles, alone with Maria, moralizes on the hypocrisy of city dwellers, on the danger of allowing passion to influence one in his choice of a spouse, and on the duty a child owes its parents. The scene ends with Maria kneeling to promise her father that she will never marry without his consent (III, i). The sentimental appeal of such a scene is obvious.

Of the ten characters in Nelson's play nine are good people, and Lord Moreland also emerges as good when he renounces his mercenary ways and consents to his daughter's marriage. Mr. Walmesley's delicacy is displayed to best advantage as he debates the ethical rightness and propriety of declaring his love to Maria. His respect for Sir Charles, whose "property" Maria (still a minor) is, decides him against revealing his passion (II, iii). The letter in which he asks Sir Charles's permission to "disclose" himself to Maria is such a one as may have come out of the many guides to letter-writing so popular in the eighteenth century (IV, i). Lady Moreland pleads with her husband to consent to their daughter's marriage to the Colonel. Mr. Moreland, a good-natured young man throughout, also tries to help his sister. Mr. Gage and Miss Peers act as choruses, proclaiming Sir Charles's benevolence on all occasions. Maria is a loving and obedient daughter. And when Lord Moreland is made to see the error of his ways by Sir Charles, the play ends on exclamations of gratitude and love all around, even Mr. Gage and Miss Peers coming in for their share of happiness when Sir Charles joins them, having known their secret attachment to one another for some time. Significantly enough, in the light of Goldsmith's remark about the "tin money" which is so lavishly given away in sentimental drama, Miss Peers is given a bill for five thousand pounds by Sir Charles, Maria adding "a few hundred pounds" to an already impressive gift. The reader is overwhelmed by speech after speech which serves to drive home the theme of the play —the happiness attendant upon filial obedience and unselfish parental love. It is hardly surprising to learn from the title page of this play that the author had written "an essay on the government of children, under the general heads of health, manners, and education." *The Affectionate Father* is nothing more than another such essay cast into dialogue form. Nelson's play is a very poor one, but it shows how the necessary emphasis for sentimental effects can be obtained.

The title page of the first printed edition of *The Honest Whore, Part II* informs the reader that he will find in the play

... The Humours of the Patient Man, the Impatient Wife: the Honest Whore, perswaded by strong, Arguments to turne Curtizan againe: her brave refuting those Arguments. And lastly, the Comicall Passages of an Italian Bridewell, where the Scaene ends.

The first major difference between Dekker's play (Middleton's part in the play is slight, if there at all) and *The Affectionate Father* is immediately apparent. Nelson's play tells one story: Dekker's tells two—and contains "comical passages." Attention must be divided between the story of the disguised Orlando Friscobaldo, Bellafront, Hippolito, and Matheo; and that of Candido and his wife. One will be expected to adjust his mood to keep pace with the alternation of scenes; to pity Bellafront and sympathize with her father in one scene, and to laugh heartily as Hippolito's gentlemen bait the patient Candido in another. There are thirteen scenes in the play; the Candido story figures in six of them. At the end, as is frequent in Elizabethan drama, the characters in both plots are brought together, but the device is largely a mechanical one, and the two stories exist independent of one another. There are twenty-one characters whose names appear in the *dramatis personae* of Dekker's play. Only seven of them are essential to the main plot, the others figuring in the Candido story or appearing, for the most part, in the final scene in the "Italian Bridewell." The appearance of so many characters whose presence does nothing to further the action of the main plot serves also to distract attention from the tender or pathetic story. In Nelson's play all the characters are essential to the one story. The last scene of *The Honest Whore, Part II* takes place in a prison, and there are very prominent elements of comedy and bawdry in that scene. Again, the obtrusion of these elements serves to counteract and weaken the sentimental effect of the fifth act with its reformations and its reconciliations. Had Dekker wished to emphasize the sentimental possibilities in the story of Bellafront and her father—and Hippolito and Matheo also, of course— he could have done so by cutting out the Candido subplot, the "Bridewell" scene, all unnecessary characters, and all comedy and bawdry. As is evident from Nelson's play he would not need to add anything to the story itself; all that would be necessary would be to exploit the story he already had by introducing little moral essays and frequent sententiousness, and by repeatedly emphasizing Bellafront's determination to remain true to Matheo, and Orlando's grief at the spectacle of his daughter's suffering. All this, climaxed by a long last scene devoted to Hippolito's repentance and Matheo's reformation and forgiveness, would have resulted in a sentimental comedy like Nelson's. The whole process would be one of a shift in emphasis and direction, the deletion of extraneous and distracting material being, of course, of primary importance in the process.

Another, very convenient way to underline the importance of emphasis, in discussions of the sentimental status of some plays, is to compare a play that has not been thought of as such with a sentimental play on the same theme. A theme popular with English dramatists is that of the gamester who reforms and gives up his passion for play. There are many such plays, too many to be treated here. Sometimes, as in the first of the group of six plays to be studied, the vice of gaming is only an incidental interest; in another play it is the basis for the whole action. The six plays under analysis are James Shirley's *The Gamester* (1635), Susannah Centlivre's *The Gamester* (1705), Colley Cibber's *The Lady's Last Stake* (1707), Charles Johnson's *The Wife's Relief* (1712), Edward Moore's *The Gamester* (1753), and Thomas Holcroft's *Duplicity* (1781). Five of the plays are comedies; Edward Moore's *The Gamester* is a domestic tragedy. Shirley's play alone has not figured in discussions of sentimental drama. The succeeding discussion will help in evaluating with a greater degree of confidence and accuracy the comments that have been made on these plays.

Allardyce Nicoll's discussion of Mrs. Centlivre's *The Gamester* occurs in a section entitled "comedies of sensibility," but little is said there about the play's sentimentalism. Bernbaum calls the play a sentimental comedy, notes the briefness of the "serious passages," and concludes that the play was "a moderately successful, but not a bold, experiment in the sentimental." F. W. Bateson, believing that sentimental drama need not be false, also calls the play sentimental comedy, but deprecates Mrs. Centlivre's attempts in that direction. He suggests that

The Gamester and *The Basset-Table*, though primarily experiments in the fashionable sentimentalism, had shown that Mrs. Centlivre's real talent lay rather in a lively reproduction of the manners and atmosphere of contemporary society. The sentiment was false, but the animation was genuine and unquestionable.[14]

Cibber's *The Lady's Last Stake* is also discussed by Nicoll under "comedies of sensibility," but there is recognition of the gayer side of the play.

Croissant says of the play that "It is a fully developed comedy of the sentimental type of this period, with its four acts of intrigue, its reconciliation at the end, and its extremely moral teaching." And he speaks of a "distinct element of pathos" in the situations of Lady Gentle and Mrs. Conquest. R. H. Barker terms *The Lady's Last Stake* "a companion piece to *The Careless Husband,* a second and more mature exercise in genteel-sentimental comedy," while Bateson, seeing the comedy as the "most serious of Cibber's plays" and calling it "primarily . . . a comedy of ideas, a problem play in embryo," recognizes and discusses the lighter side of the play. Bernbaum attaches great importance to Cibber's play in the development of sentimental comedy, reading a seriousness into the play which may or may not be there.[15] It is evident, however, that both plays—Mrs. Centlivre's *The Gamester* and Cibber's *The Lady's Last Stake*—have been consistently thought of as sentimental comedies.

Charles Johnson's adaptation of Shirley's *The Gamester* has not excited much comment. The play is indeed poor and merits the obscurity to which it has been relegated. Genest devotes a few pages to a resumé of Shirley's and Johnson's plots and concludes that the latter was "on the whole . . . a good play." Agreement with Genest's verdict on the play is, of course, a matter of individual taste. Nicoll discusses *The Wife's Relief* or *The Husband's Cure* under the general heading of "comedies of sensibility," and states that "there is no question here but that the aim of the author was sentimental," adding that for "over four acts the play might be taken for a Restoration comedy."[16] Despite the paucity of comment on the play, it possesses a real value for present purposes. Thomas Holcroft's *Duplicity*, his first comedy, is discussed by Nicoll under "sentimental comedy." The serious action is recounted, mention is made of the purely comic element, and Nicoll concludes that the play is "an excellent comedy of sentimentalised manners."[17] Since Holcroft falls just outside the chronological limits of Bernbaum's work, there is no discussion of any of that writer's plays. His name does come up, however, in Bernbaum's conclusion:

The leadership in comedy devolved upon Cumberland . . . , Thomas Holcroft, and the younger George Colman,—all writers of the sentimental school. Usually they tried to enliven their comedies with some laughable situations and one or two humorous personages, but it was their sentimental conception of life that determined the main action of their plays and the motives of their chief characters. (p. 267)

Finally, Edward Moore's *The Gamester*, probably the most famous of the plays under examination, is a domestic tragedy. It is discussed as such by Nicoll, who does not, however, think of it as sentimental drama. The most complete account of the play is to be found in J. H. Caskey's study of Moore's life and works. Moore's models, or sources, were *A Yorkshire*

Tragedy and Aaron Hill's *The Fatal Extravagance*,[18] but he complicated the plot somewhat and introduced what Caskey calls "a sentimental comedy sub-plot" in the story of Lewson and Charlotte. Holcroft's *Duplicity* is thought to be indebted to Moore's play, and Caskey concludes that the later writer, consciously or unconsciously, made *The Gamester* "into a sentimental comedy" (p. 118). With the various comments on these plays in mind it should be possible to gain further insight into the problem of sentimental drama—especially with reference to discussions of the problem by earlier writers—in the comparison that follows.

The first thing that strikes one is that Shirley's play has never been termed sentimental, but that Johnson's close adaptation has. If the distinction is justified, it should be relatively simple to isolate those elements which make the later play sentimental. It must be noted that Johnson uses Shirley's dialogue freely, changing words here and there but keeping the sense. There are three plots in Shirley, as many in Johnson; Shirley's bawdry is less than Johnson's; and the comedy in the earlier play is not more prominent than in the later. Johnson combines Sir Richard Hurry of the serious-romantic subplot of Shirley's play and Old Barnacle of the purely comic third action into one character, Sir Tristrum Cash, "a humorous old Fellow." In Johnson's play Sir Tristrum is tricked into allowing his niece Teraminta to marry Valentine, and he goes out swearing to bring a "Bill in Chancery" against his dupers. In Shirley, Sir Richard Hurry voluntarily gives up the idea of forcing Beaumont to marry his daughter, and he joins Beaumont to Violante, whom the latter loves (V, ii). The older play is the sentimental play so far as this episode is concerned—if there must be a decision as to sentimentalism at all. Penelope, the ward of Wilding (in Shirley), makes her first appearance with these words (she is being courted by her guardian):

> Pray collect
> Yourself, remember what you are, and whose;
> You have a virtuous gentlewoman, think
> Upon your faith to her. (I, i)

Arabella, cousin to Riot (in Johnson), under the same circumstances, treats his importunities in the following fashion:

ARAB. I'll not be made Love to.
RIOT. You shall hear how Beautiful you are.
ARAB. You'll Flatter me—
RIOT. I swear I won't.
ARAB. Do, Cousin, you'll oblige me infinitely—Oh, to be handsomely flatter'd is so happy an Amusement, 'tis like a gay Dream, which if one was never to be wak'd from, wou'd be very near the real Injoyment—(I, ii)

This is Arabella; a coquette, good-hearted enough probably, but somewhat mercenary, and very much the lady of fashion. Shirley's Penelope, it should be admitted, must not be judged only by the few words quoted. She is an entirely likeable, far from mealy mouthed young woman herself.

Thus far the evidence would suggest that Shirley's is the sentimental play, not Johnson's. The evidence against this conclusion is not impressive. Johnson cuts out the gaming scenes in Shirley, gives Horatio (Shirley's Beaumont) a set speech against "intoxicating wine" (IV, i), and makes just a trifle more of the fifth-act repentance of Riot (Shirley's Wilding). Here are the two declarations of repentance:

WILD. I am asham'd; pray give me all forgiveness.
        I see my follies; heaven invites me gently
        To thy chaste bed: be thou again my dearest,
        Thy virtue shall instruct me. . . . (V, ii)

RIOT. I am Tongue-ty'd in my Guilt—my Follies glare upon me in their full Light—This Conviction in my Mind, gives me Hopes I shall amend— Can you, my Dear, forgive me?—My future Life shall pay the mighty Debt I owe thy Vertue, with eternal Love; Heav'n kindly invites me back to thy Chast Arms, nor will I ever stray again—no, not in Thought.
. . . .
RIOT. I own I may be Blind with too much Light, but I see so well at present to be fully satisfy'd that the Libertine's Joys are all short, and false, as Feaverish Dreams, wherein the whole Animal Oeconomy is miserably torn and distracted, to support a momentary Delirium—Nor can the most extravagant Voluptuary, in all his expensive Pursuits, possess a blessing like a good Wife.
                    He therefore who wou'd have his Pleasures last,
                    And, while a Mortal, Food of Angels taste
                    A Circling Round of lasting Heav'nly Charms,
                    Must find 'em in a Virtuous Woman's Arms. (V, iii)

Johnson echoes Shirley in one phrase, elaborates upon the repentance by giving Riot a few more sentences, and winds up the play with Riot stating the moral. The addition of the moral, explicitly stated in the closing lines of verse in Johnson's play, cannot seriously be suggested as an important difference between sentimental and non-sentimental comedy. The differences between the two plays are so slight that if one is considered sentimental, both must be. Neither play is, however, a sentimental comedy, and that because of the presence of three widely different plots, the relative lack of emphasis on the "gamester" action, and the intrusion of the comic and the bawdy into the serious action—as well as its presence in the secondary action or actions (Johnson having tried clumsily to join Shirley's two secondary plots into one).

Both Mrs. Centlivre's *The Gamester* and Cibber's *The Lady's Last Stake* have been called sentimental comedy. There is no need, as with Shirley and Johnson, to compare the plays one with the other, although the conclusion arrived at for each play may be the same for the same reasons. Mrs. Centlivre's main plot concerns itself with Valere, addicted to gambling, and Angelica, who loves him, and marries him when he gives up his vice. A secondary action centers about Lady Wealthy, young widowed sister of Angelica, who desires to marry Valere, but who finally marries her faithful lover, Mr. Lovewell, when the latter saves her reputation. Minor interests are to be found in Valere's uncle's unsuccessful wooing of Angelica, and in the unmasking of the Marquis de Hazard, who is revealed to be an adventurous footman trying to make his fortune. This brief recital of plot interests indicates that the playwright was not too much concerned to focus attention solely on the serious action. There are some scenes which further the plot not at all; they are actually diversions. Thus, in Act IV there is a scene in which Valere dices with a number of gamblers, and for three pages one is treated to a dice game, replete with the jargon of the game, and serving no observable purpose. Again, in Act III occurs a scene in which Valere, fresh from a winning streak at play, faces his creditors, a tailor and a milliner, and denies having any money. The tailor pleads his wife's approaching lying-in period as the reason for needing money, and the milliner asks for her money that she may give her daughter the dowry she promised the bridegroom-to-be. Valere pays neither. Here was an opportunity to show Valere as a good-hearted young man, touched by the needs of others, and such evidence of his essential goodness might have made his eventual reformation more credible. Finally, and significantly, the play ends with the unmasking of the bogus Marquis de Hazard (plain Robin Skip) who is mocked at, and kicked by Valere. A country dance follows, and then Valere—almost an afterthought on the part of Mrs. Centlivre, one might say—speaks the moral.

Other considerations exist which make one chary of accepting Mrs. Centlivre's play as sentimental comedy. The play contains a large element of the purely comic—Hector, Valere's valet; Mrs. Security, a female pawnbroker; Cogdie, a gamester; the bogus Marquis de Hazard; and even Dorante, Valere's uncle, being conceived as comic characters. Incidents like the Marquis de Hazard's footmen entering to bring a succession of billet-doux to their employer are comic diversions which do not advance the plot. The bawdy element, not very prominent, is present in one song and in humorous references to the practice of "keeping." Anti-sentimental notes are also present: Lady Wealthy parodies the lover who throws himself at his mistress' feet and offers to kill himself if she will not favor him, and the same Lady calls Mr. Lovewell's "sentimental" language "grave stuff." Even Valere's protestations to Angelica are not allowed to pass without some satiric comment:

VAL.   I do confess I am a Wretch below your Scorn; I own my Faults and have no Refuge but your Mercy.
FAV.   In the old Strain again—   [Aside]

Favourite is Angelica's maid and has, presumably, been present at previous such scenes. During the course of the play Angelica dons man's attire to enter a gaming house and win her picture back from Valere at play. Mrs. Bracegirdle, in a "breeches" role, has little place in a sentimental comedy.

Nor are other reasons to suspect the appropriateness of the term "sentimental comedy" in relation to *The Gamester* far to seek. Lady Wealthy agrees to marry the good, grave Mr. Lovewell, struck by his concern for her honor. The manner in which she accepts his proposal of marriage is far from sentimental.

L. WEAL.   Bless me, is the Man mad? Here would be a strange Leap indeed, from Mortal Odds into Matrimony. No, no; a little longer Time must try you first.

Mr. Lovewell renews his plea, and Betty, Lady Wealthy's woman enters.

L. WEAL.   Betty, come to my Aid; here's an audacious Man will marry me, in spite of my Teeth, this very Instant.
BETTY.   O Madam, the luckiest Moment in the World, I have been just looking on *Erra Pater,* and there's the happiest Conjunction—And the Chaplain sauntering about the Gardens ready for Employment.
LOV.   Nay, look not back, your Eyes consent, and I'll have no Denial.
L. WEAL.   Well, this is the maddest Thing.

And so a marriage is entered upon in a scene which faintly echoes the end of Mirabel and Millamant's famous marriage-bargaining scene. Another extremely important criterion has been overlooked by those who have thought this play sentimental comedy. There is practically no appeal to the emotions. Valere's reformation makes some appeal to the emotions, it is true, but it is alone in this respect. What is more, his reformation is preceded by a comic bit of business as he tries to brazen out the loss of the picture with which Angelica had told him never to part. Angelica, of course, has the picture herself, having won it from him in disguise. Almost immediately after the reformation and forgiveness scene there ensues the comic revelation of the true identity of the spurious Marquis. The appeal to the emotions in the one sentimental scene in the play is thrust between two pieces of comic business. If the sincerity of the author has any place in a final judgment on the sentimental quality of a play, one must rule against Mrs. Centlivre again. One last remark: there are no tears in *The Gamester*. This is not to suggest that sentimental comedy cannot exist without tears, but it is the rare sentimental comedy that does not make use of them.

Cibber's *The Lady's Last Stake* has two plots, linked by characters that appear in both. The plot which gives the play its title contains some elements of the sentimental, but it is really the other action which has attracted the term sentimental to the play. This second action tells of the misunderstandings between Lord and Lady Wronglove, their near separation, and their reconciliation through the efforts of Sir Friendly Moral—whose name is adequate description of his character. The longer, more elaborate action contains the reformed-gamester theme. Lady Gentle is an inveterate gambler whose chastity is being plotted against by Lord George Brilliant. He wins a large sum of money from her, and she is about to surrender her person to him—the "last stake" which she has wagered and lost—when a mysterious stranger enters the room and gives her the money to redeem her honor. Lord George tries to force her to his will when she is saved by Mrs. Conquest, disguised as her own hypothetical twin brother, who forces Lord George to go out and fight a duel. Lord George is set upon by thieves outside the house, and the disguised Mrs. Conquest is wounded as she helps him fight off his assailants. Mrs. Conquest's identity is revealed and Lord George, thinking her fatally wounded, asks that he be allowed to marry her that her reputation be saved. Thereupon Mrs. Conquest gets up and reveals that the whole business—robbery, wound, and all—had been a ruse concocted by herself. She offers to release Lord George from his marriage proposal, but he cries out

Since you provoke me then, prepare to start, and tremble at my Revenge—I will not only marry thee this Instant, but the next spiteful Moment insolently bed thee too, and make such ravenous Havock of thy Beauties, that thou shalt call in vain for Mercy of my Power. Ho! within there! call the Chaplain.

A situation which could so easily have been made to degenerate into the mawkishness which is the mark of the true sentimentalist is saved by what may be termed "bedroom" humor. As Lord George embraces the protesting Mrs. Conquest she exclaims "Oh!—Quarter! Quarter! O spare my Periwig." Sentimentally conceived heroines do not think of their coiffure at moments like these. There is no need to elaborate the point; the denouement of the main plot is handled comically.

It is the other action, however, which is conceived sentimentally, and which would make a sentimental comedy if it were isolated from the Lady Gentle-Lord George-Mrs. Conquest story. Lord George is a close friend to Lord Wronglove and is on hand frequently to engage in bawdy dialogue with him. There is one other reason for hesitating to call the Lord-and-Lady-Wronglove action sentimental, having already decided that the whole play cannot be called sentimental comedy because of the juxtaposition of the two interests. Lord Wronglove is trying to seduce Miss Notable, a young chit of fifteen years, who knows what she is about and delights in trickery. It might be mentioned here that Miss Notable, best described as a "sexy" little thing, falls in "love" with Mrs. Conquest when the latter dons breeches for her disguise, the revelation of the disguise finally subjecting Miss Notable to no little ridicule. Miss Notable indulges in very suggestive language, and is the object of equally suggestive conversation by Lord Wronglove and Lord George. The climax of the Lord-and-Lady-Wronglove story comes in their reconciliation by Sir Friendly Moral. This is in true sentimental style. It is, however, the only sentimental scene in a play full of intrigue, bawdry, and humor, and it is followed immediately by a short scene between Miss Notable and Mrs. Conquest, the latter in her breeches disguise and the object of the former's desire. It seems scarcely reasonable that the presence of one scene, sentimental as it may be, should allow one to call a whole play a sentimental comedy when so many elements antagonistic to sentimentalism are present in the same play. The objection that the scene in which Lady Gentle, having lost her "last stake," pleads with Lord George not to dishonor her, is sentimental can be easily refuted. It would have been sentimental if Lord George generously refused to take advantage of his unfortunate victim. Instead, her debt having been paid by the mysterious stranger, he tries to rape Lady Gentle, scorning to be fooled into pity by her tears.

Cibber's dedication contains some interesting comments. He says that "a Play without a just Moral, is a poor and trivial Undertaking," he denounces gaming as "a Vice that has undone more innocent Principles than any one Folly that's in Fashion," and he expresses the hope that some women will be persuaded by their husbands to forswear gaming because of his play. Even the casting of *The Lady's Last Stake* is of particular interest. Cibber was a frequent gambler at the time, had been addicted for some years, and was to continue to gamble for many years to come;[19] yet he played the part of Lord George Brilliant. Thus, a known gambler played a gamester in his own play, avowedly written against gaming. Nance Oldfield, playing the part of Mrs. Conquest, appears in "breeches," a costume designed to bring into some relief the bodily charms of the actress who wears it. Mrs. Cross played the hoydenish Miss Notable, fifteen years old, of whom Lord George says that "before she's five weeks older, she will be totally unqualified for an ape-leader" (i.e., she will have lost her virginity). It develops that Mrs. Cross had earlier enjoyed some rather dubious notoriety. She was one of a number of young girls who had been employed to recite very suggestive prologues and epilogues in the closing years of the seventeenth century,[20] and she had run off to France with a Baronet—evidently without benefit of clergy.[21] Is it too much to suggest that Mrs. Cross as Miss Notable, who is the object of the bit of dialogue quoted—as well as others in a similar vein—was being capitalized upon by Cibber, counting on knowledge of her escapade of eight years ago when she was still as "green" as Miss Notable is made out to be in the play? In 1705, two years before *The Lady's Last Stake*, Mrs. Cross was given a benefit performance, playing Florimel in Dryden's *Secret Love*,[22] proof that she was still before the public. Possibly this delving into the history of actors and actresses may seem a needless and worthless refinement, but it helps to reconstruct some part of the reaction of the audiences which saw the play in 1707.

One final point is to be made in connection with Cibber's play. If Cibber had been a true sentimental writer, it seems unlikely that he would have introduced a direct thrust at one of the most sentimental scenes in one of his earlier "sentimental" comedies. Yet he does precisely that in *The Lady's Last Stake*. In IV, i, he introduces a critique of the famous steinkirk scene in his *Careless Husband*. In this earlier play, one must remember, Sir Charles Easy is discovered by his wife asleep near Edging, her maid. Sir Charles's periwig is off, and Lady Easy covers his head with a steinkirk to prevent his catching cold. He awakens, realizes the full extent of his wife's goodness, and a reconciliation follows. The critique of this scene that appears in *The Lady's Last Stake* is quoted in full.

LA. WRONG. What is the Play to-day?

MRS. HARTS. The—the—*Husband*, something—the *Careful Husband*, I think, Madam.

LA. WRONG. The *Careful*; the *Careless Husband*, you mean sure—tho' I never saw it.

MRS. HARTS. Yes, yes, Madam—it's that Play, that my Lady Wear-breeches hates so, that I saw once, Madam—where there's a Lady that comes in, and catches her Husband fast asleep with her own Woman, and then takes her Handkerchief off her Neck, and then goes softly to him—

LA. WRONG. And strangles him in his Sleep?

MRS. HARTS. No, Madam.

LA. WRONG. O, strangles the Woman.

MRS. HARTS. No, Madam, she only lays it gently over his Head, for fear he should catch Cold, and so steals out of the Room, without so much as offering to wake him.

LA. WRONG. Horrid! And what becomes of the poor-spirited Creature?

MRS. HARTS. O! Madam, when the Gentleman wakes, and finds that his Lady has been there without taking any notice of it to him, he grows so sham'd of his Wickedness, and so sensible of her Vertues, that he afterwards proves the civilest Gentleman, and the best Husband in the World to her.

LA. WRONG. Foh! were I an Husband, a Wife with such a tame enduring Spirit wou'd make me scorn her, or, at best, but sleep at her groveling Vertue—(IV, i)

It is impossible to reconcile this scene—and the various other considerations discussed—with the designation of *The Lady's Last Stake* as sentimental comedy.

Edward Moore's *The Gamester* is a thoroughgoing example of sentimental drama. It is, of course, a domestic tragedy, and as such there is no comedy in it—although domestic tragedies with comic elements are not unknown. The play is free from bawdy language. The action is single; there are no subplots that demand to share the attention of reader or spectator. Caskey, comparing Moore's play to Aaron Hill's *The Fatal Extravagance*, objects to the greater complexity of plot demonstrated by *The Gamester*. He writes:

In some respects Moore loses by it—the emphasis is distributed, and a considerable part of the reader's attention [Caskey has anticipated one's very phraseology] must go to the outcome of the love of Charlotte and Lawson, and to the detection of the villainy of Stukely.[23]

Some account of the plot will help. Beverley has been reduced to near poverty by his addiction to gambling, but his wife has continued loving and faithful despite the efforts of Stukely, ostensibly Beverley's friend, to win her to his lust. It is Stukely who has cheated Beverley of his money. Beverley's sister Charlotte is in love with Lewson, he with her. Beverley goes through his own money, his sister's fortune, his wife's jewels, and the reversion of his uncle's estate. Stukely plots to have Lewson killed and Beverley arrested for his murder. Beverley is jailed, and takes poison. At the last minute Lewson turns up alive—Stukely's accomplices having refused to kill him—and word arrives that Beverley's uncle has died and left him his sole heir. Here again is the sentimental device of allowing good news to arrive just too late. Beverley dies in a scene reminiscent of the prison scene in Lillo's *George Barnwell*. The objection that attention is diverted from Beverley by the Charlotte-Lewson subplot and the villainy of Stukely is true only in a limited sense. Charlotte and Lewson do not figure in a subplot at all; they are inextricably bound to the only plot in the play—so, too, is Stukely. Unregenerate villainy is not inconsistent with sentimental drama; even Waldron's sentimental comedy

The Prodigal,[24] nothing but Hill's *The Fatal Extravagance* with a happy ending, does not go so far as to cause its villain to repent. Charlotte's fortune and happiness are part of the sentimental picture as a whole, and Lewson plays an important part in the plot. It is he who is responsible for revealing Stukely's true nature. Unity of effect is consistently maintained. Indeed, Oxberry, commenting on the play, can say that

Beholding this play is like gazing at a funeral procession of a mile in length, without a single break in its melancholy monotony; for, the slight attempt at an underplot, in the loves of Lewson and Charlotte, is too trivial, and partakes too much of the general character of the composition, to afford the spectator any mitigation of the mental torture he is compelled to undergo.[25]

Another remark of Caskey's deserves comment. It must be understood that he is concerned only with the dramatic effectiveness of the play; he is not arguing for or against it as sentimental drama in the passage which follows:

The story of Lewson and Charlotte is a sentimental comedy sub-plot; the faithful lover and the faithful sister get their reward, and Moore may be justly charged with injuring his plot by contriving to save all the virtuous characters from harm. (pp. 106-07)

The recognition that the Charlotte-Lewson interest—though one must repeat that it is not a subplot—is of the sentimental comedy type strengthens rather than weakens one's own contention that the play demonstrates real unity of effect. The fact that Moore saves the virtuous characters from harm only further enhances the sentimentalism of his play.

Other features of *The Gamester* further warrant its being called sentimental drama. Beverley is a weak but essentially good young man, gentle and loving with his wife, too confident in the goodness of human nature to suspect Stukely despite the fact that he has been warned against him. The play contains a character whose emotional appeal is irresistible—the faithful old family servant. One speech of this good old man's is enough to indicate how Moore exploits the character. Jarvis, the old servant, comes to Mrs. Beverley to offer his savings to the master who has dismissed him:

Is he indeed so poor, then?—Oh! he was the joy of my old heart—But must his creditors have all?—And have they his house too? His father built it when he was but a prating boy. The times that I have carried him in these arms! And, Jarvis, says he, when a beggar has asked charity of me, why should people be poor? You shan't be poor, Jarvis; if I were a king, nobody should be poor. Yet he is poor. And then he was so brave!—Oh, he was a brave little boy! And yet so merciful, he'd not have killed the gnat that stung him. (I, i)

The whole scene should be read. It is not necessary to prove the sentimentalism of this play, but it is important to point out in what respects it differs from non-sentimental plays on the same theme. Characters in *The Gamester* weep easily, and there is frequent mention of tears. A song is introduced (III, iv), and it develops to be what one might call the sketch for another sentimental drama. In fact, one might go so far as to suggest that it tells the story of Charles Johnson's *Caelia*[26]—in barest outline, of course. Mrs. Centlivre also introduces a song in her "sentimental" comedy, but its appeal is a bawdy one. Dawson, a minor character and one of Stukely's accomplices, expresses compassion when he turns Beverley over to the officers (V, i) and it is Dawson's (and Bates's) scruples against murder which save Lewson's life. Throughout there is not a single note which jars with the sentimental conception of the play as a whole. Indeed, in III, iii, Beverley's lying down on the hard stones of the street, determined to spend the night in contemplation of his miserable state, yields precedence to few other scenes for sheer sentimental appeal.

Caskey states, one recalls, that Holcroft made Moore's *The Gamester* into a sentimental comedy in his own play, *Duplicity*. Comedy *Duplicity* certainly is; whether it is sentimental comedy is, however, another matter. The serious action can be summarized very briefly. Sir Harry Portland gambles away his and his sister's fortune and is about to take his life when his friend Osborne, who had won all his money, confesses that the whole affair had been only to reveal to him the horrors of gaming. A happy ending finds Sir Harry marrying Clara and Osborne marrying Melissa, Sir Harry's sister. The very comic subplot depends on the old theme of mistaken identity. Sir Hornet Armstrong, whimsical uncle to Sir Harry, seeing Clara at Bath, is struck with her beauty and wit. Hoping to match her with his nephew, he inquires her identity of Squire Turnbull, a country lout, who so misunderstands him as to believe that it is his own sister to whom Sir Hornet refers. Consequently the Squire and Barbara, his sister, come up to London; he to woo Melissa, she to make a match with Sir Harry. The hilarious complications which arise from this confusion of identities are fully realized by Holcroft, and his play is enjoyable despite the sentimental part. Clara, incidentally, is wooed by her sixty-seven year old guardian, much to Sir Hornet's outspoken amusement and the old man's discomfiture. Clara, a sprightly, witty young woman, mimics Barbara's country dialect and rustic simplicity to perfection. Sir Harry, the "sentimental" hero—and this is worth noting—joins in the fun at the expense of the Squire and his sister, even to the extent of taking part in a parody of a country wooing. Among the minor characters is Mrs. Trip, a descendant of Sheridan's Mrs. Malaprop, whose doctor has told her that she is in danger of declining "into a liturgy" which may lead to her death from a "fit of apostacy." Timid is a mild "humor" character whose tag-line is "lackaday," and Squire Turnbull is given to larding his speech generously with old saws and proverbs.

Holcroft has gone back to the kind of comedy that Cibber wrote in the early years of the century—four acts of fun and intrigue and one act (often not the whole act, at that) devoted to a sentimental conclusion. The vice of gaming is almost incidental to the plot of *Duplicity*; it achieves some prominence only in the fifth act. As a consequence there is no attempt to evoke an emotional response until the play is in its closing act. The first tears shed in the play come in the last act—and tears, or expressions of grief, are meat and drink to the sentimentalist. Scene-by-scene analysis of *Duplicity* would clearly show the preponderance of comedy in the play. Here, as with Mrs. Centlivre's and Cibber's plays, one must conclude that *Duplicity* is not a sentimental comedy, and that easy generalizations made on the basis of some attempt at sentimentalism in a play are not particularly trustworthy. Holcroft has left us a statement of his intention in the preface to *Duplicity*. Although he says that

Whatever the execution may have been, the intention of this Comedy is of far nobler nature than the mere incitement of Risibility: the vice it pretends to correct is become truly enormous; and I would rather have the merit of driving one man from the gaming-table, than of making a whole theatre merry.

he also says that

The English Comic Drama has long been renowned for humour; and when, about fourteen years ago, the French Comedie Larmoyante, or, as we call it, Sentimental Comedy, was introduced, the complaint was, that we had lost all the spirit of our old writers, and were dwindled into mere translators. The town was in this temper when Dr. Goldsmith's Comedy of *She Stoops to Conquer* was produced, in which, humour, alone, seems to be the chief intention of the Author, and which gave a fatal blow to mere sentimental dialogue. The success of this piece rouzed later writers from the soft slumbers of the heart, and wit and humour became commodities in great request. The road to fame, though difficult, was obvious; and it would have been unpardonable for a young traveller, at his first out-set, so far to have mistaken, as not to have attempted it. The difficulties and dangers have increased, however, in a vast proportion. I need only mention the *School For Scandal;* and every discerning critic will immediately recollect how, and why.

This latter statement does not sound like the credo of the author of sentimental comedies.

It is to be hoped that the amount of time spent in analyzing these various "gamester" plays has made clear how important a consideration emphasis can be in discussing sentimental drama. The choice of plays on a common theme is an arbitrary one; the same procedure could just as readily be followed in analyzing a number of plays based on different themes. The differences between sentimental drama and that which is not is probably more easily seen, however, when two plays that have the same theme are used for purposes of comparison. In any event, to recapitulate briefly, final decision on the sentimentalism of a play must not now neglect the criteria—repetition and prolongation, eschewal of the humorous and the bawdy, and emphasis and direction—which have been demonstrated to be of great importance in any such decision.

Chapter VI. OTHER CRITERIA

CERTAIN DISTINGUISHING FEATURES of sentimental drama cannot be isolated and examined as easily as those treated in the preceding discussion. It is relatively simple to point out passages in which a sentimental effect is obtained by the dramatist's deliberate prolongation of a scene or situation, and it is equally simple to cite scenes and whole plays in which a sentimental effect is avoided by the timely introduction of comic and bawdy elements. The importance of emphasis and direction is demonstrable by examination of certain plays which have a common theme but which are or are not sentimental because of the stress laid on the tender or pathetic part of the play. These criteria can be studied objectively, but it is not always possible to achieve any great degree of objectivity in discussing the criteria now introduced for consideration. Many plays seem to exhibit all, or most, of the features of sentimental drama. These same plays do not evoke any sentimental response because their chief concern is quite obviously with interests other than the sentimental. Conspicuous in this category are many Elizabethan tragicomedies in which the dramatist is interested in intrigue, in unusual sexual relationships, in multiple disguises, in poisons which do not deprive of life, and in a number of other situations that contain opportunity for striking effects. Potentially sentimental scenes are neglected as the dramatist concentrates upon action rather than upon emotion.

Often an early English play not only seems to contain all the elements of sentimental drama but even seems to contain them in greater measure than do later, eighteenth-century examples of the genre. Yet these earlier plays cannot properly be called sentimental for the reason that they demonstrate a naïveté, a primitiveness, and a traditional quality which is absolutely foreign to sentimental drama. Sentimental drama is almost always sophisticated and deliberately calculated; simplicity and sincerity seldom have a place in it. Following logically upon the preceding statement comes the very important consideration that plays of obvious artistic distinction and integrity cannot be called sentimental drama. The very essence of sentimental drama is to be found in its artificiality, its improbability, and its illogicality. Contributing largely to these elements is the inevitable presence of false or exaggerated emotion, a feature which is enough to prevent any serious play from achieving artistic distinction or integrity.

Despite an abundance of sentimental situations and speeches in it, there is one Elizabethan play whose author does not appear to be interested in producing sentimental effects. *A Knack to Know an Honest Man,* of unknown authorship, was entered in the Register of Stationers' Company on November 26, 1594. It appears as a new play in Henslowe's Diary on October 22, 1594, and twenty-one performances are recorded from that time to the third of November 1596, proof that the drama enjoyed some popularity.[1] Since it is not one of the more widely read Elizabethan plays, a summary of its plot follows. The scene is Venice. Some shepherds witness a duel between two gentlemen, Lelio and Sempronio, erstwhile friends but now enemies because of the latter's unsuccessful attempt on the virtue of Annetta, Lelio's wife. Lelio wounds Sempronio and flees, believing him dead, and Sempronio is borne off by Philip, the hermit. Servio, avaricious uncle to Sempronio, secures sentence of death on Lelio, and banishment and confiscation of goods for any who aid Lelio in any way. Subsequently Lelio is seen sheltered by his father-in-law, Brisheo. At this point Sempronio appears, disguised as an old man, and is taken into the service of Fortunio, son of the Duke of Venice. Fortunio and Marchetto, a Senator, enter Lelio's home to search for him (a reward of 1000 crowns has been set on his head). Marchetto asks to enjoy Annetta's favors, and is scornfully repulsed; so, too, is Fortunio when he tempts Lucida, Lelio's daughter. Marchetto and Fortunio retire. Brisheo is banished for helping Lelio to escape; he leaves two sons, Orphronio and Zepherius. Sempronio, acting as Fortunio's messenger, offers Lucida riches if she will satisfy the young nobleman's lust. She refuses, and Sempronio applauds her virtue. Fortunio and Marchetto now plan to use violence. When they try to force their way in at night they are stopped by Brisheo's sons, warned by Sempronio. Fortunio is wounded, and Orphronio and his brother are taken prisoner. They are released by Phillida, Servio's daughter, in love with Orphronio.

Meanwhile Lelio, fighting for the Duke of Florence, and Brisheo, fighting for the rival Duke of Milan, meet in the battlefield, embrace, and bring about a reconciliation between their leaders. Brisheo's sons come to Lelio, demanding that he return to Venice to lift the sentence of banishment on their father. They threaten Lelio with their swords, but are fiercely upbraided by their father. Left alone, Lelio decides to return to Venice to provide for his daughter by having her turn him in for the reward on his head. Servio recognizes Lelio and arrests him. When Lelio is brought before the Duke he is sentenced to death for the murder of Sempronio, but at the last moment Sempronio throws off his disguise and he and Lelio are reconciled. Brisheo's sons, arrested for their attack on Fortunio, are released when he confesses the fault was his and asks that they come to no harm. Brisheo, returned from banishment, is asked to pay a fine. As he is penniless, his life is in danger until Lucida pays his fine out of the reward money given to her because Servio had waited three days before turning Lelio over to the authorities. Phillida and

Orphronio are joined, Fortunio wins Lucida, and Servio is made to restore Sempronio's goods, which he had inherited.

Even in skeletal outline some of the opportunities for sentimental treatment are apparent. Three major themes run through the play:

1. Sempronio's repentance and the help he gives to the virtuous in distress. (He acts, by the way, as a moralizing chorus.)

2. The inviolable chastity of Annetta and Lucida. (Annetta's virtue is attempted by both Sempronio and Marchetto; she repulses both. Lucida is tempted by Fortunio, but she is equally impregnable.)

3. The friendship of Brisheo for his son-in-law, Lelio. In his first appearance in disguise Sempronio takes leave of Philip, the hermit, in the following vein:

> Here is that Venice that beheld me fond,
> Here is that Venice that shall behold me wise,
> Looke how thy science hath disguisde these lookes,
> So hath thy councell reconcilde my heart,
> I hate all the worldly pompe, I scorne lewd lust,
> This tongue from tempting in dishonest love
> Shall labour to releeve the innocent . . . (ll. 297-303)

He takes the name of Penitent Experience, and is instrumental in saving Lucida from Fortunio's intended violence. Earlier he encourages the girl to refuse Fortunio's riches, the lure set for her chastity. He also helps the impoverished Orphronio and Zepherius and advises them to lead a "sober decent comely life." It is he who brings Fortunio to see the evils of his ways, and it is he, of course, who acts as the final *deus ex machina*.

The chaste Annetta and her equally chaste daughter Lucida withstand the lust of the powerful Marchetto and Fortunio. Annetta replies to Marchetto's "Grant me possession of thy private bed" with

> Awaie dishonest man, abuse not me,
> My povertie is happines to me,
> So long as vertue guides and governe it,
> Come Lucida, beware of subtill men.
> Fly from these Sirenes that inchant chast hearts,
> Come let our toiling fingers get us bread,
> Before suspect should preiudice our names. (ll. 458-64)

This speech is not unlike that of Mrs. Haller in Kotzebue's sentimental *Stranger*. Although the circumstances are different, the sentiments expressed are the same:

To the labor of my hands alone will I owe my sustenance. A morsel of bread, moistened by the tears of penitence, will suffice my wishes, and exceed my merits . . .[2]

Brisheo's love for Lelio is so extreme as to be incredible, but unlike the brief passage in Shakespeare's *Two Gentlemen of Verona* where Valentine offers Sylvia to Proteus, this friendship is emphasized enough to warrant one's assumption that the anonymous dramatist is exploiting the relationship. Brisheo helps Lelio to escape; the two meet on the battlefield and lay down their arms; Brisheo threatens to disown his sons when he learns that they are trying to force Lelio back to Venice on his account; and when he discovers that Lelio has returned to Venice he threatens to kill his sons unless they bring Lelio back to him. When Lelio is sentenced to death, Brisheo resolves to die with him. On all these occasions Brisheo has something to say about the obligations of true friendship. One example should suffice. Brisheo is asked if he knows the penalty for aiding Lelio. He replies

> All this I knew, but none of this I feare,
> True friendship lightneth all these burdenous harme
> If Lelio be escapt I feare no wants,
> My exile to me is libertie,
> Go fruites of nature, I will leave you heere,
> Go toward children, thrive among my friends,
> Glut you with my excess of Vanities,
> Feed your uncleane desires by spoiling me,
> I wreake them not, so Lelio live to me.
> Not irkesome age, not lims with sicknes tir'd,
> Nor you my sonnes, nor all my other friends
> Not fortune nor intreate shall keep me backe. (ll. 563-74)

As though all this had not been enough, the playwright includes a scene in which Orphronio and Zepherius ask two Senators, in turn, to give them financial aid now that their father's fortune has been confiscated. The Senators, formerly helped by Brisheo, refuse in the approved *Everyman* formula. Phillida, Servio's daughter, who, it will be remembered, set Brisheo's sons free, asks the Duke to take her life instead of her father's, doomed to die for his negligence in letting the two escape. When the Duke offers to have Phillida strangled, Servio, represented as an avaricious old villain, cries out "Oh pardon the daughter, let the father dye." Even he is not entirely devoid of humanity.

All the characteristic features of sentimental drama are here. What is more, there is hardly any comedy or bawdry in the play. Gnatto, servant to Lelio, attempts some feeble witticisms, but they are very few and occur in one scene in isolation (ll. 621-61). And yet the anonymous playwright's handling of the sentimental scenes is curious. He devotes enough time to them to warrant the assumption that he is interested in them, but he does not dwell upon them at sufficient length to make it reasonably certain that he is working for sentimental effects. Here is one of the borderline cases where it is difficult to put a finger precisely on the elements which keep the play from being sentimental. Some considerations, however, may help to explain one's feeling that the play is not sentimental. It is very episodic, and its interests are diverse. As in later tragicomedies, the emphasis falls primarily on what the characters do or are reported to have done. Too many strands of action are present for any one of them to receive the emphasis that is observed in more sophisticated plays where the author telegraphs his intention and prepares the reader or spectator for the big scene toward which he has been leading. In short, there is a naïve quality about this play which is probably best seen in the inclusion of little episodes which do not further the action and which have their origins in tradition. The scene in which Brisheo's sons are refused help when they are in need, as has already been said, is an example. Reminiscent of medieval moralities, it is so brought in that one feels sure the dramatist is confident his use of the scene will be welcomed because of its familiarity to his audience. An indefinable, almost impersonal, quality, as in folk literature, prevents us from thinking of a sentimental manipulator.

The idea implicit in the word "naïve," used to describe *A Knack to Know an Honest Man,* is worth further discussion. Eighteenth-century writers of sentimental drama have often left evidence, either in the plays themselves or, more importantly, in other writings, of their own feeling about the genre in which they wrote. Often letters and essays, or critiques of other plays, contain corroboratory evidence of the writer's sincerity in writing sentimental comedy. More often there are indications that belief and practice did not coincide. These casual references may or may not be used in deciding the sentimental quality of a particular play of a particular writer. It is sufficiently obvious that a hard-headed, uncharitable man can write a sentimental play in which he extols the virtue of charity. If it is known that this hypothetical writer is uncharitable, it may be assumed that his celebration of charity is insincere. There is no way of knowing, however, that Elizabethan dramatists whose private lives and correspondence are lost to us were sincere or insincere in their celebration of certain virtues. It becomes dangerous to state categorically that in this scene or another a particular Elizabethan playwright is being hypocritical because it seems impossible that he should be so naïve as to believe in the ideals he extols. Times change, and what may now seem mawkish sentimentality may not have been that at all three hundred years ago. But this idea is not precisely expressed; an example may serve to make the whole matter much clearer.

The Pleasant Comedy of Patient Grissil, by Dekker, Chettle, and Haughton is a dramatic version of the old story which one finds in

Boccaccio and Chaucer. It was already an old story in the fourteenth century, and when the trio of Elizabethan playwrights took it up in 1600 it was so familiar, so much a part of popular tradition, that it is safe to speak of it as folklore. The Grissil (Griselda) story, in its essentials, is well known, but the treatment afforded it by Dekker and his collaborators must be reviewed. Grissil, of poor extraction, is wed by a Marquess. She is a model of loving humility. For no reason except a desire to try his wife's patience, the Marquess decides to subject her constancy and love to a trial. He announces his intention in these words:

> So dearly love I Grissil, that my life
> Shall end, when she doth end to be my wife.
> FURIO. 'Tis well done.
> MAR. Yet is my bosom burnt up with desires
> To try my Grissil's patience. (II, ii)

In the light of the Marquess' expression of love for his wife, the nature and extent of the trial to which he subjects her is fantastic. Grissil is accused of pride, and made to tie an attendant's shoelaces. She is ordered about like a servant, and her father and brother are banished. She gives birth to two children, and her husband charges her with adultery, forbidding her to touch them. Soon she is driven from court in the rags she was wearing when she came to wed the Marquess. Her children are taken from her and sent away to be brought up. Finally, after years of separation from her husband, she is called back to court to wait upon the Marquess' bride-to-be, and she is made to give up her wedding ring to the Marquess' new love. Grissil bears all these trials with patience, never ceasing to love her husband. Her constancy is rewarded when the Marquess reveals that his bride-to-be is their own daughter and takes Grissil back as his wife.

Apart from the indignities that Grissil is forced to undergo, one is struck by the length of time the trial involves. Making allowances for child marriages, it is a conservative estimate to say that the trial lasted at least ten years, an incredible time for the Marquess to deny himself the love of his wife. The whole trial is, of course, incredible. It is a fairy tale, a story of the people, known for centuries and belonging properly in a never-never world of fantasy. One must not ask for logic in a fairy tale, nor must one expect the inhabitants of this legendary realm to act and feel like people of the workaday world. To speak of sentimentalism in connection with this play is to lose sight of the fact that it was never meant to represent real life. When one turns to the eighteenth century and comes upon a play in which a husband mistreats a virtuous wife by neglect, by clandestine affairs with other women, by gambling away her fortune, or by any one of a number of other credible deviations from his duties and obligations as a husband, one is in the world of events that find their way daily into the newspapers. When this eighteenth-century husband repents and is forgiven, it is then time to start thinking of sentimentalism.

This naïve or primitive quality is present in many plays of the Elizabethan period. Heywood's plays often contain themes reminiscent of the moralities. Sir Charles Mountford and his sister Susan seek help of their uncle, of a friend, and of a tenant without success—the Everyman story again (*A Woman Killed With Kindness*, III, iii). Of Heywood's *Royal King and Loyal Subject* Tucker Brooke says:

It is nursery-tale morality, which Heywood reinforces by his subplot: Captain Bonville, likewise returning from the wars and in apparent destitution, finds his false friends disloyal and his true friends more devoted than before.[3]

In this last play Heywood combines a male "Griselda" story in the main plot with the Everyman theme in the subplot. *The Blind Beggar of Bednal Green* has a trial by combat (V, i), and knowledge that the husband in *A Yorkshire Tragedy* is demoniacally possessed is necessary for a proper understanding of the terrible murders he commits. A whole body of Elizabethan drama based on magic and on charms and incantations falls into this category of plays which rely upon primitive or traditional materials.

There is, as well as a degree of naïveté, a degree of sophistication or stylization, which militates against sentimentalism. Fletcher's *The Faithful Shepherdess* is a play in which this trait can be seen; and it must be recalled that the play conforms to the model definition of sentimental drama originally set up.[4] At the very center of Fletcher's pastoral is the theme of inviolable chastity, a theme so old that one is at a loss to suggest its origins. The preoccupation with chastity is so popular a theme that an enormous body of literature, both dramatic and nondramatic, would be lost if works built upon it were suddenly to disappear. One must realize that a particular kind of dramaturgy is being dealt with in a discussion of plays like *The Faithful Shepherdess*, that a different set of techniques is being used from that which obtained in eighteenth-century sentimental drama. In Elizabethan plays, as in eighteenth-century sentimental comedies, chastity plays an all-important part. The difference in treatment is understandable in the light of the desired end-effect. Elizabethan dramatists of the school of Fletcher were interested in moral problems which lent themselves to the introduction of striking scenes and situations. Taking chastity as one of their basic themes, they attempted to work out all the possible variations on it, not for the sake of the theme itself, but for the sake of the pyrotechnical display involved in the working out of those variations. The emphasis was upon action, the *scene à faire*, rather than on the emotion. Taking the same theme as their point of departure, eighteenth-century dramatists worked out all possible variations which would tend to emphasize and bring into bold relief the emotion, or emotions, they were bent on exploiting. Action with them was secondary, a means to an end. The desire to exploit action and striking situations is present in *The Spanish Gypsy*, and it is this emphasis, among other things, which saves that play from being sentimental. This is the chief difference which distinguishes tragicomedy from sentimental comedy.

Another consideration which cannot be slighted in distinguishing between sentimental and non-sentimental drama is the kind of language used. Differentiation between the language of sentimental drama and drama that is not sentimental involves a judgment on sincerity or artificiality of expression, and this is not always easy to make. Sometimes, however, it is possible to say with some degree of assurance that in a particular speech or speeches the dramatist is insincere because he has employed phrases or expressions which have become trite from constant usage. A serious play of today whose dialogue contained utterances such as "Unhand me, villain," "Go, and never darken my threshold again," or "Better death than dishonor" could only be ridiculous, yet these speeches were once taken seriously. The situations which prompt such treatment are cheapened by triteness of language, and there can be no respect for the product of a writer who does not trouble to invest a familiar situation in fresh language. But judgment on the sincerity and freshness of language in treatment of familiar situations or themes is doubly difficult in considering drama as remote as that of the Elizabethan age. Inevitably one has the impulse to think in terms of the twentieth century and not in those of the sixteenth or seventeenth. What is old and hackneyed now may have been newly minted when it found its way into an Elizabethan play, but it is almost impossible to repress the impulse to label it trite because of the associations it arouses. Clariana, in *Love's Cruelty*, by James Shirley, is caught by her husband in the act of adultery with his friend Hippolito. She tries to defend herself by asking "what woman is/Without some stain?" and Hippolito asks to be spared that he may "wash off" the "shame" and "leprosy" on his name (IV, i). The words "stain," "shame," "leprosy" in this context strike a modern reader as trite. They have a familiar ring that sometimes defies efforts to place them in a particular play or novel. The words are so familiar that their recognition does not even make an impression on the reader's consciousness. Did Shirley's audiences, however, recognize them as familiar and trite words which had been used again and again in similar scenes? One hesitates to answer that question. When, more than two hundred and fifty years later, a father says to his disobedient daughter "Away, base wretch! stain to your father's honor and his peace" (*Lindor and Clara*, III, ii), the word "stain" becomes suspect, particularly in a play which abounds in other, equally time-worn, words and expressions. One can be quite confident that by 1791 much of the language in *Lindor and Clara* was recognized for what it is—trite and insincere.[5]

"The man who wrongs that lady is a villain—Draw!" cries out a character in Richard Cumberland's *The West Indian* (IV, iv). In another of Cumberland's plays the simple question "Where do you dwell?" is answered in the following fashion:

I have no house, no home, no father, friend, or refuge, in this world; nor do I at this moment, fainting as I am with affliction and fatigue, know where to find

a hospitable door. (*The Fashionable Lover*, III)
It might be difficult to recall exactly where speeches like these have been read or heard before, but they summon up vague memories of similar speeches in similar situations, and they leave one with a sense of dissatisfaction. Play after play of the sentimental genre demonstrates this triteness of language. Emilia, of Mrs. Griffith's *The Platonic Wife*, is indignant that her character should be impugned: "My character, Sir, is far above the reach of malice, nor has the tongue of slander ever yet pronounced my name" (II, i). Lord Winworth speaks of "the anguish of a rejected passion" (*False Delicacy*, II, i); Lucy Waters calls herself "the basest, the falsest of womankind" (*The Brothers*, II, v); and in one speech of Mr. Gage's occur the phrases "infant beauty," "lovely babe," "emblem of innocence," and "sweet resemblance of your sweet mother" (*The Affectionate Father*, I, ii). Examples need not be multiplied. The difference between this artificial and trite language of sentimental drama can be best seen by comparing two speeches made under almost exactly similar circumstances. Joseph Richardson's *The Fugitive* has already been compared to its model, Beaumont and Fletcher's *The Coxcomb*.[6] In both plays the heroine, insulted by her drunken lover who does not recognize her upon the night fixed for their elopement, finally forgives him and accepts him as a husband. Viola speaks to Ricardo:

> For God's sake urge your faults no more, but mind!
> All the forgiveness I can make you, is,
> To love you; which I will do, and desire
> Nothing but love again; which if I have not,
> Yet I will love you still. (*The Coxcomb*, V, ii)

Julia speaks to Young Manly:

. . . and now, Manly, may a poor persecuted fugitive hope at last for a happy asylum from the severities of her fortune? Shall I trust myself again to the precarious direction of so fickle a guide—yes, I will trust, most confidently trust thee, for where there is generosity as the foundation virtue in a man's nature, the memory of a woman's sorrows will secure her against a repetition of the cause of them, nor with such a mind, can her affection fondly bestowed ever be quite hopeless of a return. (*The Fugitive*, V, v)

Another of the remarkable and exasperating elements of the language employed by sentimental dramatists is what has already been briefly mentioned and compared to the language of letter-writing manuals. Unlike domestic tragedy, sentimental comedy usually selects its characters from the well-to-do upper middle class or from the nobility, and these characters are made to speak "genteely." In fact, the term "genteel comedy" is sometimes substituted for "sentimental comedy" in the eighteenth century. James Nelson's play, quoted above, provides a few examples. A son greets his mother after an absence of years with "Honoured Madam, I rejoice to see you look so well," and another character protests: "Pardon the verbal remark, Madam; but I should think that a nobleman's table would rather demand the term elegant than hospitable." It is obvious that etiquette has entered the drama. But other passages from other plays offer themselves; the difficulty is which to quote, which to omit. Richard Cumberland, often accorded the dubious honor of heading the sentimental school in the latter years of the century, generously gives characters of high and low classes the same kind of dialogue. Belfield, Jr., of *The Brothers*, says, "I doubt not your discretion, and shall implicitly surrender myself to your guidance." Here, as elsewhere, the circumstances do not matter. Sophia, of the same play, requires "in a husband, good morals, good nature, and good sense; what has all this to do with contiguous estates, connected interests, and contested elections?" The reader will not miss the artful alliteration of that last series. Lucy Waters, of humbler station, addresses Sophia,

Yes, amiable Sophia, you was unrivall'd in his esteem; and I, who persuaded you to the contrary, am the basest, the falsest of womankind; every syllable I told you of his engagements to me was a malicious invention: how cou'd you be so blind to your own superiority, to give credit to the imposition, and suffer him to depart without an explanation? (II, v)

Lucy and Sophia, daughter of Sir Benjamin Dove, are sisters under the skin.

In Hugh Kelly's characters delicacy of thought, feeling, and language—sometimes admirable, sometimes false—is prominent. One of the young ladies in his *School For Wives* (1775) speaks: "The peculiarity of your father's temper, joined to my want of fortune, make it necessary for me to keep our engagements inviolably secret; there is no merit, therefore, either in my prudence, or in my laboring assiduously to cultivate the good opinion of the General" (I). But the characters in his *False Delicacy* easily bear the palm. Lord Winworth (another almost allegorical name, it will be noted) delivers himself of the following:

Since your final disapprobation of those hopes which I was once presumptuous enough to entertain of calling your ladyship mine, the anguish of a rejected passion has rendered me inconceivably wretched; and I see no way of mitigating the severity of my situation, but in the esteem of this amiable woman, who knows how tenderly I have been attached to you, and whose goodness will induce her, I am well convinced, to alleviate, as much as possible, the greatness of my disappointment. (II, i)

It is useless to try to describe the effect of such stilted phraseology; it speaks for itself. Fortunately, Kelly was not entirely unaware of the absurdities of "false delicacy," and there is the temptation to see parody or at least deliberate exaggeration in speeches like these.

The emotion, or response, or reaction that is most often described as sentimental is that in which there is an element of enjoyment as well as of grief, or pity. Sir Leslie Stephen speaks of sentimentalism as "the name of the mood in which we make a luxury of grief." Joseph Wood Krutch suggests that the submission of the hero of sentimental romance "draws a pleasant tear from the the eye of the beholder." And Steele speaks of a "joy too exquisite for laughter."[7] These descriptions of the sentimental response are accurate, and it is interesting to note the presence of the same idea in various plays. The last lines of the prologue to Ford's *The Broken Heart* suggests that the play may have been based on an incident in real life, and concludes

> . . . if words have cloth'd the subject right,
> You may partake a pity with delight.

In John Banks's *The Unhappy Favourite*, the Countess of Essex, describing the joys of her nuptial night, speaks of her tears and joy:

> . . . I sigh'd, and wept for Joy, a showre of Tears,
> And felt a thousand sweet, and pleasant fears,
> Too rare for Sense, too exquisite to say. (II)

Luxuriating in grief characterizes the heroine of Philip Francis' *Eugenia*:

> I never shall have Cause to weep again,
> And I'll enjoy it now. (IV)

Harriet, in Mrs. Elizabeth Griffith's *The School For Rakes*, frequently given to weeping, says that "Joy has its tears, as well as grief" (II). Monimia, in Otway's *The Orphan*, asks that she be left alone to her "beloved despair" (IV, ii). In George Colman the Elder's *The English Merchant*, a character describes the meeting between father and daughter in these words: "First they wept for grief; then they wept for joy; and then they wept for grief again" (IV). Interestingly, the drama critic for the *Gentleman's Magazine* chose this feature of the play for comment, speaking of "a luxury in tears that laughter can never taste" (March, 1767, p. 130). Jarvis, in Edward Moore's *The Gamester*, announces good news with: "I have a tale of joy for you, and my tears drown it" (V, ii). And in Edward Young's *The Brothers* (1753) one character queries "How exquisite is Pleasure and Pain?" and is answered with "Joy and Sorrow dwell too near" (V). This deliberate mingling of joy and tears occurs too often in sentimental situations to be neglected.

Similarly, the statement that sentimental drama makes an appeal to the emotions rather than to the intellect has found its way into many definitions of the genre. The statement is vague enough in itself, and, it may be objected, may apply to all drama. Exceptions might be suggested, but there would be the inevitable quibble about definitions of "intellect" and "emotion." It seems wiser to point out specific passages in which the sentimental dramatist appeals to the emotions alone, and the non-sentimental dramatist appeals to the emotions, true, but also to the intellect. Chaste maidens whose virtue is besieged are frequent in drama. In Shirley's *Love's Cruelty* the chaste Eubella reproaches Hippolito, who has been trying to persuade her to give herself to the Duke:

> Is chastity and innocence no treasure?
> Are holy thoughts and virgin purity
> Of so small value? where is your religion?
> Were we created men and women to
> Have a command and empire o'er the creatures,
> And shall we lose our privilege, our charter,
> And wilfully degrade ourselves of reason
> And piety, to live like beasts, nay, be such?
> For what name else can we allow ourselves?
> Hath it been held in every age a virtue
> Rather to suffer death than stain our honour?
> Does every sin strike at the soul and wound it,
> And shall not this, so foul, as modesty
> Allows no name, affright us? Can the duke,
> Whose wicked cause you plead, with justice punish
> Those by his laws that in this kind offend,
> And can he think me innocent, or himself,
> When he has played the foul adulterer?
> Princes are gods on earth, and as their virtues
> Do shine more exemplary to the world,
> So, they strike more immediately at heaven,
> When they offend. (II, ii)

Eubella appeals to reason. Man is superior to the other creatures. Shall he, then, bring himself to the level of the beasts by surrendering one of his sovereign gifts? How can the Duke pretend to dispense law when he himself violates the law? Compare this with a similar situation in Mrs. Charlotte Lennox's *The Sister*. Miss Courtney is approached by her brother—who does not know her—acting as the agent of Lord Clairville, who is prepared to "keep" her. She cries out

No more, Sir—this insult is too plain. (turns and weeps) Oh! why am I thus weak?—indignation, scorn, contempt would better become me. (II)

and follows her first words with some sententious moralizing. Others of Shirley's women are logicians. Lady Peregrine repulses Lord Fitzavarice's advances, determined to be true to her absent husband. Her answer to Lord Fitzavarice's importunities makes its appeal both to the emotions and the intellect.

>   . . . not your estate,
> Though multiplied to kingdoms, and those wasted
> With your invention, to serve my pleasures,
> Have power to bribe my life away from him,
> To whose use I am bid to wear it. Be yet just,
> And seek no further to pollute the stress
> Of my chaste thoughts; I'll rather choose to die
> Poor wife to Peregrine, than live a king's
> Inglorious strumpet; can you think, my lord,
> Should I give up my freedom to your bent,
> And for the pride of wealth, sell woman in me,
> (For she must lose that name that once turns whore,)
> Could I arrive at impudence enough
> To come abroad, and not be mov'd to hear
> My shame from every tongue, but scorn my infamy,
> (As 'tis the nature of this sin to strengthen
> Itself still with a greater,) could you think,
> If no religion can correct your wildness,
> Another's price, or pleasure, would not buy me
> Even from your arms? there is no faith in lust,
> And she that dares be false to one she loves,
> Will twine with all the world, and never blush for't,
> Kiss, and betray as often. Think on this,
> And call yourself home. (*The Example*, III, i)

Sentimental heroines do not try to argue their way out of situations like these by telling their would-be seducers that they may deceive them as well as their own husbands. Another of Shirley's women, Celestina, shames the Lord who would have her as his mistress by an elaborate analogy between her virtue and his coat of arms (*The Lady of Pleasure*, V). One cannot help feeling that the bewildered Lord, unaccustomed to such argumentation, gave in from sheer inability to match Celestina's dialectic.

This appeal to reason in scenes which might well rely for their effect on an appeal to the emotions alone is present in other dramatists as well as in Shirley. Dekker, in *II Honest Whore*, shows Infeliche shaming her husband Hippolito by pretending inconstancy, hearing his rebukes, and then turning on him with proof of his real inconstancy (III, i). Unfaithful husbands in eighteenth-century sentimental comedy are usually met with a shower of tears from their much abused but still adoring spouses. (A notable exception is to be found in Hugh Kelly's *The School For Wives*, III). Later in *II Honest Whore* Dekker has Bellafront and Hippolito argue the advantages and disadvantages of a life of prostitution. Hippolito reminds Bellafront that he won her away from prostitution "with one parley," and he now proposes to "beat down" her chastity "with the same ordnance," "the power of argument." Bellafront agrees, and the debate—for it is really that—is on (IV, i). In Webster and Middleton's *Anything For A Quiet Life* an unscrupulous and ambitious lawyer named Knaves-bee offers to persuade his wife to satisfy the lust of wealthy Lord Beaufort. Mistress Knaves-bee goes to Lord Beaufort's home in compliance with her husband's wishes—she knows for what purpose, and is determined to remain chaste. Pretending a strong sexual desire for Lord Beaufort's young page she promises to satisfy him if she may only enjoy his page first. Lord Beaufort is furious at the thought that he should be made "procurer" to his servant, and Mistress Knaves-bee seizes upon this as an opportunity for analogizing. If, she says, you have done worse already by bribing my husband to be a "Pander to his own wife," you certainly should not hesitate to pimp for your servant (III, i).

Comparison of a cold, unemotional speech in one play with a speech designed only for emotional effect in another play points up the difference even further. The circumstances are approximately the same; the periods are the Restoration and the late eighteenth century—by coincidence the two plays are exactly one hundred years apart. Olivia, of Thomas D'Urfey's *The Virtuous Wife* (1680), repulses the advances of the rake Beauford in the following words:

In fine, sir, by way of advice, let me tell ye—you do but swim against the stream, and vainly dash against the rock of my Constancy; therefore desist in time, do; Marry, grow vertuous, and love honestly;
> Look gravely, say your prayers, think on Hell,
> Your Ill luck comes by Whoring, so farewell. (V)

There is no appeal to the emotions in this speech; it is the speech of a self-sufficient woman who does not need pity or sympathy—she can even win back her errant husband by her own resourcefulness, as she proves convincingly in the play. Cecelia of Sophia Lee's *The Chapter of Accidents* (1780) is a true sentimental heroine. When Harcourt, pretending to be an agent for somebody who desires her for his kept mistress, makes Cecelia an offer, the shocked girl cries "Good heavens! to what an insult have I exposed myself." She then "bursts into tears, and sinks into a chair," and her next speech makes even clearer that she is not the woman that D'Urfey's Olivia is.

... Return, sir, to your vile employer, tell him, whoever he is, I am too sensible of the insult, tho' not entitled to resent it—tell him, I have a heart above my situation, and that he has only had the barbarous satisfaction of adding another misery to those which almost over-whelmed me before. (V)

There is in this speech a definite bid for pity which is noticeably absent from the analogous speech by Olivia. Olivia's words are hard, cold, even somewhat comic; Cecelia's are weak and emotional—intended to arouse pity for her distressed state. It must not, of course, be understood that the difference between sentimental drama and non-sentimental drama lies in the emotional appeal of the former as against the intellectual appeal of the latter. There is an appeal to the emotions in almost all drama. The point is that scenes which might easily become sentimental are sometimes saved by the presence of an appeal to the intellect. Where one is asked to think logically the possibility of a sentimental response tends to disappear.

One important question remains to be discussed. The term "sentimental tragedy" has been used to describe certain plays of the Elizabethan period.[8] It is necessary to distinguish between the great tragedies of the period and the tragedies which fail to achieve greatness. It is almost impossible to discuss this problem without falling back upon references to this dramatist's genius as opposed to its absence in that dramatist, but some general remarks can be made. The whole question is extremely complex, but the criteria that have been suggested in the present work can be applied to a certain extent in seeking to establish the difference between true tragedy and "sentimental tragedy." More often these same criteria, like almost all others, are inadequate. Although they become useful in examining the kind of tragedy that has been called sentimental or pathetic, their applicability to true tragedy is, at best, of dubious value. There is a possible confusion in terms here. There is great tragedy, *Hamlet*, *Lear*, *Macbeth*; there is true tragedy, *The Duchess of Malfi*; and there is sentimental tragedy, *The Maid's Tragedy* and *The Broken Heart* and the later tragedies of dramatists such as Banks, Southerne, Otway and Rowe.

Any statement about Shakespeare's plays usually ends with an embarrassed bow to his genius. Always the feeling exists that there is something inexplicable about his art, and use of that sufficiently nebulous term "genius" affords a loophole. *Hamlet*, for instance, is one in the tradition of revenge plays, but it is a revenge play like no other that has been written. Recognition of stock situations, characters, conventions, and ideas is simple, but how does one explain why this much-used material is transformed into something different and great? The answer is, obviously, genius. If pity and terror are aroused by true tragedy (and great tragedy, of course—these terms have the value of convenience only in this discussion), only pity is aroused by sentimental tragedy. Sentimental dramatists are not concerned to arouse terror. Some critics might wish to distinguish between "pity" and "pathos," the second being reserved for tragedies like Rowe's, for instance. Actually, such a distinction involves a difference in degree rather than kind. The death of Jane Shore, of Lady Jane Grey, or of Calista arouses a degree of pity which has been termed pathos because it is felt that the death of a Hamlet, a Macbeth, or a Lear involves a degree of pity which is far greater. Great tragedies are rare; tragedies like Rowe's are common. One can say "What a pity!" or something equally banal, even if sincerely felt, when the protagonist of a sentimental tragedy meets his end; one cannot say anything adequate at the death of Lear. The average man can usually conceive of himself as the hero of a sentimental tragedy, but it would be an act of presumption to think of himself as a Hamlet. In the first identification there is a person-for-person equation; in the second there is the more humbling equation in which one finds himself the first number of a geometric progression which ends in infinity. This, essentially, is what one critic says of Chaucer's *Troilus*:

Of such a character, so easily made happy and so easily broken, there can be no tragedy in the Greek or in the modern sense. The end of *Troilus* is the great example in our modern literature of pathos pure and unrelieved. All is to be endured and nothing is to be done. The species of suffering is one familiar to us all, as the sufferings of Lear and Oedipus are not. All men have waited with ever-decreasing hope, day after day, for someone or for something that does not come, and all would willingly forget the experience. Chaucer spares us no detail of the prolonged and sickening process to despair: every fluctuation of gnawing hope, every pitiful subterfuge of the flattering imagination, is held up to our eyes without mercy. The thing is so painful that perhaps no one without reluctance reads it twice. In our cowardice we are tempted to call it sentimental.[9]

In comparison with the kind of drama under analysis, Chaucer's *Troilus* decidedly does not deserve to be called sentimental.

The preceding remarks are of a very general nature, but they may have the virtue of clarifying some of the present writer's views on the difference between tragedy that is not sentimental and tragedy that is. Immediate interest centers on those tragedies which may be called sentimental or pathetic. A number of scholars have spoken of the sentimentalism of Banks, Southerne, Otway, and Rowe. The editor of Banks's *The Unhappy Favourite* says that the plays of that dramatist "were animated by a spirit of tearful sentimentalism." Dodds concludes his study of Southerne with the following statement:

Historically, then, Southerne stands as the strongest link between Restoration and eighteenth-century tragedy—more specifically, between Otway and Rowe. The tragedy of all three was concerned preeminently with piteous love; it was inclined to be domestic, feminine, and emotional; in it the Elizabethan influence was strong. Like Otway and Rowe, Southerne softened the tragic conflict to one of pity, and thus prepared the way not only for later prose, bourgeois drama, but for the final triumph in comedy of the Sentimental Muse.

Montague Summers says of Otway's *The Orphan* that it "is a domestic tragedy, and it is easy to understand why its tender sensibility should have made it so great a favourite throughout the eighteenth century. In many ways Monimia cannot fail to remind us of Richardson's heroine, the 'divine Clarissa.'" And J. R. Sutherland describes Rowe's plays in which "the whole tone is shriller and more feminine. The blustering hero is replaced by the weeping heroine; the bold, challenging incident gives place to the sentimental situation."[10] Other critics have also found the sentimental element prominent in the work of these men.

A few of the features of tragedy as written by these men may be mentioned briefly; full discussion and quotation would necessitate another book. The first thing that strikes one is the fact that most of the tragedies of these writers are "she-tragedies"; women are the protagonists, or they are very prominent in the pathetic situations. Thus, Southerne's *Oroonoko* is not properly a "she-tragedy," but Imoinda plays a very important part in the play. Tears and references to tears figure largely in these plays. References to children for pathetic purposes are frequent, and more than once they are brought upon the stage for the extra emotional effect that they are sure to produce. Revelling in emotion for its own sake is undoubtedly the chief distinguishing characteristic of the personages in these tragedies. One recalls particularly the closing scene of Act IV of Otway's *The Orphan*; another excellent example is to be found in Banks's *Vertue Betray'd* (III, i). The protagonists of these tragedies accept death and defeat in a spirit of acquiescent submission that is foreign to great tragedy. The tremendous conflict which is at the heart of great tragedies is absent from these plays. And the note of final triumph even in the moment of defeat and death is also conspicuously absent.

Sutherland says of Rowe's audiences that they "were to leave the theatre filled with pity rather than awe" "as far as it lay in his power to compel them."[11] In final analysis one can only repeat that great tragedy must have a protagonist who transcends mere mortality as it may rub elbows with us in the street. The protagonists of sentimental or pathetic tragedy are kept from achieving greatness by their recognizably exaggerated humanity, and nowhere is this brought home to us more clearly than in those scenes where far too much is made of emotions which we ourselves are familiar with from personal experience. Perhaps, as so many others have suggested, this is the reason why great tragedy is not written today. Our tragic protagonists look too much like ourselves and they react too much as we ourselves would react—even when they are kings and queens.

The question of what constitutes sentimental drama is complex, and attempts at rigid definition are fruitless. There is always the exception to the general rule. Too often there are borderline plays in which it is difficult to state with any degree of assurance that here one finds sentimentalism and here one does not. In the present work the intent has been to select plays which seem to demonstrate clearly the point being made. There are so many plays in which a definite decision—this is a sentimental play, or this is not a sentimental play—would involve one in endless argument. It is, for example, almost impossible to draw the line of demarcation between what can be called prolonged treatment of a situation and what one is willing to call brief treatment of the same situation. Obviously, if the difference, stated statistically, is between two lines and two pages, the decision is simple. If, however, the difference is between one page and three pages, then one has to think in terms of more and less prolonged treatment. Again, if a reformation speech is disposed of in four lines in one play, and is allowed twenty lines in another, the difference is still small enough to permit one's speaking of brevity of treatment in both plays. As has been said, no one criterion, taken alone, can be complete justification for deciding whether a play is sentimental. So, too, is it with the element of comedy and bawdry in potentially sentimental situations. It is a very nice question to decide just how much comedy and bawdry are needed to save a scene or play from becoming sentimental. Some plays—*The Tender Husband*, for instance—seem to the present writer clear-cut cases of potential sentimentalism being avoided by enough comedy and bawdry in the right places. In other plays the decision is not so easily made. These remarks are an acknowledgment and a warning. Sentimental drama presents a problem that has more ramifications than seem to have been realized by many scholars. The criteria that have been analyzed in this work are supplementary aids in arriving at a closer understanding of the problem. They are not an open sesame.

Chapter VII. POPULARITY OF THE GENRE

THE ATTEMPT TO GAUGE the popularity of a play, a playwright, or a school of dramatic writing with any great degree of accuracy some one hundred and fifty to two hundred years after the event is probably doomed to failure. The causes that make such an undertaking so formidable are many; fortunately they have already been admirably described and lie ready to hand for quotation. In his study of "The Reputation of Wycherley's Comedies as Stage Plays in the Eighteenth Century" Emmett L. Avery writes

First of all, the repertory system, it is apparent, afforded ample opportunity for the revival of old plays, especially because, during most of the century, the theaters presented a daily change of fare except during the run of a new piece or of a newly revived one; even so, during most of the century a frequent change of bill was the prevailing custom, and often there might be a different play presented on each night for a week, two weeks, or even longer periods. The frequency with which plays reappeared was an indication of their drawing power. On the other hand, because this system was utilized year after year, because play succeeded play day after day, and because comment upon stage performances was not so frequent or so systematically organized as in the newspapers and periodicals of more recent times, commentators upon theatrical matters in the early years of the eighteenth century often took the system for granted and did not discuss the reasons for the retention or absence of plays in the repertory. If a play returned to the stage after a long absence, it might be commented upon, but those plays—like Vanbrugh's or Wycherley's or Etherege's—which were subject to presentation season after season were very seldom discussed, for the regularity of their appearance apparently did not stimulate analysis or discussion of them. The theatrical audiences in the mass were also relatively inarticulate in leaving for posterity a record of their impressions of plays seen and heard. Because Samuel Pepys is an exception in that respect, we are very grateful for the entries in his diary concerning the stage in the 1660's, but there is no Pepys to guide us through those years when Wycherley's plays had their greatest post-Restoration vogue. There are the facts relating to their performances, but comment is relatively scarce.

Yet, over a long period of time, a repertory theater offers a pattern for the performances of each play, a pattern which is in itself an indication of the reputation of the play. The repertory, in turn, represents the external evidences of the tastes which dominate the decade, the half-century, or the century. A play gains or declines in frequency of performance, and it may vanish altogether. The pattern offers clues to the reputation of the play, but the pattern and vogue of a drama are the more difficult to comprehend because of the many variables and unknowns of the theaters: the effect of the weather on attendance upon this or that evening or week or month; the deterring or stimulating effect of the political situation upon interest in plays; the effect of an important or exciting domestic situation—the South Sea speculation, for example; the power of a given actor or actress to command an appreciative audience in almost any part the player undertook; the share which singing, dancing, and instrumental music offered between the acts or after the main play had in attracting spectators; the vogue of the afterpieces—especially farce and pantomime—in relation to the legitimate play of the evening; the effect of a too-frequent repetition of a play, whether in a run or in performances scattered throughout a season, in giving us an erroneous conception of its drawing power; the ability of the playwright's name to attract or repel an audience, and the effect of the composition of an audience—the mixture of "persons of quality," of citizens, of footmen, or of apprentices (the enthusiasm of the last-named often disturbed men of business)—upon the selection of plays and upon the reputation of playwrights. Unfortunately, many of these matters can not now be determined with accuracy, for the clues are lost in the minutiae which compose the life of previous centuries and which are not sufficiently recorded to enable us to reproduce completely the life and times of the past.[1]

When it is a matter of determining, not the reputation of one playwright with a limited canon, but an entire genre during a period of some fifty years the difficulties are multiplied again and again. And, finally, the task is rendered more complex, and possibly thankless, by the fact that scholars often disagree on the very canon of sentimental drama.

Not only should a decision be made on the sentimental or non-sentimental status of particular plays, when possible, but it is necessary also to distinguish, as indeed some have distinguished, between two kinds of sentimental drama. Richard Cumberland's modern biographer expresses this difference as the separation into "two indefinitely merging classes, the serious, tearful type, similar to the French comédie larmoyante, and the lighter drama, less oppressed by sentiment, and relieved by comic scenes, like the comédie bourgeoisie, and still more like the English domestic drama, which developed through Steele, Cibber, and Lillo."[2] This difference between French and English sentimental drama is also remarked upon in the *Westminster Magazine*'s review of the Rev. Mr. O'Beirne's *Generous Impostor*, adapted from *Le Dissipateur* of D'estouches. The writer finds that the French "will sit, not only with patience but pleasure, to hear long sermons of morality in a sentimental comedy. An English audience requires characters of humour, smart repartee, sallies of wit and pleasantry, poignant satire, and variety of incidents, all so happily combined as to form an agreeable whole" (November, 1780, p. 577). It may be remembered that Hugh Kelly tried to "steer between the extremes of sentimental gloom, and the excesses of uninteresting levity" (see above, p. 7), evidence enough that he recognized the existence of a school of dramatic writing more sentimental than his own. A sentimental dramatist *malgré lui*, Thomas Holcroft also saw the difference between schools of sentimentalism and remarked upon it, among other places, in his review of Frederick Reynolds' *The Rage*. Holcroft writes in the *Monthly Review* for March, 1795, that Reynolds "is much more studious of the means of exciting laughter than of interesting the heart . . . Amusement is the thing required; and, provided we laugh, we inquire but little concerning probability. Aware of this propensity in the public mind, Mr. R. has turned his efforts to its gratification; and with no inconsiderable success" (pp. 332-33). And Allardyce Nicoll who, incidentally, discusses *The Rage* quite properly as exemplifying one kind of sentimentalism, finds not only two but three "distinct tendencies" in sentimental comedy: "There are the relics of the Cibberian genteel comedy, aiding in the intensification of that 'high' note in comedy against which Goldsmith raised the flag of rebellion; there is the often mawkishly pathetic theatre of Cumberland, intent upon raising a sigh and calling forth a tear; and there is the more revolutionary humanitarian drama which is seen at its best in the plays of Mrs. Inchbald and of Thomas Holcroft" (*1750-1800*, p. 154). Holcroft would doubtless have placed Reynolds' *The Rage* in Nicoll's first category. It is abundantly clear, hence, that generalizations concerning sentimental drama must be careful to differentiate among its kinds.

In addition to the necessity for recognizing different kinds, and sometimes different degrees, of sentimentalism in drama there is the imperative need to establish a canon of acted drama as opposed to drama written for the "closet." The Reverend Charles Jenner knew that his adaptation of Diderot's *Le Père de Famille* could not possibly succeed on the stage, so he designed his *Man of Family* (1771) for the reading public, remarking that "the amusements of the stage and the closet cannot be brought to coincide" (see above, pp. 4-5). William Kenrick's *The Duellist* (1773), a comic adaptation of Fielding's *Amelia*, was driven off the stage, but the author congratulated himself in an Advertisement to the third edition of the play in the same year (indeed, in less than two months) that his piece met with a "favourable reception" "in the closet." The reading public of the second half of the eighteenth century was becoming increasingly more demanding in its desire for moral literature, a fact consistent with the growth of a large body of readers from the middle and lower classes. All the reasons for the popularity of particular plays with this new public are not always discoverable; that they insisted on a large infusion of the moral element allows of no argument. The three thousand copies of Hugh Kelly's *False Delicacy* sold on the day of publication and the four large editions of Goldsmith's rival play, *The Good-Natur'd Man*, published in less than three weeks, do not make it necessary to assume a fickle reading public nor even one divided into two camps, though the latter possibility is probably nearer the truth. Kelly offers plenty of humor in his comedy, and certainly, Goldsmith's play cannot properly be described as immoral. The failing Richard Cumberland "presented" his comedy, *The Sailor's Daughter* (1804), "to the Public, trusting it may find favour in the Closet, whatever it may be likely to experience on the Stage" (Advertisement). Sometimes, as was true with James Nelson's *The Affectionate Father, A Sentimental Comedy: Together with Essays on Various Subjects* (1786), the dramatic form was used to enliven the moral lesson without any thought of representation on the stage. In July, 1788 the drama critic of the *Monthly Review* distinguished between plays designed for the stage and those aimed solely at readers and concluded, of Nelson's play, that "This mode of conveying instruction is well chosen; the characters are produced in action, and may therefore be attended with a better effect than in the way of essay-writing" (LXXIX, 85). And the reviewer of *The West Indian* in the *Critical Review* for 1771 "saw it performed with pleasure; but . . . forebore to give our judgment till we had dispassionately perused it in the closet" (XXXI, 112). Their confrère of the *Town and Country Magazine* held the same distinction in mind as he reviewed the drama of the day. Of Mrs. Griffith's *The Times* (1779) the *Town and Country* critic wrote, "it is by far too sentimental for the stage, which requires wit and humour in Comedy, as well as whimsical and laughable situations, of which this piece is entirely destitute. In fine, tho' we think it would have afforded good ground-work for a sentimental Novel, it is not calculated for dramatic representation" (XI, 660). And although Joseph Richardson's *The Fugitive* (1792) was successful on the stage, the *Critical Review*'s account of the play concluded with these words: "It always gives us pain not to confirm the plaudits of the theatre; but, when the author appeals also to the reader, *his* opinion must be given independent of the splendor of the scene and the excellence of the actors" (Ser. 2, vol. V, p. 102). As one would expect, "sentimental comedies were relatively more successful in the sale of printed copies than in the record of performances on the stage."[3]

Although there are many obstacles to an accurate evaluation of the popularity accorded sentimental drama, some avenues of approach to the problem still exist. The most obvious of these is the dramatic reviews in eighteenth-century periodicals; but here, as elsewhere, a caveat must be entered. Sometimes the reviewers were bound by editorial policy; thus, the *Town and Country Magazine* was anti-sentimental—to put it mildly. Again, a particular reviewer, sympathetic to sentimentalism, might cause one to get a somewhat distorted view; this is partially true of Dr. John Hawkesworth, regular drama critic for the *Gentleman's Magazine* in the 1760's and an occasional reviewer for the *Monthly Review*. Taken as a whole, however, the end impression gathered from an examination of a number of reviews from the leading periodicals of the time should be fairly trustworthy. Some indication of the tastes of audiences may be gained by quotation of prologues and epilogues attached to plays that are, or have been called, sentimental. The presence of anti-sentimental or apologetic prologues and epilogues affords curious evidence of the mixed appeal of sentimental drama. It is tempting to conjecture a segment of the London playgoing public, of say the last three decades of the eighteenth century, which went to the theatre to laugh at the absurdities of the extremer forms of sentimental drama. Since these same prologues and epilogues were often written by the dramatists themselves, it is difficult to see any great sincerity in the sentimentalism of their plays. This fact does not, admittedly, affect the box-office popularity of the genre; it does, however, reflect adversely on the seriousness and depth of the sentimental attitude in the century. A final, and more accurate, measure of the success of sentimental drama in the theatre resides in the calendars of the playhouses. By examination of the number and kinds of plays put on in a season fairly definite conclusions are possible.

The phenomenon of anti-sentimental or apologetic prologues and epilogues accompanying sentimental plays can be treated first, as its implications are most obvious. There is no point in quoting Garrick's attacks on sentimental drama in the prologues or epilogues he wrote for Hugh Kelly and other practitioners of the genre. Garrick's opposition can be taken for granted; it is the curious stand assumed by men like Richard Cumberland and others which is of immediate interest. It will probably be enough to quote the pertinent passages from a few of these prologues and epilogues with only a minimum of comment. Cumberland wrote nonsentimental comedies; one of these, *The Impostors* (1789), has an epilogue, earlier quoted, which pokes fun at the kind of comedy he usually wrote, that upon which he had built his reputation.

> Oh, rot your delicacy!—Give me fun,
> Sir Balaam Blubber cries . . .

and then,

> I come to laugh, or I come here no more.

and again,

> Not a Miss Biddy—she is all for feeling,
> For Sentiment, for sighing, sobbing, kneeling;
> Rope ladders she admires and closet scenes,
> Escapes, surprizes, hudlings behind screens,
> And ever when two meanings mask the jest,
> Miss Biddy's purity picks out the best.

145

Although Cumberland is satirizing different elements in the audience, it is significant that he does not omit the sentimental Miss. Another sentimentalist, the novelist Henry Mackenzie, author of the widely admired *Man of Feeling*, also tried his hand at the drama. His one comedy, *False Shame, or The White Hypocrite*, was unsuccessful on the stage. In his Prologue Mackenzie stated that he would "pay his court" to the rival sisters who "walk the comic stage," the one laughing and gay, the other, serious and prudish. The interest here lies in the gay sister's words

"You sister Grave-Airs!" said the laughing Muse,
"Who stalk with stately pace on high-heeled shoes,
Whose face demure was formed to whine and cry,
You give us precious stuff for comedy,
In fine long words your moral truths rehearse,
"And turn the Ten Commandments into verse.
Your *drames* from France such sweet heroics teach,
Make tailors tragedise, and ploughmen preach.
Your tags of tragedy, your ahs! and ohs!
Your fine-spun sentiments, and wire-drawn woes,
Shew us how comical it is—to weep!
And how diverting—to do what—to sleep!"

Mrs. Griffith's *School For Rakes* (1769) enjoyed some contemporary popularity. The printed play has two epilogues; one, by Henry James Pye, makes fun of the predicament of the sentimental heroine:

A foolish girl! so near to throw away
Love, rank, and reputation, in a day.
And all for what? from prejudice, in truth,
Tho' christened delicacy, now, forsooth.
If (sentimental nonsense thrown aside)
To cards and politics, she had applied,
For common cares, her soul had been too great.

Later in the century, in the prologue to Frederick Reynolds' comedy *How to Grow Rich* (1793), the author

shakes his head, and owns he sometimes fears,
The muse of smiles may join the muse of tears?
Together read the sweet pathetic page,
And banish joke and laughter from the stage;
'Till comedy, quite sentimental grown
Doffs her light robe, to wear the tragic gown.
Draws from the virgin's breast hysteric sighs,
And thinks to weep—is all the use of eyes!
Still may each rival muse her pow'r maintain,—

With smiles Thalia best supports her reign:
To start the tear and palpitate the heart
Justly demands her Sister's nobler art!
Each has her charms, and while to nature true,
Each finds impartial advocates in you.
If these fair rivals, jealousy forgot,
Should once embrace, and tie the friendly knot;
Mirth must retire and hide her dimpled face
Convuls'd with laughter, at the strange embrace;
Our bard discarded, must his jokes forego,
And Vapid's frolics, yield to Werter's woe!

Cumberland, Mackenzie, Mrs. Griffith (or Henry James Pye, himself a playwright), and Frederick Reynolds, described by Allardyce Nicoll as "next in importance" to Hugh Kelly as a "sentimental author" (*1750-1800*, p. 131)—all took occasion to satirize extreme sentimental drama and its audiences. They were not alone, of course, in deprecating the sentimentalism of their own work.[4]

In the period in which sentimental drama was revived (1750-67), suffered attack (1768-72), and finally "triumphed" (1773-80), dramatic criticism had become a fairly regular feature of the leading periodicals. Printed plays, at least, were reviewed, and some of the criticism in a few of the newspapers and periodicals was of plays in representation. Thanks to the growing reading public many plays found their way into print, and we have the recorded opinion of contemporary critics upon which to help base our inquiry. It would be unnecessarily exhaustive to chart the responses of every critic to every sentimental play from 1750 to 1780, even if one had access to the rarer magazines and newspapers. Some notion of the trends in dramatic criticism of sentimental drama can be obtained in C. H. Gray's *Theatrical Criticism in London to 1795* (New York, 1931), but the focus of that work is much broader than our own. The field of investigation must be narrowed. Taking, then, those three periods which are said to mark the revival, subjection to attack, and final triumph of sentimental drama, and examining the critical reaction to key plays in the sentimental canon for each period (the authority is Bernbaum) in four leading periodicals, one should arrive at a representative contemporary opinion. Since this opinion would be relatively meaningless taken in isolation, without any reference, that is, to contemporary reaction to non-sentimental drama in these same periods, some quotation of reviews of one or two of these non-sentimental plays is needed. The four periodicals to be used are the *Gentleman's Magazine*, the *London Magazine*, the *Critical Review*, and the *Monthly Review*.

Three plays are of importance in the revival of sentimental drama from 1750 to 1767: these are William Whitehead's *School For Lovers*

(1762), Mrs. Sheridan's *Discovery* (1763), and the elder Colman's *English Merchant* (1767). It would not be pertinent to follow the critics in all their little cavils; the important thing is to see how they respond to the sentimentalism of these plays. Hawkesworth wrote of the *School For Lovers* that "the dialogue is natural and spirited; the sentiments are chaste and elegant; and some of the situations are touching and tender in the highest degree" (*Gentleman's Magazine*, p. 161). The *London Magazine*, like the *Gentleman's*, summarized the play and allowed itself to remark only on a plot full of "delicacy and sentiment" (p. 264). The *Monthly Review* was more reserved; the play is "rather a Conversation-piece than a Comedy. The Conversation is, however, natural, decent, and moral; and if the work does not abound with all the variety of business, plot, scenery, character and humour, which are requisite to gratify the tastes of an English audience, it is, nevertheless, not an uninteresting performance; and may certainly rank among those which are distinguished by the appellation of Genteel Comedy" (p. 158). The fullest criticism of the play is found in the *Critical Review*:

The reader must not expect to meet with much witty repartee, or great violence of humour, in this performance. Nor will the eye be entertained with a variety of shifting scenes, nor the imagination transported by a hurry of business; yet these are the articles on which the success of a modern comedy, in a great measure depends . . . Although there is nothing in the *School for Lovers* to elevate, surprize, and excite loud bursts of laughter; the delicate reader will find in it abundance of entertainment . . . The dialogue is easy, natural, and genteel, and the situations are extremely interesting. (XIII, 137-38)

The critics liked the play, on the whole, and for the same reasons. Two of them, however, state that this is not the kind of play English audiences found gratifying. And the writer for the *Critical Review* assured "the delicate reader" of "an abundance of entertainment" free from "loud bursts of laughter."

Mrs. Sheridan fared worse in the periodicals. The *Gentleman's Magazine* (1763, p. 99) promised an account of her *Discovery* in its next; the promise seems to have gone unfulfilled. The *London Magazine* praised its language, sentiments, and parts of the fable, but protested that "to many scenes abounding with the comic humour, there are added almost two whole acts of the pathetic." And it went on,

We have no objection to the muse of comedy's sometimes raising her voice: But must confess that we rather admire her smiles than her tears. In the present case, in particular, we could have wished she had not taken on so very grievously; especially as it is the tragick part of this deep comedy that has chiefly occasioned the writer to violate the unity of the fable . . . The last act is rather a Richardsonian narration than part of a dramatic action . . .

148

The magazine then concludes that there was "sufficient matter for a comedy," but that "the serving on the tragic had embarrassed the whole" (XXXII, 94-95). And when the play was revived in 1776 the same magazine, through its reviewer, a champion of sentimental comedy, was even more severe (XLV, 49). The critic for the *Monthly Review* characterized the comedy as "sentimental and moral in the conduct, easy and correct in the language, various and entertaining in the characters: the greatest fault we observe throughout the whole, is the language and languor of some of the scenes, which almost deviate into preaching," adding that these last have been "pruned in the representation" (XXVIII, 167). Here is an interesting point: one does not always have, in the printed version of these plays, the plays as they were acted; sometimes the more sentimental parts were "pruned in the representation." It is unfortunate that there is such meager information on this important matter. Cumberland's *The Brothers*, for further example, was successful only, according to the *London Magazine* (1769, p. 601), because of excellent representation and "judicious mutilations" by Colman. The *Critical Magazine* afforded *The Discovery* great praise, but pointed also to the chief criticism of the play, which was "censured by many as too grave, the latter part of it especially, approaching to what the French call the *Comédie Larmoyante*. For our own parts, we think the use and excellency of the moral resulting from it makes us ample amends for its gravity; and if the critics still insist on it, that *serious* cannot be called *comic* scenes, we will . . . say, that this is no *comedy*, but something better" (XV, 112). In sum, the critics are agreed that the play has its merits, but they censure the very part of the play that makes it sentimental comedy.

When Colman the Elder, two years after translating Terence, produced his *English Merchant* (1767) he capitalized on the popularity of sentimental drama. As a theatre manager he knew what audiences wanted, and he demonstrated that he could satisfy their demands; the *English Merchant* won the praise of the critics far more than any other sentimental play of this period. Hawkesworth was lyrical in his enthusiasm and Johnsonian in his style: "A more general objection to this piece is, that it does not much provoke laughter; it must, I think be admitted, but to those who can taste higher pleasure this defect is abundantly attoned. There is a luxury in tears that laughter can never taste; but these luxurious tears are perhaps less the tribute of pity to distress, than of virtue to virtue; they are an effusion of tenderness, complacency, admiration and joy excited by generous passion, untutored benevolence, and unexpected felicity" (*Gentleman's Magazine*, p. 130). The *London Magazine* did not "pretend to determine" how far "the piece may bear the test of severe criticism," but "if sentimental speeches, together with a mixture of true humour, devoid of the least tincture of obscenity or immorality, can please an audience, this cannot fail of having a happy effect" (XXXVI, 142-43). Garrick, reviewing the play for the *Monthly Review*, laid aside his anti-sentimentalism for the moment, almost surely in deference to his collaborator of the year before—his and Colman's *Clandestine Marriage* appeared in 1766. He praised the play and remarked that though "a vein of comedy runs through the whole play . . . yet the distresses of *Amelia* and her father make the comic muse *raise her voice* in many of the scenes, and give a variety which is not to be met with in the lower species of the drama, or in that, which the French call *Comedie Larmoyante*" (XXXVI, 225). It will be noted that Garrick carefully distinguishes this play from the extreme, French school of sentimental drama. The *Critical Review* lauded the play in much the same terms as the others. "Perhaps no comedy was ever produced upon the stage with a more moral tendency, or less offensive to decency, than the English Merchant. We enter with concern into the fate of the virtuous characters, and we can see that the author's feelings are always in the right place" (XXIII, 215). The reception accorded this play corroborates one's opinion that there is no need for any sincerity in the writer of sentimental drama; the clever man of the theatre can send sentimentally inclined critics into veritable raptures without himself really sharing their beliefs. It might be remarked, in passing, that Colman thought his play could draw without an afterpiece and was sadly disappointed.[5]

Curiously, the three most popular non-sentimental comedies in this period are headed by Colman's *Jealous Wife* (1761). The other two, *The Way to Keep Him* (1760) and *All in the Wrong* (1761), are by Arthur Murphy. Hawkesworth, a champion of sentimentalism, reviewed *The Way to Keep Him* for the *Gentleman's Magazine*. His praise is proof, if proof be required, that sentimentalism in the drama lived side by side with, say, comedy of manners and that both were appreciated by the same critics and audiences—often in the same play, at least to the extent to which these can ever be reconciled. Hawkesworth writes

This piece is written in the spirit of true comedy. It is comic not only in the dialogue, but in the action, yet perfectly pure from quaint repartee and farcical buffoonery: The *manners* are comic, and the dialogue and incidents are comic, as expressive of the manners; all is natural and characteristic. If any objection can be supported against this piece, it must be that some of the incidents are not sufficiently probable. This however, if it be allowed, is an objection that will lie against every dramatic piece upon the stage; the improbability is not such as can in any degree lessen the pleasure of the representation, or invalidate the moral, and it cannot therefore derogate from the merit of the piece so much as from the candour of those that shall urge it (p. 74).

The *London Magazine* confined its critical comment to the statement that the play possessed "a very great share of the more delicate part of the *vis comica*" (p. 42). The *Monthly Review* detected distinct echoes of *The Way of the World* but conceded that "on the whole, however, this comedy is well written; the sentiments are for the most part chaste and elegant; the incidents natural and diverting; the characters drawn from the life, and the fable well conducted" (XXII, 144). The *Critical Review* was more captious, finding the dialogue "spirited" but "not very natural," protesting that Lovemore's morals were too loose "even for an honourable libertine," wishing the character of Mrs. Lovemore had been "more strongly marked" in the part "which was disgusting to the husband," and criticizing the final reformation as "too abrupt and violent" (IX, 142-43).

Murphy's other comedy of this period, *All in the Wrong* (1761) received less critical attention, being merely listed in the *Gentleman's* and *London Magazines*. The *Monthly Review* gave it only a paragraph, concluding that the author had "given us a Comedy, which bids fair to maintain its footing upon the English Stage" (XXV, 473). And most of the seven pages given over to the play in the *Critical Review* rehearse the plot; the last paragraph contains the critic's judgment: "Though this performance is not high-seasoned with wit and repartee, which seem in a great measure exiled from modern comedy, the situations are artfully adapted to the stage; the characters are well marked; the reflections solid and judicious; the dialogue is decent and easy, and the moral happily enforced" (XII, 437). The reviews of Murphy's two comedies reveal nothing startlingly new. Possibly the most that can be said is that non-sentimental comedy, marked, it is true, by "chasteness" and "decency," was certainly not being entirely supplanted by its lachrymose rival.

If Murphy's plays merely held their own with the sentimental comedies of this period, the same is not true of Colman's *Jealous Wife* (1761). Its popularity exceeded even that of the same dramatist's sentimental *English Merchant*. Again one finds the drama critics, cordial as they are to sentimental drama, opening wide their arms to welcome a good comedy in the older tradition. Hawkesworth summarizes the plot and concludes that the play "loses more than almost any other, by being thus reduced to a mere narrative, without the character and humour that appears in every part of the dramatic dialogue. Upon the whole, this piece is a very high and a very rational entertainment; having, as a Comedy, few equals, and no superior" (p. 54). The review of this play was, as in the *Gentleman's*, the leading article of the February *London Magazine*. Two scenes are quoted and the remainder of the play summarized, but there is no criticism. The *Monthly Review* acknowledges the virtues of the play as an acting piece, but "not withstanding the general applause with which this comedy has been represented on the stage, we shall venture to appeal from the people in the theatre, to the same people in their closets" (XXIV, 181). Judging the *Jealous Wife* as a closet play, then, the critic finds Colman's characters and manners disappointing. Yet, in summation, the critic is more generous with his praise than with his censure. "There is a good deal of humour and keen ridicule in this piece, interspersed with many sensible reflections which show a knowledge of life: and it abounds with those changes and contrivances which surprize and entertain an audience," he writes. "But," and censure has the last word, "the Author's talent seems to lie in caracature [*sic*]: he is very happy in hitting off strong marked features, but cannot command those soft and delicate touches which form an agreeable and finished picture" (p. 192). "From the thundering peals of applause with which this performance hath been received on the theatre" the reviewer for the *Critical Review* flattered himself that he would enjoy it in the closet; he, like his fellow critic of the *Monthly Review*, was disappointed. He admits, however, that, as far as "the entertainment of the audience" is concerned, "few plays have been better calculated for this purpose, than is the comedy now lying before us" (XI, 132). But he finds fault with the characterization of the jealous wife, with the use of soliloquies, and with the dialogue. And, after cataloguing these faults again in his last paragraph, he concludes that Colman's play "contains a great deal of good sense, salutary satire, humour, contrivance, incident, and all that forms the *jeu de theatre*" (p. 141).

In this period of the revival of sentimental drama (1750-1767) critics were, then, enthusiastic about sentimentally conceived plays; they looked for chastity of sentiment and language; they applauded virtue. But they also deprecated excessive gravity and moralizing; they were conscious, despite their efforts to gloss over the fact, that comedies should excite laughter; and they had not wilfully shut their eyes to the virtues of non-sentimental comedy. They applauded Colman's *English Merchant* cordially; they were equally, if somewhat grudgingly, appreciative of his *Jealous Wife*. And they are witnesses to the popularity *in the theatre* of the latter play; they do not remark the same phenomenon for the former. Their criticism of the *Jealous Wife*, the best comedy of those years, is rather picayune, insisting as it does on studying the play in the closet. When sentimental plays are subjected to criticism based only on stage representation they, too, often make a poor showing.

The next period, that in which sentimental drama is attacked (1768-1772), saw the immense popularity of Goldsmith's *She Stoops To Conquer*, one of the more memorable farces of the English stage. When modern critics claim this play for the sentimental canon it is time to call a halt to sane inquiry, for further discussion is impossible. To record contemporary critical reaction to Goldsmith's play is unnecessary; it is easily available elsewhere. The reader should, however, remember that this *is* the period of *She Stoops To Conquer* while he reads the reviews of the three outstanding sentimental plays of this period. The plays are Mrs. Griffith's *School For Rakes* (1769), and two comedies by Richard Cumberland: *The West Indian* (1771) and *The Fashionable Lover* (1772). Hawkesworth reviewed Mrs. Griffith's play in the *Gentleman's Magazine* and in the *Monthly Review*. The review in the latter has already been quoted in a different connection (see above, p. 74); that in the former is essentially the same. Hawkesworth observes that there are "many tender and some cheerful scenes in this piece; but the distress is not naturally produced, and the comedy arises chiefly from the strange conduct of Harriet's aunt, an absurd Welchwoman, proud of family, fond of quality, silly, and opinionated" (p. 199). The *London Magazine* criticized the conduct of the fable, the manners, and the diction; commented on the absence of any new characters; found the moral "excellent"; and pronounced the sentiments " 'tho not new in many places, . . . in general, very just, and such as do honour to the benevolence of the writer" (pp. 59-63). The *Critical Review* also found weaknesses in the fable, but owned "that the sentiments of honour and virtue, which fall from the mouth of Mr. Frampton, are such as ought to reform the manners of the most dissolute" (XXVII, 223). Here one discovers the curious dilemma in which some of these critics found themselves. They could sympathize with the sentimental dramatist at the same time that they deplored the expedients to which he was put to entertain his audiences, and as a result one often gets a kind of vacillating criticism which pitches upon the morality as a subject for praise and censures, or seeks to justify, poor or incongruous elements in these sentimental pieces.

Yet it is in this period in which sentimental drama is attacked that Richard Cumberland's *West Indian* (1771) was produced and won tremendous popularity. This play is usually acclaimed by modern scholars as the best example of sentimental comedy; contemporary critics also found much to praise in it. Hawkesworth reviewed it for the *Gentleman's Magazine* and the *Monthly Review*. In the former he censured the play for certain weaknesses, yet concluded that many "parts are exceeding comic, and many very tender; from faults, it is by no means free, but with all its imperfections on its head, take it for all in all, we have not often seen it's [*sic*] like, nor is it probable we should see it's like again" (p. 126). In the *Monthly Review* he said much the same:

We think that there are few pieces intended for the stage that, upon the whole, have more merit than the West Indian. The plot is complicated without confusion or perplexity; the characters are strongly marked, yet natural; the dialogue is sprightly without labored turns of epigrammatic wit; and the sentiment is at once elevated and tender. It excites a curiosity strongly interested, and has so blended the pathetic and ridiculous, that if the spectator or reader has sensibility and discernment, he will be kept almost continually laughing with tears in his eyes" (XLIV, 142).

This is tribute indeed! Yet the critic for the *London Magazine* set himself up a score card and commented on the various aspects of the play; he did not let his heart run away with his head. The fable was "incongruous, improbable, inaccurate"; the characters "by no means new"; the diction "not unexceptionable"; and the manners "violated glaringly." But the moral was "excellent"; the sentiments in "many places do honour to humanity—they are often new—generally striking—and always the dictates of benevolence.—They merit and receive the greatest approbation"; and the play "pleases very much" in the representation (pp. 13-16). The *Critical Review* assumed knowledge of the plot and confined itself to quotation of two scenes, one to "open the character of the West Indian," the other to exhibit "the comic manners of Major Dennis O'Flaherty, who for this month past has filled the theatre with repeated convulsions of laughter" (XXXI, 113). The reviewer agreed with others that he "never received greater pleasure from any comic performance of modern date, either in the closet or on the stage" (p. 116). The critics were only repeating the plaudits of audiences which kept the play going for a run of twenty-eight days without an afterpiece, if we can accept Cumberland's word for it. Much of the play's success, possibly even most, is directly attributable to Garrick's efforts. He "changed scenes, rewrote speeches, and, from his wide experience, made the play better suited to the stage."[6] And it was Garrick who decided what actors were to play the important roles of the West Indian and the comic Major O'Flaherty.

The success of *The West Indian* was not to be repeated in Cumberland's later career as dramatist. His very next comedy, *The Fashionable Lover* (1772), suffered in comparison with the earlier play. The gist of Hawkesworth's criticism of the comedy in the *Gentleman's Magazine* resides in these words:

It pleases like a fairy-tale, and its excellence consists in producing an interest by the violation of Nature. But a writer, who has been able to warm the heart and to melt it, in spite of improbabilities perpetually recurring, both with respect to character and incident; who has interested the passions in the cause of virtue, and endeavoured to correct the vices and follies of a dissolute age, at the very moment when he is administering to its pleasures; has no reason to be ashamed of his performance, and may well set both the envy and the accuracy of criticism at defiance (p. 81).

In short, Hawkesworth is saying that Cumberland's heart is in the right place, and criticism may go and be hanged. The *London Magazine* thought the play "no despicable effort of genius," but some "improbabilities, some abrupt and precipitate steps, there are in it. The sudden reformation of Lord Abberville, the discovery made by Napthali, the Jew, the hasty departure of Tyrrel from Miss Aubrey, all these circumstances are perhaps a little unnatural" (p. 73). The *Monthly Review* found "less spirit" in it than in *The West Indian* but judged it to be "more correct, more chaste, and . . . a more moral performance" (XLVI, 168). And the *Critical Review*, favorably impressed on the whole, summed up its feelings by confessing that though "the piece be not entirely void of blemishes," yet "it contains many strokes of humour and sentiment, which command our approbation" (XXXIII, 85). The critics seem embarrassed, conscious perhaps that the author of *The West Indian* of the previous year could not have written a play of little or no intrinsic merit. Their praise of *The Fashionable Lover* is awkward, left-handed.

Perhaps it may be well to quote here a few sentences from an essay on the drama in "The British Theatre," a regular department in the *London Magazine*, beginning in June, 1767. The essay in question appeared in July, 1768 and makes a point worth considering, especially since the writer had proved friendly to sentimental drama.

The theatrical productions of the present time, though so generally ridiculed by the pert, or the inconsiderate, are nevertheless founded upon good sense, and have a manifest view to promote the laudable ends for which the stage was originally erected.—If therefore the public mind is so well disposed as to prefer them to those glittering compositions of wit and licentiousness, which formerly gave so much satisfaction, he must be an enemy to virtue who speaks of them with disapprobation on account of their gravity.—By condemning sentimental pieces, we reason against the sense of our own conviction, and nothing can be a stronger argument of a bad heart, than a willingness to be entertained at the expence of morality.—From this I would by no means infer that the abortive endeavours of stupidity are to be encouraged, because they may be written with a good design.—Dulness will always be exposed to contempt, and the wretched execution of a blockhead be treated with derision, however meritorious his motive; but where men of *real* talents give us a connected *interesting* fable, where they conduct that fable judiciously, and present us not only with an instructive but an entertaining picture of life, it is the business of every benevolent spectator to give the strongest marks of applause, and the kindest thing that can be said of those who censure it for being grave, is, that they are wholly destitute of understanding. (p. 340)

The distinction between poor plays written on a moral design and the equally moral productions of dramatists of some talent who, moreover, entertain as well as instruct is central to any discussion of sentimental comedy. The element of the entertaining, synonymous, it would seem, with the comic, is what rescues the better plays of the latter half of the eighteenth century from the limbo of deserved oblivion.

It remains now to examine the critics' reaction to the three sentimental comedies in the period of the genre's "triumph," 1773-1780. The plays are Mrs. Cowley's *Runaway* (1776), Mrs. Griffith's *The Times* (1779), and Mrs. Lee's *Chapter of Accidents* (1780). *The Runaway* was not reviewed in the *Gentleman's Magazine* and was given little attention by the *London Magazine*, which spoke of "a strange jumble of incident [by which] poetic justice is done to all the parties" (p. 71). The critic did, however, expect "much rational entertainment" from Mrs. Cowley's "future labours" (p. 72). The *Monthly Review* quoted extensively from the play, concluding that without "much strength of fable, force of character, novelty of sentiment, or humour of dialogue, a certain delicacy pervades the whole, which in some places interests and attaches us, and in all places induces us to overlook greater deficiencies" (LIV, 217). The *Critical Review* observed that the "characters are generally supported with propriety and spirit, through several interesting situations; and though we meet not with a very high degree of the *vis comica*, our attention is so agreeably engaged, that we never find room to regret, and hardly even to be sensible of its absence" (XLI, 239).

The Times attracted even less critical attention than had *The Runaway*. It was not reviewed in the *Gentleman's Magazine*, the *London Magazine*, or the *Critical Review*. The *Monthly Review* was relatively unimpressed:

As to *the Times*, they are but faintly coloured in this draught of them. Mrs. Griffith views with too much delicacy the foibles of her own sex, and is too little acquainted with the irregularities of the other, to mark them with sufficient force and accuracy. We think, however, that the scene of the rout is rather too coarse a picture of the assembly of a woman of fashion; and that the characters of Mr. and Mrs. Bromley are too openly profligate, even to carry on their frauds and impositions. Lady Mary and Louisa are amiable and tender; and indeed the genius of the Writer seems to delight in touches of sentiment rather than strokes of humour." (LXII, 246)

It is apparent that this reviewer was not overly struck by the excellences of Mrs. Griffith's comedy. In the absence of reviews of the play in the periodicals being used in this study, that from the *Town and Country*, already quoted, may be repeated here. *The Times* "is far too sentimental for the stage, which requires wit and humour in Comedy, as well as whimsical and laughable situations, of which this piece is entirely destitute. In fine, tho' we think it would have afforded a good ground-work for a sentimental Novel, it is not calculated for a dramatic representation" (XI, 660).

The next play marks, according to Bernbaum, "the final triumph of sentimental comedy over its enemies" (p. 265). Mrs. Lee's *Chapter of Accidents* (1780) did not, however, cause any great stir among the critics. The *Gentleman's Magazine* reviewed the play in its January, 1781 issue.

The only note of criticism of any kind was a protest against bringing a character like Cecelia, who had given herself to Woodville without benefit of clergy and yet was rewarded at the end, on the stage (p. 33). The *London Magazine* merely gave a resumé of the plot but offered no critical comment. The *Monthly Review* remarked that the "title of *The Chapter of Accidents* is in some sort an apology for a romantic fable; we shall not therefore too sincerely examine the *probability* of the incidents. The dialogue, though not perfectly pure and natural, is often enlivened by humour, and ennobled by sentiment" (LXIII, 361). But the reviewer quotes approvingly a bit of the anti-sentimental prologue by Colman the Elder, a bit that characterizes hero and heroine as so "full of virtue, *some of it runs over!*" (p. 360). And, to complicate matters, he quotes one of the sentimental scenes in the play, praising the "address and delicacy" with which the author handled it (p. 362). The *Critical Review* gave the play one paragraph:

This is, it seems, the first dramatic performance of a very young authoress, and, considered as such, has great merit; some of the accidents, which are taken from a comedy of Diderot's, are interesting and agreeable, and, as we are informed, were received with applause in the representation. To the sentiments and diction of this comedy many objections might be made, but it would answer no end to point out faults which it is now too late to amend, more especially as we would not wish to discourage a young writer, whose first attempt promises so well, and from whom the public have reason to expect much pleasure and entertainment in future productions. (L, 396)

The reviewer for the *Westminster Magazine* may be impressed into service to supply the deficiency of the *London Magazine*. He too is shocked by the character of a "frail woman" as the "principal subject of comedy," but once this "defect be overlooked . . . the piece abounds with such business, perplexity, and humour, as must ever be agreeable to a common audience. The characters of Bridget the waiting-maid, and Jacob the footman, are drawn with a boldness which gives them claims to originality. The errors and incidents are well imagined; and if they were made to succeed each other with more rapidity, would furnish a good deal of merriment" (VIII, 410).

As the writer for the *Westminster Magazine* acutely observed, the truth of the matter is that *The Chapter of Accidents* would be a more enjoyable low comedy, "agreeable to a common audience," if the mawkish sentimentality of intercalary scenes did not interrupt the rapid succession of comic situations. This is an unfortunate play to select as the mark of "the final triumph of sentimental comedy over its enemies," for it possesses more of the characteristics of those same enemies than it does of the genre for which it stands. The most that can be said for it is that it maintains the moral or sentimental note doggedly in the midst of a welter of farcical and comedy-of-intrigue elements. It *is* a chapter of accidents, with mistaken identities, disguises, immorality, and the old device of marrying a cast-off whore to an unsuspecting and conniving knave. Each of the sentimental characters is set off by an anti-sentimental character. There are, by actual count, more broadly comic scenes than there are sentimental, and the final scene, dear to the thoroughgoing sentimentalist, is compounded of sentimental and anti-sentimental notes plus the necessary unravelling of a complicated plot. The triumph of sentimental comedy is Pyrrhic, or, if a play on words be permitted, at best moral.

Not only were the three sentimental plays of the period 1773-1780 received with little, if any, critical acclaim; their popularity was far overshadowed by Sheridan's *The Rivals* and *The School For Scandal* as well as by Mrs. Cowley's *The Belle's Stratagem*. At the risk of being accused of opinionatedness, the present writer has little patience with scholars who make much of the sentimentalism of the subplot in *The Rivals* or of the character of Charles Surface in *The School For Scandal*. But it is not even necessary to adduce these plays as evidence of the greater popularity of non-sentimental drama in this period. One need only review the reception given Mrs. Cowley's *The Belle's Stratagem*—and it will be remembered that in this same period her sentimental comedy *The Runaway* (1776) provoked only qualified praise—to see that sentimental comedy had by no means been left in triumphant possession of the field. *The Belle's Stratagem*, first produced in 1780, was not published until 1782; only the *Monthly* and *Critical Reviews* noticed the play. The *Monthly Review* praised and censured; it thought the main plot conducted with "adroitness, elegance, and vivacity," but objected to the "underplot" "unfortunately grafted on it"; the play "contains many lively traits of character, as well as lucky bits of wit and humour," but the manners and dialogue seem "gathered from novels and newspapers" rather than "transcribed . . . from the book of Nature"; and yet, "on the whole, the Comedy of *The Belle's Stratagem* approaches much nearer to dramatic excellence, than any other piece yet produced by Mrs. Cowley" (LXVI, 291-92). The *Critical Review* gave Mrs. Cowley's comedy a very short paragraph only, but for a reason other than lack of interest:

The merit of this piece, which has already been in possession of the stage for two seasons, is so universally known and acknowledged, that it is unnecessary for us to say anything more concerning it, than that it is the best dramatic production of a female pen which has appeared since the days of Centlivre, to whom Mrs. Cowley is at least equal in fable and character, and far superior in easy dialogue and purity of diction. (LIII, 314)

The critic for the *Monthly Review* found *The Belle's Stratagem* better than *The Runaway*; the critic for the *Critical Review* went further and claimed for Mrs. Cowley's comedy a pre-eminence over the efforts of any other female dramatist—this includes Mrs. Sheridan, Mrs. Lee, Mrs. Griffith, Mrs. Lennox *et al.*—since the time of Susannah Centlivre.

The statement of the *Critical Review* that *The Belle's Stratagem* had held the stage for two seasons suggests an examination of runs (not necessarily consecutive) and revivals of the plays in the three periods in the advance of sentimental drama from 1750 to 1780. Some further light may be had on the immediate and subsequent popularity of these plays, even if the guide to be chosen, the Reverend John Genest's *Some Account of the English Stage, From 1660 to 1830,* cannot always be trusted for complete and accurate information. This is particularly true of Genest's record of revivals. He is, however, still the best single authority available, and he can be assumed to be catholic in his errors or omissions. The nature of this evidence is best presented by a table of figures:

Revival, 1750-1767

		Run	Revivals
Sentimental	*The School For Lovers*	12 times	revived twice, last in 1794
	The Discovery	17 times	revived 4 times, last in 1806
	The English Merchant	14 times	revived 5 times, last in 1789
Non-Sentimental	*The Way to Keep Him*	10 times	revived 14 times, last in 1818
	All in the Wrong	10 times (in the summer)	revived 10 times, last in 1824
	The Jealous Wife	20 times	revived 18 times, last in 1829

Attack, 1768-1772

		Run	Revivals
Sentimental	*The School For Rakes*	13 times	revived once in 1776
	The West Indian	28 times	revived 4 times, last in 1807
	The Fashionable Lover	15 times	revived 4 times, last in 1818
Non-Sentimental	*She Stoops To Conquer*	12 times	revived 12 times, last in 1825

159

Triumph, 1773-1780

		Run	Revivals
Sentimental ?	The Runaway	about 17 times	never revived
	The Times	9 times	never revived
	The Chapter of Accidents	14 times	revived 9 times, last in 1823
Non-Sentimental	The School For Scandal	20 times[7]	revived 8 times, last in 1825
	The Belle's Stratagem	28 times	revived 4 times, last in 1818

Any scholar using Genest for an extended inquiry will be able to point to an occasional revival of plays which, from his index, would seem to have enjoyed no favor after their first season; similarly, however, one can add considerably to the number of revivals of, for example, *The Belle's Stratagem*—the hope of the present writer is that errors and omissions will cancel themselves out.

Certain obvious conclusions can be derived from this table. The sentimental comedies in this thirty-year period enjoyed runs from a respectable, but by no means unusual, nine nights for a new play to the unusual twenty-eight granted *The West Indian*. Non-sentimental comedies of the same period enjoyed runs from ten to the phenomenal sixty-five performances (see note 7) of *The School For Scandal*. The outstanding successes were *The School For Scandal*, *The West Indian*, and *The Belle's Stratagem*, the latter two running about equal. *The Jealous Wife*, another non-sentimental comedy, with a record of twenty nights, also proved more popular than the sentimental plays of this period, with the exception of *The West Indian*. As far as lasting success, measurable in terms of number of revivals and the latest date of revival up to 1830, is concerned, the non-sentimental plays easily prove more popular. And it is hard to resist adding that two plays of this period are constantly being revived to this day; *She Stoops To Conquer* and *The School For Scandal* bid fair to become, if anybody should insist that they still are not, classics of English drama.

The next question that proposes itself is inevitable: what plays formed the staple article of diet for theatre audiences? Obviously, the bare examination of runs and revivals of the plays selected for study gives no hint as to the other kinds of plays and theatrical entertainments which made up the body of the theatrical calendars. Since sentimental drama is said to have triumphed in the period 1773-1780 and thereafter, a breakdown of the theatrical calendars for each fifth year from 1775 to 1800 should demonstrate, or at least indicate, how far-reaching this ostensible victory was. A few words as to method are in order. The *Gentleman's Magazine* gives the theatrical calendars for Drury Lane, Covent Garden, and the Haymarket quite regularly in this period; the calendars for 1775 and 1785 are incomplete—the former lacks eleven months and the latter lacks two. The *Westminster Magazine* gives a fuller calendar for January, 1775 and provides the statistics for February and September of the same year; unfortunately it gives no theatrical calendars for 1785. Using these two periodicals as a basis, then, the total number of acting days, not plays, for each year has been computed. Also computed was the number of plays that can be called sentimental. The guides here have been Bernbaum, Nicoll, and Genest; the last's descriptions are usually full enough to allow a judgment without the necessity of reading countless plays. Wherever a play could not be identified by the use of these authorities, and where the title even remotely suggested sentimentalism, the play was included in the sentimental canon. "Operas" were not included, as being a genre not strictly dramatic. Often, indeed almost always, plays which the present writer does not look upon as of the sentimental canon have nevertheless been accorded that dubious distinction in deference to Bernbaum or Nicoll. Older plays, i.e. *The Provoked Husband, The Orphan, Oroonoko, Isabella, George Barnwell*, etc., have been included in the canon also; so, too, have been Rowe's she-tragedies.

Since statistics form the substance of this analysis, another table is called for:

Year	No. of Acting Days	Performances of Sentimental Plays
1775 (Jan., Feb., Sept.)	109	12
1780	463	54
1785 (without Nov. and Dec.)	325	43
1790	486	91
1795	446	132
1800	490	168
	2319	500

The results cannot be misinterpreted: most notably, there is an increase in the number of performances of sentimental plays from 1790 on; and about twenty per cent of all performances in the period are of sentimental plays. The plays which make up the remaining eighty per cent of the dramatic fare in these years are of a number of different genres, ranging from farce to tragedy and including comic opera, melodrama,

Gothic drama, revivals (of Elizabethan, Restoration, and earlier eighteenth-century plays), adaptations (from earlier English plays and from French drama), comedy of manners, and almost every other conceivable kind of dramatic entertainment. Some of the most popular plays of this period are non-sentimental. Mrs. Cowley's *Belle's Stratagem*, as has already been pointed out, was the hit in 1780. In 1785 Thomas Holcroft's translation and adaptation of Beaumarchais' *Mariage de Figaro*, Englished to *The Follies of a Day*, proved the most popular play of the year, with some twenty-two performances. Mrs. Inchbald's comedy, *I'll Tell You What*, was acted twenty times in this year, and it is a far cry from her revival of elements of Restoration comedy to the lachrymosities of earlier senti- mental comedies. James Cobb's comic opera *Strangers At Home* was acted fifteen times in this year. And it was the same dramatist's *Haunted Tower*, described as a Gothic opera, that enjoyed the greatest success in 1790: fifty-seven performances that year and a total of eighty performances for its first two seasons. Another great favorite in 1790 was Colman the Younger's *Battle of Hexham*, with fifteen performances in that year after twenty in 1789. Genest describes the play as "a jumble of Tragedy, Comedy and Opera." Frederick Reynolds' *The Dramatist*, with twenty-eight performances, was the leading sentimental play of 1790. Audiences in 1795 divided their applause and approbation among a number of plays. Foremost of these were Frederick Reynolds' sentimental comedy *Specu- lation* and *The Mysteries of the Castle*, variously described as melodrama and Gothic drama, by Reynolds and Miles Peter Andrews. James Cobb scored another, less outstanding, success with a melodramatic opera titled *The Cherokee*, and John O'Keefe's non-sentimental comedy *Life's Va- garies* was acted seventeen times in its first season. Richard Cumberland's *Wheel of Fortune*, its hero superbly acted by Kemble, went to some eighteen performances. And Holcroft's *Deserted Daughter* accounted for another of the thirteen performances given over to sentimental drama. The offerings that achieved an appreciable measure of success in 1800 were, if anything, even more varied than those in 1795. Indeed, it is almost impossible to classify some of the plays; Nicoll, for example, describes Thomas Morton's *Speed the Plough* as "a sentimental melo- dramatic comedy." This play was, incidentally, the greatest success in 1800. Next in popularity, as measured in terms of the number of times it was acted, came Sheridan's adaptation from Kotzebue, the tragedy *Pizarro*. Both it and Reynolds' *Life*, a sentimental comedy, were acted twenty- seven times. Also sharing the honors of the season were Kemble's *Point of Honor*, listed by Nicoll as a "Drama" and described by Genest as "tragedy rather than comedy," and Cumberland's melodrama, *Joanna of Montfaucon*.

The fact that emerges most clearly from the foregoing analysis is that theatre-goers in the last few decades of the eighteenth century were as eager for variety as those of any other century. This conclusion may seem anticlimactic, but it is a necessary corrective to the view that those years saw a triumph of the sentimental spirit. Nothing could be farther from the mark. And, it is necessary to repeat, the kind and extent of the sentimentalism in the plays of this period differ greatly from those of some of the earlier and less adroit specimens of the genre.

The remaining question, that of the sincerity of the writers of sentimental drama, admits of more precise conclusions. The need to examine this aspect of sentimentalism in the drama results from the sweeping generalization with which Bernbaum concludes his study of "the drama of sensibility." His work leaves the student with the impression that the chief writers in the genre were thoroughgoing sentimentalists in principle as well as in practice. He finds that in the period 1773-1780 the "leadership devolved upon Cumberland (who resumed his work in the 1780's), Thomas Holcroft, and the younger George Colman—all writers of the sentimental school. Usually they tried to enliven their comedies with some laughable situations and one or two humorous personages, but it was their sentimental conception of life that determined the main action of their plays and the motives of their chief characters" (p. 267). This statement inspires the belief that the ablest writers of this kind of comedy were themselves convinced of the truth of the view of life expressed in their work. Elsewhere, both in this chapter and earlier, the present writer has suggested the contrary; support is to be had in more exhaustive studies of the sentimental triumvirate set up.

The dramatist who most nearly satisfies the condition of believing sincerely in the sentimental view of life found in his plays is Richard Cumberland. Stanley T. Williams writes of him that while "far from being insensible to the applause of his audiences, he nevertheless believed sincerely in the mission of sentimental comedy to reform abuses, and to correct English prejudices." And yet he feels that Cumberland's superiority over other writers of sentimental comedy is owing to the fact that, "sunk in sentiment as he seems, he is less under the sway of the tearful muse than Kelly or Holcroft." Another reason for Cumberland's greater worth, for Williams, resides in his dialogue, which "attains occasional eminences of wit not equally apparent in his rivals' drama."[8] But Cumberland was not above ridiculing sentimental comedy, as is evident from the prologue to *The Impostors* and from an occasional remark in the plays: "You are as dull as a sentimental comedy" (*A Note of Hand*). It would seem, of course, that he is directing his remarks against the ultrasentimental school. Cumberland is credited with some fifty plays by Williams; all the comedies, twenty-six in number, "may be regarded as comedies of the sentimental type."[9] This indiscriminate lumping of all the comedies together gives a distorted perspective; a number of them are not sentimental, unless any play not markedly immoral is to be looked upon as of the sentimental genre. Williams himself later writes, of *The Choleric Man,* that "a character named Old Nightshade bore the brunt of the critics' assaults, and seemed to violate all the decorum of sentimental comedy."[10] Allardyce Nicoll states that *The Impostors* shows how "Cumberland could, at least for a time, escape from his prevailing sentimental mood and present dialogue designed for the single purpose of raising laughter" (*1750-1800,* p. 176). He also speaks of *The School For Widows* and *The Box-Lobby Challenge* in which Cumberland "seemed to be moving still farther away from true sentimentalism" (*ibid.,* p. 127). And Bernbaum describes *The Choleric Man* as a play in the comic, as opposed to the sentimental, vein (p. 251). Another scholar points out that in his novel *Henry,* Cumberland protests against the sentimental, against the typical heroine in the novel of "melodramatic sentimentality," and against the idea that the hero in these novels must always be good.[11] Even Cumberland, it is clear, had reservations about the sentimental view of life; that these reservations focused about the matter of possible over-emphasis may be partly granted.

With Thomas Holcroft there is no need for the qualifying statement. The two scholars who have studied the man and his work most closely are agreed that he was not a sentimentalist in principle, whatever the ostensible direction taken by his writings. Elbridge Colby, editor of Holcroft's autobiography, discussing the years 1782-1794, can write

The purely sentimental comedy had gone, possibly laughed off the stage by the subtle ridicule of *The School For Scandal.* Holcroft considered it "a puling, rickety, unhealthy brat," and used social satire with serious intent, to improve the world across the footlights, and not merely to produce light laughter. He left no doubt in his prefaces that his principles were doctrinaire. That plays written with such bare-faced preaching should have been successful is strange. And they were successful.[12]

One need not agree with the statement that "sentimental comedy had gone"; the importance of this passage lies in its revelation of Holcroft's opinion of the genre. And it is to be hoped that the homiletic in drama, and in Holcroft's plays, must not always be linked with the sentimental. It should, however, be remarked that Holcroft was not opposed to comedy's drawing forth tears. In his review of Mrs. Inchbald's comedy, *Each One Has His Faults* (1793), from which Colby quotes only the "unhealthy brat" passage, Holcroft opposes "mere sentimental comedy" but he declares that "of all the delights which comedy can give, that of exciting tears and laughter by the same thought is supreme" (*Monthly Review,* XCI, 302-03). In his reviews of other "sentimental" plays he is usually noncommittal rather than at all enthusiastic. Even more unmistakable is Virgil Stallbaumer's statement of Holcroft's position. Holcroft was a satirist who wrote at a time when sentimentalism was demanded; he recognized the trend of the times and compromised as best he could with it. For Stallbaumer it "seems abundantly established that all of Holcroft's prepossessions, talent, and theory, were in keeping with the comic spirit" rather than with the sentimental.[13] Holcroft wrote sentimental plays, but his heart was decidedly not in the effort and he turned to another dramatic genre before long.

George Colman the Younger would seem to have inherited his views on comedy from his father. Like the elder Colman (at least after about 1765), the younger stressed the comic elements in his plays and paid his devoirs to the contemporary taste for sentimentalism by the inclusion of the already well-worn devices of sentimental drama. His fourth play, *Inkle and Yariko* (1787), sometimes referred to as an opera by his contemporaries, "clearly belongs in the sentimental tradition," according to J. F. Bagster-Collins who continues

It rises above the general level of its type in at least three qualities: swiftness of movement; an engaging freshness and good humor which strongly suggests that Colman was fully aware of the absurdity of much of the whole affair; and an authentic ring of sincerity in Sir Christopher Curry's execration of slave traffic carried on by Englishmen, an indictment short, direct, and simply phrased, without the bathetic exaggeration so often evident in the drama of the period. Inkle's rapid reformation in the last act, like that of Belcour in Cumberland's *The West Indian,* is characteristic of the ultra-sentimental school, but it is well motivated and psychologically probable. Colman seems, on the whole, to have struck a good bargain with sentiment, and with the audience which demanded it, by clinging firmly to his well-developed sense of humor.[14]

The impression one gets from this analysis is that the only real concession to current sentimentalism is in the final reformation of Inkle, but even here, as Bagster-Collins points out (p. 33n), the choice of this ending seems to have been haphazard. The songs interspersed in the play and "completely irrelevant to the plot" (p. 35) suggest that sentimental drama as a pure genre was of relatively short duration and depended more and more on the admixture of other kinds of drama, until it becomes critically short-sighted to speak of sentimental drama when one is actually discussing melodrama or Gothic plays in which sentimental elements and devices are present. The fact is that Colman the Younger, and Holcroft as well, wrote comparatively few sentimental plays; they attempted, however, many other kinds of drama. Indeed, Allardyce Nicoll lists *Inkle and Yarico* as a comic opera, and Bagster-Collins says of *The Poor Gentleman* that "in many respects it is really a melodrama" (p. 136). It might also be well to point out here that Cumberland, Holcroft, and Colman the Younger all wrote one or more Gothic dramas, and "Gothic drama—even plays like those by Lewis, which contain an elaborate diablerie—is thoroughly moral; indeed we shall see that the Gothic was virtually 'converted into a school of virtue' such as Mrs. [Hannah] More had imagined might be established."[15]

It is not, hence, mere hair-splitting to insist that drama after 1783 be regarded as essentially heterogeneous rather than essentially homogeneous. More simply put, it is a question of emphasis again: whether it is more strictly accurate to speak of the presence of some sentimentalism in the bulk of the dramatic output after this period or to maintain that sentimentalism dominates the scene and other elements are the intruders. After all, it must be constantly remembered that after the Restoration, drama could only go in one direction; it could hardly become *less* moral, it had perforce to become *more* moral. The immorality, sometimes too much exaggerated admittedly, of the years 1660-1685 was a freakish phenomenon born of a combination of circumstances that would be hard to parallel again in history. And yet some scholars have suggested the heroic play as an ancestor of sentimental drama, so that even during the Restoration some of the responses evoked by sentimental drama are discernible. The question of the sincerity of Dryden in one of his heroic plays, for example, is as pointless, really, as the same question in connection with Cumberland, Holcroft, or Colman the Younger. When these writers were sincere in their efforts they did not write sentimental comedies, for the two are irreconcilable by very definition. When sincerity is invoked, it is time to discard all talk of sentimentalism and look for another term. Sentimentalism is to be found in the mawkish attitudinizings of the inferior-gifted moral ladies and, sometimes Reverend, gentlemen who chiefly capitalized on an undiscriminating reading public. The theatre-going public sought, and the theatre managers provided, entertainment of various sorts; in comedy that deserved the name the principal aim was to amuse, albeit the didactic-moral strain was usually present as a minor accompaniment.

NOTES

Chapter I. SENTIMENTAL DRAMA "DEFINED"

1. *The Correspondence of Samuel Richardson*, edited by Anna Laetitia Barbauld, 1804, IV, 282-83. The same loose use of "sentimental" persisted throughout the century. I have come upon sentimental spies, spouters, magazines, exhibitions, conversation, diaries, journeys (other than Sterne's) and liberties in the literature of the century. My favorite is a description of a well-known courtesan as "the sentimental Mrs. Eliot" in the *Morning Post* for January 27, 1776.

2. "The Gentleman" No. VI, in *Prose on Several Occasions* . . . , 1787, I, 208-10.

3. Preface to *The Town Before You*, 1795 (2nd ed.).

4. *Quarterly Review*, CCXLI (1924), 418.

5. "The Reformer" No. 10 (March 31, 1748). In the *Daily Advertiser* for March 21, 1737 a notice of Fielding's *Historical Register* ends thus: "N.B. All Persons are desir'd to cry at the Tragedy and laugh at the Comedy, being quite contrary to the present general Practise." I owe this last to Prof. James L. Clifford.

6. "Gray's Inn Journal" No. 91 (July 13, 1754).

7. See Robert B. Heilman, "The Sentimentalism of Goldsmith's *Good-Natured Man*," in *Studies for William A. Read* (Baton Rouge, 1940), pp. 237-53, and W. F. Gallaway, Jr., "The Sentimentalism of Goldsmith," *PMLA*, XLVIII (1933), 1167-81.

8. *The Elements of Dramatic Criticism*, 1775, pp. 141-42.

9. Chapter XIII of Ernest Bernbaum's *Drama of Sensibility* is entitled "Sheridan and the Final Triumph of Sentimental Comedy, 1773-1780." Subsequent references to this work will appear in the text.

10. *A Complete History of the Stage*, 1795, V, 277.

11. "On the Provinces of Dramatic Poetry," in *Works*, 1811, II, 74, 94, 95.

12. *Works*, 1801, I, 142. The poem was written in 1787.

13. Quoted in Virgil Stallbaumer, "Thomas Holcroft: A Satirist in the Stream of Sentimentalism," *ELH*, III (1936), 42-43.

14. *The Life of Richard Cumberland* . . . , 1812, I, 281.

15. "Thoughts on Comedy," in *Works*, 1798, II, 320-21.

16. *Correspondence*, ed. W. S. Lewis (New Haven, 1944), X, 301 and XI, 103.

17. See Adams, Croissant (2), Krutch, Ristine, Schorer, Smith (2) in my bibliography.

Chapter II. THE "DEFINITION" TESTED

1. F. T. Wood, "The Beginnings and Significance of Sentimental Comedy," *Anglia*, LV (1931), 373.

2. *Elizabethan Drama* (Boston and New York), I, 27-28.

3. Edith Birkhead, "Sentiment and Sensibility in the Eighteenth Century Novel," in *Essays and Studies by Members of the English Association*, XI (1925), 97-98.

4. C. M. Scheurer, "An Early Sentimental Comedy," *Anglia*, XXXVII (1913), 125.

5. "The Normality of Shakespeare Illustrated in his Treatment of Love and Marriage," *The English Association Pamphlet No. 47*, Sept. 1920, p. 7.

6. "Shakespeare and the Unhappy Happy Ending," *PMLA*, XLII (1927), 751; *Shakespeare's Satire*, 1943, p. 88; *Comic Characters of Shakespeare*, 1946, pp. xiv, 73, and 3; *Shakespeare's Portrayal of the Moral Life* (New York, 1902), p. 169; "Shakespeare, Marston and the Malcontent Type," *MP*, III (1905-06), 287; *Modern English in the Making* (New York, 1928), p. 163; *Character Problems in Shakespeare*, 1922, pp. 55 and 98, 56, and 196; *Shakespeare, His Mind and Art* (3rd ed.) (New York, 1881), pp. 68, 119 and 121, and 150; *The Influence of Beaumont and Fletcher on Shakespeare* (Worcester, Mass., 1901), p. 139.

7. *English Tragicomedy*, pp. 112, 114, 122; *Fletcher, Beaumont and Company* (New York, 1947), p. 238; (New York, 1948), pp. 573 and 575; Theodore Spencer, *Shakespeare and the Nature of Man* (New York, 1943), p. 190.

8. *Anglia*, LV, 377-78.

9. "Thomas Heywood," in *Selected Essays 1917-1932* (New York, 1932), p. 157; ed., *A Woman Killed With Kindness*, 1897, p. xvi; *The Influence of Beaumont and Fletcher on Shakespeare*, p. 104; ed., *A Woman Killed With Kindness*, 1917, p. cxvi; *Thomas Heywood*, (New Haven, 1928), p. 82; *Thomas Heywood, Playwright and Miscellanist* (Oxford, 1931), p. 236.

10. "Thomas Heywood," *Anglia*, XXXVII (1913), 237; J. S. P. Tatlock and R. G. Martin, *Representative English Plays* (2nd ed.) (New York, 1938), p. 156; "*A Woman Killed With Kindness*," *PMLA*, LIII (1938), 147.

11. *The Bourgeois Elements in the Drama of Thomas Heywood* (Princeton Doctoral Dissertation), 1922, pp. 26, 27, 31, 107, 111 and 142.

12. H. W. Wells, *Elizabethan and Jacobean Playwrights* (New York, 1939).

13. Willard Thorp, *The Triumph of Realism in Elizabethan Drama, 1558-1612*, Princeton Studies in English, No. 3 (Princeton, 1928), p. 88.

14. One might cite Wronglove in Charles Johnson's *Caelia*, Belfield, Sr., in Richard Cumberland's *The Brothers*, and, if Cibber's *Love's Last Shift* be thought of as a thoroughgoing sentimental comedy, Loveless. Mercour, in Francis' *Eugenia* is vicious throughout and unrepentant at the end. There may be others.

15. Lord Falconbridge, speaking of Scarborow:
> —would I had a son
> Might merit commendation equal with him.
> I'll tell you what he is; he is a youth
> A noble branch, increasing blessed fruit
> Where caterpillar vice dare not to touch   (Act I)

16. The play has been so susceptible to misreading that it becomes obligatory to correct a number of misstatements that have been made about it. Wood, *Anglia*, LV, 378 speaks of Scarborow's "misconduct" which forces him to marry Katherine, and he states baldly that "Clare dies of grief." A. H. Quinn's edition of *The Faire Maide of Bristow* (Phila., 1902), p. 27, has the following statement: "In *The Miseries of Enforced Marriage* we have another rascal-in-ordinary, William Scarborow, who deserts his betrothed, Clare, and marries Katherine for the money she will bring him." Actually, Scarborow is an amiable young man who is forced to desert Clare. There is no mercenary motive for his marrying Katherine. Charles J. Sisson (*Le Goût Public et Le Théatre Élisabéthain* . . . [Dijon, 1922], p. 168) is in error when he writes:
> De meme Wilkins, qui met en scène les préliminaires du crime que représente *The Yorkshire Tragedy*, change le dénouement de l'histoire de Calverley et de sa femme et donne une fin heureuse aux amours de Scarborow et de Clare par un procédé familier de la comédie romanesque. Tout comme Hero dans *Much Ado about Nothing*, Clare est décidément une héroïne de roman et elle ne meurt que pour renaître au bon moment.

Clare dies by her own hand ("—and with one sin,/Done by this hand, end many done by him." Act II), and she very certainly does not come to life again. Montague Summers (ed., *Works of Aphra Behn*, 1915, III, 4) declares that Clare "dies tragically of a broken heart."

17. *Dramatic Works*, 1760, I, 296.

18. In *The Shakespeare Apocrypha*, ed. by C. F. Tucker Brooke, 1908, p. 260.

19. *The Prodigal*, by F. G. Waldron, 1794.

20. See J. A. Symonds, *The Renaissance in Italy* (New York, 1935), II, 770 and L. E. Lord, *A Translation of the Orpheus of Angelo Poliziano and the Aminta of Tasso*, 1931, p. 63.

21. *Pastoral Poetry and Pastoral Drama*, 1906, pp. 254 and 262.

22. *Thomas Southerne, Dramatist*, Yale Studies in English, No. 81 (New Haven, 1933), p. 213.

23. *English Tragicomedy*, pp. 194 and 195.

Chapter III. Repetition and Prolongation

1. *Comedy and Conscience*, p. 192.
2. *Plays of the Restoration and Eighteenth Century*, ed. by Dougald MacMillan and Howard Mumford Jones (New York, 1931), p. 343. Cibber gives Loveless the last speech in the play, and it serves to drive the sentimental lesson home.
3. See Kittredge, ed. *As You Like It* (Boston, 1939), p. 173, the note on l. 137 of IV, iii.
4. See above, p. 23. Compare the reformation of Louisa in Cibber's *Love Makes A Man*, partially based on *The Custom of the Country*.
5. "Thoughts on Comedy," from *Works*, 1798, II, 320.
6. Editor, *The Complete Works of John Webster*, 1927, III, 22-23.
7. *James Shirley, Dramatist* (New York, 1915), p. 253.
8. See Ristine, *English Tragicomedy*, pp. 135-39 for a discussion of Shirley's tragicomedies.
9. I should note I, i, pp. 295-96; III, i, pp. 310-14, 315-16, 320; IV, iii, pp. 346-49, and V, ii, pp. 357-59, ed. Gifford and Dyce, 1833, III.
10. (New York, 1914), pp. 71-73. For the period of the Restoration see David S. Berkeley, "The Penitent Rake in Restoration Comedy," *MP*, XLIX (1952), 223-33.
11. See below, pp. 170-171, n. 34.
12. Alfred Harbage, *As They Liked It* (New York, 1947), p. 178.
13. V, pp. 56-58. I have used the edition of 1786, printed for W. Lowndes and W. Nicoll. See J. H. Caskey, *The Life and Works of Edward Moore*, Yale Studies in English, LXXV, 1927, pp. 29-50 for a full discussion of *The Foundling*.
14. V, ii. See Brents Stirling, *The Populace in Shakespeare* (New York, 1949), p. 167, and Mowbray Velte, *The Bourgeois Elements in the Drama of Thomas Heywood*, 1922 (Published Princeton Doctoral Dissertation).
15. See *The Unhappy Favourite*, ed. by T. M. H. Blair (New York, 1939) and Nicoll, *1660-1700*, p. 156.
16. F. S. Tupper, "John Banks, A Study in the Origins of Pathetic Tragedy," Unpublished Harvard Doctoral Dissertation, 1935.
17. See Forsythe, *The Relations of Shirley's Plays to the Elizabethan Drama*, p. 67, for a list of these "renunciation" scenes.
18. In *The School of Shakespeare*, ed. Richard Simpson, 1878, I, 161. Simpson compares Vernon's "all the right I have / In fair Nell Curtis I resign to thee" to Valentine's "All that was mine in Sylvia I give thee" (*Two Gentlemen of Verona*, V, iv).
19. Nicoll, *1750-1800*, p. 259 notes that this play was acted in the provinces.
20. R. D. Havens, "The Sentimentalism of *The London Merchant*," *ELH*, XII (1945), 184.
21. IV, iv; and V, i.

Chapter IV. Eschewal of Humor and the Bawdy

1. Baltimore, 1943, II, 500-502.
2. Preface to *The Conscious Lovers*.
3. Epilogue to *The Lying Lover*.
4. Preface to *The Conscious Lovers*.
5. New York, 1913 (Authorized Translation by C. Brereton and F. Rothwell), pp. 4-5.
6. The hand-lists of plays appended to Nicoll's histories of eighteenth-century drama offer a convenient check system. One finds seventeen women and one Reverend gentleman (James Miller) connected with the theatre as writers for the period 1700-1750. For the next fifty years Nicoll lists sixty-seven women dramatists, eighteen Reverend gentlemen, and one Bishop (Thomas L. O'Beirne). In both lists there are people who are really only on the periphery of the acted drama with translations, dramatic tales, and closet drama. (Possibly some of the men listed as "Dr." in these

lists were divines; there seems little need to pursue the matter so closely.) Further differentiation may be made in the character of the women who wrote for the theatre in both periods. One need only compare the life and works of Mrs. Centlivre and Mrs. Heywood with those of Mrs. Elizabeth Griffith and Mrs. Hannah More.

7. A. M. Clark, *Thomas Heywood, Playwright and Miscellanist*, p. 22 and *passim*.

8. *The Triumph of Realism in Elizabethan Drama*, pp. 90-91.

9. *Anglia*, LV, 375; *Thomas Heywood*, pp. 243-44; *English Dramatic Literature*, 1899, II, 608-09.

10. In *The Old English Drama*, 1824-5 (vol. I), I, i, p. 4. Each play is paged separately.

11. III, ii, p. 45. See also pp. 10, 11-12, 19, 22-23, 58, 63-64, 72, 79, and 85-89. The last is the scene in which Young Arthur, starving and despairing of any help, is succored by his wife, whom he does not recognize.

12. *Laughter*, p. 140.

13. Roberta F. Brinkley, *Nathan Field, The Actor-Playwright*, Yale Studies in English No. 77 (New Haven, 1928), p. 79.

14. One should also note that Steele's confrontation and reconciliation scene contains definitely comic elements (V, i, pp. 252-53, Mermaid ed.). Pamela (Letter 54) thought the scene "very ridiculous." Her remarks on the morality of Steele's play are worth reading. In *Amends* one might list these as "sentimental" speeches: pp. 438-41, 442-45, 449, 451-52, 463-65, 474-75, 478-80 in the Mermaid *Nero and Other Plays*.

15. Dedication to Mr. Addison.

16. Howard H. Dunbar, *The Dramatic Career of Arthur Murphy* (New York, 1946), p. 105.

17. *David Garrick, Dramatist* (New York, 1938), p. 238.

18. Krutch, *Comedy and Conscience After the Restoration*, Chapt. IX, *passim*.

19. Bernbaum, p. 170. Nicoll, *1700-1750*, p. 200, calls it a "moral-immoral" comedy.

20. M. Maurice Shudofsky, "Charles Johnson and Eighteenth Century Drama," *ELH*, X (1943), 149. The possible relationship of this play to Richardson's *Clarissa* is interesting.

21. Shudofsky, *ELH*, X, 154-55.

22. Caskey, *Life and Works of Edward Moore*, p. 37 has been my guide in this discussion.

23. See pp. 24-25, 34, 42-3 particularly. I have used an edition of 1786 (Printed for W. Lowndes and W. Nicoll).

24. This is the last scene in Vanbrugh's fragment, pp. 166-68 in Bonamy Dobrée's edition of Vanbrugh's plays, 1927, III.

25. 1774 ed., IV, i, p. 128. See also III, i, p. 105 and II, i, p. 100.

26. See above, pp. 29-30.

27. See above, p. 23.

28. Despite the description, "A Tragedy," on the title page. The only death is that of the heroine's would-be seducer.

29. References are to the Mermaid *Massinger*, vol. II.

30. References are to the play as printed in *Plays of the Restoration and Eighteenth Century*, ed. by Dougald MacMillan and Howard Mumford Jones (New York, 1931).

31. Aaron Hill, *Dramatic Works*, 1760, II, 383-84.

32. See Bernbaum, pp. 50-52; DeWitt C. Croissant, "Early Sentimental Comedy," in *The Parrott Presentation Volume* (Princeton, 1935), p. 62; Nicoll, *1660-1700*, p. 256.

33. Kathleen M. Lynch, "Thomas D'Urfey's Contribution to Sentimental Comedy," *PQ*, IX (1930), 259.

34. Nicoll, *1660-1700*, p. 264, n. 2. Nicoll also makes a slip in interpretation. Speaking of "distinct features of . . . sentimental comedy" in *Love For Money*, he says, in the note referred to: "Particularly in V, iii; Meritton, hearing that Mirtilla has become rich, has scruples about marrying her, for fear he should be accused of intriguing after her money." In the scene commented on by Nicoll, Meritton's words would lead one to believe him possessed of the scruples attributed to him, but his speech, on Mirtilla's exit, reveals his true nature. He says: "I should be fool indeed, if I should lose thee for all my seeming sullenness, I know she's fast, therefore play this game,

that hereafter she mayn't twit me with her benefits, Riches corrupt the mind, some Women must be serv'd so." This is decidedly *non*-sentimental.

35. R. S. Forsythe, *A Study of the Plays of Thomas D'Urfey*, Western Reserve Studies, Vol. I, No. 2, p. 69. Forsythe commits the same error made by Nicoll. He writes: "In V, 3, (p. 49), Meritton shows some serious scruples about marrying the now-rich Mirtilla."

Chapter V. EMPHASIS AND DIRECTION

1. Victor adds a different sub-plot of his own, but he makes it so integral a part of the main action that it is really a misnomer to call it a sub-plot. What is more, Victor's additions add to, rather than take away from, the sentimental interest.

2. *Thomas Heywood, Playwright and Miscellanist*, p. 312.

3. *The Early Middle Class Drama, 1696-1774*, (Lancaster, Pa., 1935), pp. 140 and 141.

4. J. H. Smith, *The Gay Couple in Restoration Drama* (Cambridge, Mass., 1948), p. 221, n. 54.

5. *Comedy and Conscience After the Restoration*, p. 150 ff.; and "Shadwell, the Ladies and the Change in Comedy," *MP*, XLVI (1948), 22-23.

6. *Mr. Cibber of Drury Lane* (New York, 1939), pp. 28-29.

7. *Dramatic Miscellanies*, 1783-4, III, 412.

8. Ed., R. W. Lowe, 1889, I, 220.

9. *A Comparison between the Two Stages*, ed., S. B. Wells, 1942, Princeton Studies in English, Vol. 26, p. 16.

10. Dodds, *Thomas Southerne*, p. 64.

11. Dodds, *Thomas Southerne*, p. 88. I take the facts of my discussion from this work.

12. See above, pp. 81 and 83.

13. Hazelton Spencer, *Elizabethan Plays* (Boston, 1933), p. 668.

14. *Eighteenth Century Drama, 1700-1750*, p. 195; Bernbaum, pp. 98-100; *English Comic Drama, 1700-1750*, p. 68. Bateson calls *The Basset-Table* sentimental, as does Nicoll (*Eighteenth Century Drama, 1700-1750*, p. 196).

15. *Eighteenth Century Drama, 1700-1750*, p. 185; *Studies in the Work of Colley Cibber*, pp. 53 and 54; *Mr. Cibber of Drury Lane*, p. 70; *English Comic Drama*, pp. 33-35; Bernbaum, pp. 103-07.

16. *Some Account of the English Stage*, 1832, II, 490-93; *Eighteenth Century Drama, 1700-1750*, p. 187.

17. *Eighteenth Century Drama, 1750-1800*, pp. 134-35. One wonders why Nicoll distinguishes between "comedies of sensibility" (*1700-1750*) and "sentimental comedy" (*1750-1800*).

18. See above, pp. 26-27 for discussion of *A Yorkshire Tragedy* and *The Fatal Extravagance*.

19. See Barker, *Mr. Cibber of Drury Lane*, pp. 12-14.

20. See A. N. Wiley, "Female Prologues and Epilogues in English Plays," *PMLA*, XLVIII (1933), 1067, n. 33; Nicoll, *1660-1700*, pp. 21, 254, and 265; and Bonamy Dobrée, ed., *The Complete Works of Vanbrugh*, I, 227.

21. Genest, *Some Account of the English Stage*, III, 153.

22. *Notes and Queries*, 3rd series, VIII, 24. See also Montague Summers, ed., Dryden's *Dramatic Works*, II, 236.

23. *Life and Works of Edward Moore*, p. 106.

24. See above, p. 168, n. 19.

25. *The New English Drama*, 1832, pp. iii-iv of the "Remarks" on the play.

26. See above, pp. 88-90.

Chapter VI. OTHER CRITERIA

1. Edited by H. DeVocht for the Malone Society, XXIII, 1910, pp. v-vi.

2. See above, p. 52.

3. "The Royal Fletcher and the Loyal Heywood," in *Elizabethan Studies and Other Essays in Honor of George F. Reynolds* (Boulder, Colorado, 1945), pp. 192-93.
4. See above, p. 28.
5. The play was acted in the provinces only.
6. See above, pp. 94-96.
7. *English Thought in the Eighteenth Century*, 3rd ed., 1902, II, 436; *Five Masters* (New York, 1930), p. 159; Preface to *The Conscious Lovers*.
8. See Chapter VI of H. W. Wells, *Elizabethan and Jacabean Playwrights*. The distinction made in Wells's work is that between genuine feeling and "sentiment" (p. 118).
9. C. S. Lewis, *The Allegory of Love*, 1936, p. 195.
10. T. M. H. Blair (New York, 1939), p. 16; *Thomas Southerne*, p. 217; ed., *Works of Thomas Otway*, 1926, I, lxxvi; ed., *Three Plays by Nicholas Rowe*, 1929, p. 21. See also the dissertation by Lewis M. Magill listed in the bibliography.
11. Editor, *Three Plays by Nicholas Rowe*, p. 23.

Chapter VII. POPULARITY OF THE GENRE

1. In *Research Studies of the State College of Washington*, XII (1944), 129-31.
2. Stanley T. Williams, *Richard Cumberland* (New Haven, 1917), pp. 309-10.
3. Eugene R. Page, *George Colman the Elder* (New York, 1935), p. 133n.
4. See Lt. Gen. Burgoyne's Preface to *The Lord of the Manor;* the epilogues to Thomas Holcroft's *Duplicity* and *The Road to Ruin;* the prologue, by Colman the Elder, to Mrs. Lee's *Chapter of Accidents;* Goldsmith's epilogue to Mrs. Lennox's *The Sister;* the epilogue to Hugh Kelly's *A Word to the Wise*. Doubtless there are others; too often plays were reprinted without prologues and epilogues.
5. Page, *Colman the Elder*, p. 135.
6. Williams, *Richard Cumberland*, p. 69.
7. Twenty times from May 8, to June 7, 1777, at which time the theatre closed; by the end of the next season Genest is able to record 65 performances.
8. *Richard Cumberland*, pp. 325, 309, and 311.
9. *Ibid.*, p. 304.
10. "The Early Sentimental Dramas of Richard Cumberland," *MLN*, 36 (1921), 163. Williams calls Cumberland's *Fashionable Lovers* a comedy of manners (p. 162); it cannot at the same time be called sentimental comedy.
11. W. H. Rogers, "The Reaction Against Melodramatic Sentimentality in the English Novel, 1796-1830," *PMLA*, 49 (1934), 100n.
12. *The Life of Thomas Holcroft*, 1925, I, xxvii.
13. "Thomas Holcroft: A Satirist in the Stream of Sentimentalism," *ELH*, 3 (1936), 43.
14. *George Colman the Younger* (New York, 1946), p. 35.
15. Bertrand Evans, *Gothic Drama From Walpole to Shelley* (Los Angeles, 1947), p. 45.

BIBLIOGRAPHY

Adams, Henry H., *English Domestic or Homiletic Tragedy, 1575 to 1642*, New York, 1943.

Alderman, William E., "Shaftesbury and the Doctrine of Moral Sense in the Eighteenth Century," *PMLA*, XLVI (1931), 1087-94.

Aldridge, A. O., "The Pleasures of Pity," *ELH*, XVI (1949), 76-87.

Allen, B. Sprague, "The Dates of *Sentimental* and Its Derivatives," *PMLA*, XLVIII (1933), 303-07.

Barker, Richard H., *Mr. Cibber of Drury Lane*, New York, 1939.

Bateson, F. W., *English Comic Drama, 1700-1750*, 1929.

Berkeley, David S., "The Art of 'Whining' Love," *SP*, LII (1955), 478-96.

——, "The Penitent Rake in Restoration Comedy," *MP*, XLIX (1952), 223-33.

Bernbaum, Ernest, *The Drama of Sensibility*, Boston and London, 1915.

Birkhead, Edith, "Sentiment and Sensibility in the Eighteenth Century Novel," *Essays and Studies by Members of the English Association*, XI (1925), 92-116.

Bowyer, John W., *The Celebrated Mrs. Centlivre*, Durham, N. C., 1952.

Burra, Peter, *Baroque and Gothic Sentimentalism*, 1931.

Calverton, V. F., "Social Change and the Sentimental Comedy," *Modern Quarterly* (1925), 169-88.

Caskey, John H., "Arthur Murphy and the War on Sentimental Comedy," *JEGP*, XXX (1931), 563-77.

——, *The Life and Works of Edward Moore*, Yale Studies in English, LXXV, New Haven, 1927.

Clark, Donald B., "An Eighteenth-Century Adaptation of Massinger," *MLQ*, XIII (1952), 239-52.

Cox, James E., *The Rise of Sentimental Comedy*, Springfield, Mo., Published by author, 1926.

Crane, Ronald S., "Suggestions Towards A Genealogy of the 'Man of Feeling,'" *ELH*, I (1934), 205-30.

Croissant, DeWitt C., "Early Sentimental Comedy," in *The Parrott Presentation Volume*, Princeton, 1935, pp. 47-71.

——, *Studies in the Work of Colley Cibber*, Kansas City, 1912. (Reprinted from the Bulletin of the Univ. of Kansas, Humanistic Studies, Vol. I, No. 1).

Dodds, J. W., *Thomas Southerne, Dramatist*, Yale Studies in English, LXXXI, New Haven, 1933.

Draper, John W., "Theory of Comic in Eighteenth Century England," *JEGP*, XXXVII (1938), 207-23.

Dunbar, Howard H., *The Dramatic Career of Arthur Murphy*, New York, 1946.

Edmunds, James M., "An Example of Early Sentimentalism," *MLN*, XLVIII (1933), 94-97.

Eloesser, Arthur, *Das Bürgerliche Drama*, Berlin, 1898.

Emery, John Pike, *Arthur Murphy*, Philadelphia, 1946.

Forsythe, Robert S., *A Study of the Plays of Thomas D'Urfey*, Western Reserve Studies, Vol. I, No. 2, 1917.

Gallaway, W. F., Jr., "The Sentimentalism of Goldsmith," *PMLA*, XLVIII (1933), 1167-81.

Garey, Doris B., "Eighteenth Century Sentimentalism . . . ," Univ. of Wisconsin, 1941 (Unpub. Ph.D. dissertation).

Hare, M. E., "Steele and Sentimental Comedy," in *Eighteenth Century Literature, An Oxford Miscellany*, 1909, pp. 5-41.

Havens, Raymond D., "The Sentimentalism of *The London Merchant*," *ELH*, XII (1945), 183-87.

Heilman, Robert B., "The Sentimentalism of Goldsmith's 'Good-Natured Man,'" in *Studies for William A. Read*, Baton Rouge, 1940, pp. 237-53.

Humphreys, A. R., "'The Friend of Mankind' (1700-1760)—an Aspect of Eighteenth Century Sensibility," *RES*, XXIV (1948), 203-18.

Kies, Paul P., "Lessing's Relation to Early English Sentimental Comedy," *PMLA*, XLVII (1932), 807-26.

Krutch, Joseph W., *Comedy and Conscience After the Restoration*, New York, 1924.

Landa, M. J., "The Grandfather of Melodrama," *Cornhill Magazine*, CXXXII (1925), 476-84.

Loftis, John, *Steele at Drury Lane*, Los Angeles, 1952.

Lynch, James J., *Box, Pit, and Gallery, Stage and Society in Johnson's London*, Berkeley and Los Angeles, 1953.

Lynch, Kathleen M., "*Pamela Nubile, L'Écossaise*, and *The English Merchant*," *MLN*, XLVII (1932), 94-96.

————, "Thomas D'Urfey's Contribution to Sentimental Comedy," *PQ*, IX (1930), 249-59.

Magill, Lewis, Jr., "Elements of Sentimentalism in English Tragedy, 1680-1704," Univ. of Illinois, 1949 (Unpub. Ph.D. dissertation).

Mignon, Elisabeth, *Crabbed Age and Youth*, Durham, N. C., 1947.

Moore, C. A., "Whig Panegyric Verse, 1700-1760, a Phase of Sentimentalism," *PMLA*, XLI (1926), 362-401.

Nicoll, Allardyce, *A History of Late Eighteenth Century Drama, 1750-1800*, 1927.

————, *A History of Early Eighteenth Century Drama, 1700-1750*, 1925.

————, *A History of Restoration Drama, 1660-1700*, 1923.

Nolte, Fred O., *The Early Middle Class Drama, 1696-1774*, Lancaster, Pa., 1935.

Page, Eugene R., *George Colman the Elder*, New York, 1935.

Pedicord, Harry W., *The Theatrical Public in the Time of Garrick*, New York, 1954.

Reed, Robert R., Jr., "James Shirley and the Sentimental Comedy," *Anglia*, Band 73 (1955), 149-70.

————, "Ben Jonson's Pioneering in Sentimental Comedy," *N&Q*, CXCV (1950), 272-73.

Ristine, Frank H., *English Tragicomedy . .* , New York, 1910.

Rodman, George B., "Sentimentalism in Lillo's *The London Merchant*," *ELH*, XII (1945), 45-61.

Rys, Sister Mary Ellen, "The Rise of Sentimentalism in Jacobean and Caroline Drama," Univ. of Notre Dame, 1954 (Unpub. Ph.D. dissertation).

Scheurer, C. M., "An Early Sentimental Comedy," *Anglia*, XXXVII (1913), 125-28.

Schorer, Mark, "Hugh Kelly: His Place in the Sentimental School," *PQ*, XII (1933), 389-401.

Shudofsky, M. Maurice, "Charles Johnson and the Eighteenth Century Drama," *ELH*, X (1943), 131-58.

Smith, John H., "Shadwell, The Ladies, and the Change in Comedy," *MP*, XLVI (1948), 22-33.

——, *The Gay Couple in Restoration Comedy*, Cambridge, Mass., 1948.

Stallbaumer, V. R., "Thomas Holcroft: A Satirist in the Stream of Sentimentalism," *ELH*, III (1936), 31-62.

Stein, Elizabeth P., *David Garrick, Dramatist*, New York, 1938.

Stroup, Thomas P., "The Princess of Cleve and Sentimental Comedy," *RES*, XI (1935), 200-203.

Times Literary Supplement, June 2 (p. 392), June 23 (p. 440), July 21 (p. 504), 1927; May 16 (p. 420) and May 23 (p. 440), 1936.

Tupper, F. S., "John Banks, A Study in the Origins of Pathetic Tragedy," Harvard Univ., 1935 (Unpub. Ph.D. dissertation).

Tuveson, Ernest, "The Origins of the 'Moral Sense,'" *HLQ*, XI (1947-48), 241-59.

Warner, James H., " 'Education of the Heart': Observations on the Eighteenth-Century Sentimental Movement," *Papers of the Michigan Academy of Science, Arts, and Letters*, 29 (1943), 553-60.

Waterhouse, Osborne, "The Development of English Sentimental Comedy in the Eighteenth Century," *Anglia*, Band XXX (Neue Folge Band XVIII), 1907, 137-72 and 269-305.

Whitford, Robert C., "Satire's View of Sentimentalism in the Days of George the Third," *JEGP*, XVIII (1919), 155-204.

Wilkinson, Andrew M., "The Decline of English Verse Satire in the Middle Years of the Eighteenth Century," *RES*, New Series III (1952), 222-33.

Williams, Stanley T., "The English Sentimental Drama from Steele to Cumberland," *Sewanee Review*, XXXIII (1925), 405-26.

——, "The Early Sentimental Dramas of Richard Cumberland," *MLN*, XXXVI (1921), 160-65.

——, "The Dramas of Richard Cumberland," *MLN*, XXXVI (1921), 403-408.

——, "Richard Cumberland's *West Indian*," *MLN*, XXXV (1920), 413-417.

——, *Richard Cumberland, His Life and Dramatic Works*, New Haven, 1917.

Wood, Frederick T., "Sentimental Comedy in the Eighteenth Century," *Neophilologus*, XVIII (1933), 37-44 and 281-89.

——, "The Beginnings and Significance of Sentimental Comedy," *Anglia*, LV (1931), 368-92.

INDEX

Where author and work appear on the same page, the entry is under the author's name only. A work whose author is known but not mentioned on the same page is listed under its title; where necessary there is a cross reference to the author. Plays of composite authorship are indexed under the name of one of the authors only; the only exception is for plays by Beaumont and Fletcher.

INDEX